Second Simplicity

The Inner Shape of Christianity

Bruno Barnhart

Drawings by Lynne Clarkin

Paulist Press

New York/ Mahwah, N.J.

The Publisher gratefully acknowledges the use of the following: Excerpts from *The Heart of the Matter* by Pierre Teilhard de Chardin. Originally published in French as *Ecrits du temps de la guerre* by Les Editions Bernard Grasset, Paris. Copyright 1965 by Editions Bernard Grasset. Reprinted by permission of Georges Borchardt, Inc. Also, copyright 1976 by Editions du Seuil. English translation copyright 1978 by William Collins Sons & Co. Ltd. and Harcourt Brace & Company. Reprinted by permission of Harcourt Brace & Company. Excerpts from *The Collected Works of C. G. Jung*. Copyright 1953– by Princeton University Press. Reprinted by permission of Princeton University Press and Routledge and Kegan Paul. Excerpts from *Collected Poems* by Wallace Stevens. Copyright 1954 by Wallace Stevens. Reprinted by permission of Alfred A. Knopf, Inc. and Faber and Faber Ltd. Excerpt from "A Christmas Hymn" in *Advice to a Prophet and Other Poems*. Copyright 1961 and renewed 1989 by Richard Wilbur. Reprinted by permission of Harcourt Brace and Company and Faber and Faber Ltd. Excerpt from "That Supreme Point" in *Imagine Inventing Yellow: New and Selected Poems of M. C. Richards*. Copyright 1991 by M. C. Richards. Published by Station Hill Literary Editions.

All Scripture citations are taken from the Revised Standard Version unless otherwise noted.

Cover and interior drawings by Lynne Clarkin

Cover design by Mike Velthaus

Library of Congress Cataloging-in-Publication Data

Barnhart, Bruno, 1931–
    Second simplicity : the inner shape of Christianity / Bruno Barnhart ; drawings by Lynne Clarkin.
      p. cm.
    Includes bibliographical references and index.
    ISBN 0–8091–3832–8 (alk. paper)
    1. Spirituality. 2. Wisdom—Religious aspects—Christianity. I. Title.
BV4509.5.B375   1998
248—dc21   98–40942
                                                 CIP

Published by Paulist Press
997 Macarthur Boulevard
Mahwah, New Jersey 07430

www.paulistpress.com

Printed and bound in the
United States of America

Contents

Acknowledgments

I am grateful to the community of New Camaldoli for their warm support during the writing of this book. Prior Robert Hale encouraged and facilitated the work. Pamela Pettinati and Lynne Clarkin read the manuscript and made valuable suggestions. Editor Kathleen Walsh of Paulist Press, with her sensitive criticism, helped to bring the book into a more readable state. Lynne Clarkin's drawings gracefully further the book's movement beyond words into the mystery.

Introduction

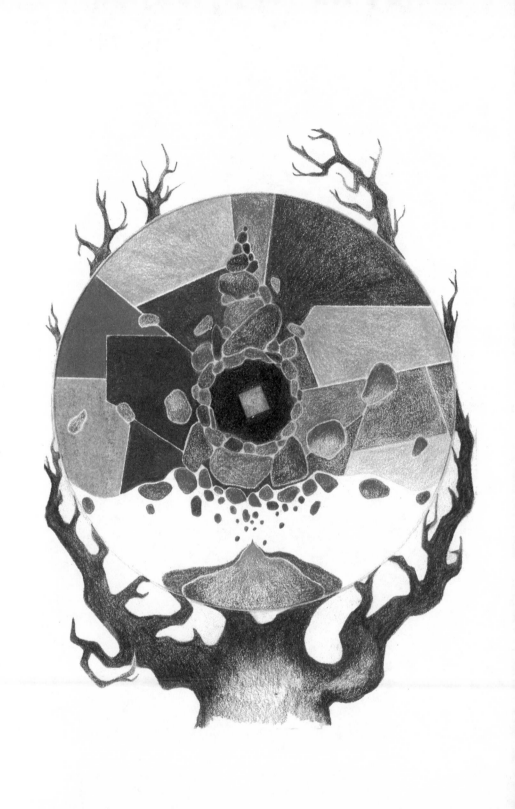

Human life in this twentieth-century Western world has seen an unprecedented expansion, seemingly in every direction. Yet we gradually become aware of a subtle loss, a vital contraction. Despite the widening of our world and of our consciousness that technological progress has brought, we may awaken, at some moment, to realize that we have been living within an invisible container: in a world subtly diminished and often without depth.

It is this growing awareness that, during the past forty years, has caused many young people in Europe and North America to go to India (or to Japan or Burma) in search of other dimensions of reality, and it has brought Hindu and Buddhist communities to flourish in the West. The perennial term for this depth of life and consciousness that has so largely disappeared from our Western civilization, and from our Western Christianity, is *wisdom*.

It was not always so. Christian spirituality, during its first millennium, understood itself as a wisdom—as a participation in the divine wisdom, which had become one with humanity in the person of Jesus Christ.

This book is an attempt to explore the world of wisdom,[1] and to map its dimensions. I shall endeavor to sketch the length, breadth, height, and depth of wisdom, and to imagine what new forms of Christian consciousness, thought, and life may come forth and flourish within these spaces that open before us, once again in our time, like an immense new world. I shall be concerned with spiritual wisdom and particularly with the ideas and intellectual structures that correspond to a wisdom (or *sapiential*[2]) consciousness.

The book's perspective is frankly a Christian one. Its purpose, however, is to outline the universal context in which a Christianity of the future will realize itself, no longer in isolation but in a participative relationship with all reality. This is the meaning of Christian wisdom as I shall trace its development here.

3

As we journey through the various provinces of wisdom, one idea (or quality of consciousness) will sound again and again as the keynote of our thought. This is unitive (or nondual) reality, and unitive experience. Unitive consciousness (awareness grounded in primal unity) is the core and "eye" of the wisdom that is our theme.[3]

The unitive vision, in turn, articulates itself, as in many ancient religious traditions, in *four dimensions*.[4] These four poles constitute a mandalic figure[5] to which I shall refer throughout the book. The two principles of unity and quaternity will consistently determine our perspective.

FIGURE 0.1

From a Christian theological perspective, this figure reflects the fundamental constellation of Trinity and Creation.[6]

FIGURE 0.2

The book's four-part structure reflects the mandalic figure, and is itself meant to express the conception of wisdom that is proposed here. This is but one of many possible ways of imagining the world of wisdom, but it is one that clearly brings to light the unrealized potential of contemporary Christianity.

The fourfold pattern is to be understood in the light of a unitive view of history: The One (God) is manifested to and participated in by created beings through Word and Spirit, the two unitive mediations of the One that are revealed in the New Testament. Through these two mediations, and their interaction in the course of history, humanity and the cosmos itself are drawn into a participation in the One. Central to this process is the human person, and then the divine-human Person of Jesus Christ, who imparts the unitive Spirit in its fullness to the world.

Each mandalic figure (see Figure 0.3) can be read as representing the totality of the Christ-mystery or the full realization (divinization[7]) of the human person. On the vertical axis, the two poles of God and Creation are paralleled in the human person by the spiritual core and the body. To Word and Holy Spirit on the horizontal axis correspond the symbolic masculine and feminine (or rational and holo-psychic/affective/psychodynamic) dimensions of the human person.

ONE represents the divine Absolute itself. Correspondingly, it also represents that unitive wisdom or *perennial philosophy*[8] (conceived here as knowledge of unitive reality), which has ever been at the heart of the Oriental traditions. This unitive Absolute is also at the heart of the Judaeo-Christian tradition, though it rarely becomes explicit in the West.

TWO corresponds to the divine Word, which, spoken in the world, has generated the traditions of Judaism, Christianity, and Islam. To this second quadrant belongs the development of the West with its polarities, its multiple fissions, its masculine bias, its genius for analysis, and its modern dialectic of critical rationality. A pervasive dualism has long characterized Western consciousness.

THREE is the dimension of dynamism, of energy, of movement, relationship, communion, personal experience, human freedom and creativity, the world of *psyche* and of the feminine. It is the principle of development, whether within the individual person, in human history, or in the evolution of the cosmos. We are always on the threshold of a great renaissance, an "Age of the

Spirit," and from our sapiential perspective this is the emerging era of a new wisdom, a *second simplicity*,[9] which integrates the developments of the creative and critical era in which we live. Meanwhile we experience the dawn of this new age in a hundred ways—related to the Spirit, to psyche, to the emerging feminine,[10] to poetry, art, and music.

FOUR returns us to earth: to the body, its death and resurrection in God. This is the dimension that always seems to elude our theories and theologies, the term we have systematically left out of our equations. It represents also the people of the earth, the poor and indigenous peoples who are invisible from within the perspective of a dominant civilization and its confident rationality.

ONE
UNITIVE DIMENSION
(SILENCE)
GOD/FATHER
JOHN'S GOSPEL
ANAGOGICAL SENSE OF SCRIPTURE
SELF/SPIRIT
SPIRITUAL
NONDUAL ABSOLUTE

TWO
CHRISTIC DIMENSION
(WORD)
THE WORD-SON
MATTHEW'S GOSPEL
ALLEGORICAL SENSE
MIND
MASCULINE
FORM

THREE
DYNAMIC DIMENSION
(MUSIC)
THE HOLY SPIRIT
LUKE'S GOSPEL
MORAL-TROPOLOGICAL SENSE
PSYCHE
FEMININE
ENERGY

FOUR
COSMIC DIMENSION
(DANCE)
COSMOS-HUMANITY
MARK'S GOSPEL
LITERAL-HISTORICAL SENSE
BODY
BODILY
MATTER

FIGURE 0.3

Four is the number of completeness and integration, the mandalic number that draws together everything that has gone before in a centered symmetry. The same fourfold pattern, visibly symbolized by the figure of the cross, represents cosmos, human person, and the fulfillment of the Christ-event through a unification of all created being in God.

Each of these four poles represents a dimension of reality and a world of human experience. As citizens of the Western world, we are inhabitants of the world of Two ("Word"); our consciousness and even our lives are often circumscribed by the boundaries of Two. It would be natural, for this reason, to begin with Two. Nevertheless, we shall begin with *One:* This is the world of the *wisdom* traditions of Asia, which is freshly opening up to us today. With this ancient and perennial wisdom, we shall embark on our journey in quest of a new wisdom.

As we begin with One and proceed through Two, Three, and Four, we should not forget that our own journey is better described as beginning within the world of the Word (Two). Our personal history is likely to start within a "Two-container," from which we then proceed outward by gradual exploration and integration of the other three worlds. The fullness of Christianity is represented by the whole mandala (see Figure 0.3)—and this figure of the fullness of the Mystery is already present beneath the letter of the New Testament writings.[11]

This book is a general sketch, a first exploration from our unitive and quaternary perspective, and I have tried not to allow the movement to halt for long in the study of any particular area. Here you will find only a few suggestions regarding contemporary emergences and movements along the four dimensions. It is the invitation that matters.

One

The Silence

Introduction

> Behold but One in all things; it is the second that leads you astray.[1]

Before thought there is a ground, a principle, a primal reality. That this reality may be realized by the human person is the principle of spiritual enlightenment and of the wisdom traditions. This unitive primal reality is our starting point.

Beneath the ordinary human ego and its operations there lies another Self, which participates immediately in the primal ground. This has been called, in the various traditions, atman, Buddha-mind, Christ-self, unity consciousness, inner man. The ascetic and monastic ways of life, with their simplicity, solitude, and silence, respond to the magnetism of the ground and of this inner Self.

The primal ground, however, is not only the focus of the spiritual seeker, but the basis of every act of human consciousness. Scientific and philosophical thought, artistic creation, human relationship, and even political activity are driven by the inner unitive principle.

The modern West, in its complex, explosive centrifugal movement, has moved further away from the primal ground, the principle, than any other society. Today we encounter its witnesses in the traditions of the East: Hinduism, Buddhism, Taoism. We shall encounter, in the various traditions, many symbols for the One (see Figure 1.1): silence, mountain and sea, wilderness and desert, emptiness, ignorance, the "beginning," and darkness as well as light.

FIGURE 1.1

1. Apophatic Spirituality

Apophatic spirituality is a seeking of absolute reality beyond all images and concepts and experiences. It is a quest for the "center," or the ground of being, in purity, in emptiness, without the mediation of particular objects or symbols.

This apophatic tradition of spirituality appears in the highly developed spiritual traditions and is embodied particularly in the various currents of monasticism. It corresponds to the experience of an ultimate unitive reality and to the *perennial philosophy*.[2]

While the apophatic is only one tradition within Christianity, it is central to Buddhist spirituality. Buddhism appears, in its original expressions, as an essentially apophatic, quasi-monastic spirituality. This pole of the Christian tradition, which corresponds to the invisible God, "the Father," to pure ultimate unitive reality and to unitive contemplative experience, is reawakened by the encounter with Buddhism today.

An early Buddhist text is typically emphatic on the unknowing that characterizes ultimate experience:

> There exists…such a state in which there is neither earth nor sea nor air; where there exists neither infinite space nor infinite consciousness and not even emptiness, neither sensation nor non-sensation; where there is neither this world nor another nor both together, neither sun nor moon. O monks, there is neither going or coming or standing still; neither is there duration or decline or growth; nothing is fixed and still, nothing moves nor has foundation. This is the end of suffering.[3]

Biblical Apophatism

The apophatism or *negative theology* of Biblical tradition is very different from that of Buddhism. Yahweh is a God who speaks and acts. Yet we read in the Book of Exodus that "no one can see God and live" (see Ex 33:18–23). Divine manifestations in the Bible are pervaded with a sense of the ineffable, of a numinous reality that exceeds and overwhelms the human capacity to understand and to articulate. Again and again, God is manifest in a sudden bursting of the confines of ordinary experience, an invasion of sheer reality. The Book of Genesis begins in the darkness of a primeval chaos; Israel is born into the wilderness of Sinai, and the New Testament will begin in the desert where the word of God resounds in the preaching of the Baptist. This God of the wilderness, of new beginnings and births from nothingness, will not be domesticated by the formulations and structures of religion.

Israel's radically apophatic attitude toward its God is expressed in an insistence on God's absolute transcendence, in a horror of idols and a prohibition of images—whether of God or of other creatures.

> Truly, you are a God who hides himself, O God of Israel, the Savior. (Is 45:15, NRSV)

Paradoxically, this assertive God, vigorously present and active in the life and history of his people, is an unapproachable God, who can be known only through his Word and worshiped only through his chosen intermediaries.

Gradually, within this perspective of absolute transcendence, a personal religion emerges in which God is known intimately as dwelling within favored persons through the divine Spirit or Wisdom, while yet remaining completely veiled in mystery.[4]

Christian Apophatism

The paradox of this God, both completely transcendent and profoundly immanent, is intensified in Christianity as the divine Spirit comes with a new depth and power to dwell within person and community. The coming of God into this world through incarnation and this gift of the Spirit finds expression in a religion that, from its beginning, moves powerfully out into the world.

In the New Testament, however, we find that the mysterious quality of the God of Israel has been deepened rather than being dissipated in this further revelation and this movement into the world. The gospels (most explicitly John's Gospel) and the writings of Paul are full of a sense of *mystery*. Indeed the Mystery is now present in the midst of these human beings, the disciples.

> ...the blessed and only Sovereign, the King of kings and Lord of lords. It is he alone who has immortality and dwells in unapproachable light, whom no one has ever seen or can see. To him be honor and eternal dominion. Amen. (1 Tm 6:15–16, NRSV)

God has become visible in Jesus Christ; God is known through the indwelling Spirit in a life of love. These are the two unitive mediations through which the human person becomes divine. God is known, ultimately, in union.

No one has ever seen God; the only Son, who is in the
bosom of the Father, he has made him known. (Jn 1:18)

No one has ever seen God; if we love one another, God lives
in us, and his love is perfected in us. (1 Jn 4:12, NRSV)

It is only centuries later, in the Christian East, that this context of mystery brings forth an explicit apophatic theology.
Pseudo-Dionysius[5] clearly sets forth the *via negativa*, or
apophatic way, and distinguishes it from the cataphatic or positive way. The "positive" approach, through images, symbols,
and concepts, offers some knowledge about God but leads only
so far. It is the "negative path," since God is essentially incom-
prehensible, that brings one finally to divine union.

The Christian apophatic way, then, is ultimately concerned
with a truly unitive experience, a movement beyond duality into
oneness with divine Reality. This new divine-human oneness,
corresponding to the Incarnation, is the heart of Christianity. It is
paradoxical, therefore, that nonduality has so rarely found
expression in Christianity[6] while it appears so clearly and explicitly in the Asian traditions.

Vladimir Lossky speaks of "that apophatism which constitutes the fundamental characteristic of the whole theological tradition of the Eastern Church."[7] Apophatic spirituality, while
much less central to Western Christianity, has survived in the
mystical tradition of the West. At the beginning of the modern
era, St. John of the Cross describes the same negative way
toward divine union. He emphasizes something presupposed
by the earlier writers: The core of this spirituality is *faith* (for
John of the Cross, faith becomes "dark contemplation") that
alone joins one with God. Here we see once again that Christian
apophatism is rooted in the New Testament.

Among the small number of really significant changes that
can occur in our consciousness is the emergence of an awareness
that reality is *open* rather than framed. Completely accustomed
to operating within one or another box, we become insensible to
the infinite possibility surrounding us. Enlightenment and liberation are gradual, with an occasional quantum leap.

Together with the sense of an unconfined reality there

emerges the awareness of an inflowing supply, an unlimited Source. We begin to conceive reality not as static but as flowing, and as continually flowing forth from within. This is true, first of all, in ourselves. Our life is welling forth at every moment from dark depths. We are continually arising, flowing upward and outward. We are usually aware of ourselves, and of reality, only at the periphery, rather than at the source. Our consciousness is peripheral, our knowing is a downstream knowing.

Silent meditation is one of the most direct ways of going upstream, against the outflowing current. But here our geometry, our metaphor, must change: The movement upstream is a descent and an interiorization. The journey is downward into the ground and inward to the center. Still we are in the realm of metaphor; we cannot speak directly of this reality of the Source.

Another way upstream is poetry.[8] Poetic discourse knows the way to the Source that is hidden within words: the path within words to the invisible Word from which they originate. The words of the poem dwell within a bright little aura, a field of energy that participates in the energy that is beginning and end. The poem is an epiphany, a little eucharist of the Word in which the cosmic communion is momentarily realized.

The opening of our consciousness to embracing Mystery, then, is an opening also to the Source. We become aware of being (and our own being) as flowing from this unseen Source into visibility. We awaken to the abundance of the Source. We become aware of reality as dynamic: as movement, emergence, as a present energy. This too is a major change in consciousness.

2. Unitive Reality, Unitive Experience

Ultimate reality, the contemplative traditions testify, is a *unitive* reality.

This "Oneness of being," in which all opposites are reconciled, is the supreme insight of the perennial philosophy. It cannot be known by reason, but where the heart is opened in faith to the supreme Reality, it is known with intellectual clarity.[9]

It is in the ancient traditions of the East—Hinduism, Buddhism, Taoism—that this unitive reality has been most fully expressed. *"That art thou."*[10] Unitive reality lives at the heart of the Western spiritual traditions, but it has rarely been expressed there with the directness and purity with which we find it in the Hindu and Buddhist literature. Explicitness with respect to pure unitive experience has been inhibited in the Judaeo-Christian tradition by a consistently firm insistence both on the distinction between God and the created world and on divinely sanctioned mediations of the relationship between God and humanity.

The New Testament, however, gives witness powerfully and repeatedly to a new presence of divine unitive reality in Jesus Christ, which, after his resurrection, is experienced in two ways by those who believe in him. The baptized person experiences a new being *in Christ*. The Christian community experiences a new *koinonia*, a new communal being in Christ and in the divine Spirit.

Here and there in the Eastern Christian writers of the first millennium, and then in the late medieval mystical-theological tradition of northern Europe (particularly with Meister Eckhart and Jan van Ruysbroeck), the personal unitive experience does become explicit. Contemplation (*contemplatio* in Latin, *theoria* in Greek), is the classical name for this unitive experience in the Christian tradition.

During one extraordinary period in history, sometime around the middle of the first millennium B.C.E., the unitive experience in its purity burst through into human consciousness. Karl Jaspers has named this time the *Axial period*.[11] This is the time at which, concurrently in different places around the earth, a personal consciousness emerged from the background of primal and tribal consciousness. The emergence took different forms in India (with the Upanishads and the Buddha, initiating two great traditions of spiritual philosophy), in China (with Lao Tzu and Confucius), in Greece (with the presocratic philosophers, then Socrates, Plato, and Aristotle), and in Israel (with the biblical prophets).

Christian understanding of contemplation has undergone a very important development during recent decades. In their encounter with the Asian traditions, Christians become aware of their own contemplative experience once again as nondual experience, as unitive experience. This is an awakening of pure consciousness, an unconditioned illumination and realization of the core of the Person, the point of a primordial oneness with God.[12] Thus contemplation itself acquires a necessary autonomy with respect to the elements and formulations of Christian faith, enabling it to interact fruitfully with Word and with church. This is a recovery of the apophatic contemplative tradition in Christianity.

The traditional Western Christian conception of contemplation is well represented by Adolphe Tanquerey's Thomistic definition: "a simple, intuitive gaze on God and divine things proceeding from love and tending thereto."[13] Typically, this Western definition presupposes a subject-object relationship between the person and God. The contemplator is "gazing upon," "attentive to" God and "divine things." This view falls short of the simplicity and immediacy, the essentially unitive character, of contemplative experience. Rather than being participated, God remains exterior to the human person even within this experience.

Some statements on contemplation by contemporary Christian writers will make clear the change in conceptualization of contemplation that has taken place since the middle of the twentieth century, largely under the influence of the Eastern spiritual traditions.

> We are being called to recover unity beyond duality as our birthright, and it is this alone which can answer the deepest needs of the world today.... This is our calling and our hope. Meditation is the only way to go beyond dualism. As long as you think rationally you will have a dualistic attitude. But when you stop the mind, you discover the unifying principle behind everything.[14]

> The contemplative life is primarily a life of unity. A contemplative is one who has transcended divisions to reach a unity beyond division.[15]

> There is a higher light still, not the light by which man gives names and forms concepts, with the aid of the active intelligence, but the dark light in which no names are given, in which God confronts man not through the medium of

things, but in His own simplicity. The union of the simple light of God with the simple light of man's spirit, in love, is contemplation. The two simplicities are one. They form, as it were, an emptiness in which there is no addition but rather the taking away of names, of forms, of content, of subject matter, of identities. In this meeting there is not so much a fusion of identities as a disappearance of identities.[16]

Contemplation is direct unitive experience of the Divine.

In both of these ways, as direct and as unitive experience, contemplative knowing is distinguished from the rational-analytical-conceptual knowing that is commonly supposed, in our modern West, to be the only valid kind of knowledge. These two qualities are essentially related: Direct experience is unitive experience, as contrasted with mediated kinds of knowledge.

3. The Maximum: Meaning of Meanings

There is one thought that cannot be thought, though all thoughts reach toward it as their limit. It is not a way, but the goal of all ways, unattainable yet completely present now. We most often encounter it through indirection, through miscalculation and loss of direction, through surprise. Here opposite ways meet.

As I am about to deal with ignorance as the greatest learning, I consider it necessary to determine the precise meaning of the maximum or greatest. We speak of a thing as being the greatest or maximum when nothing greater than it can exist. But to one being alone does plenitude belong, with the result that unity, which is also being, and the maximum are identical; for if such a unity is itself in every way and entirely without restriction then it is clear that there is nothing to be placed in opposition to it, since it is the absolute maximum. Consequently, the absolute maximum is one and it is all; all things are in it because it is the maximum. Moreover, it is in all things for this reason that the minimum at once coincides with it, since there is nothing that can be placed in opposition to it. Because it is absolute, it is in actuality all possible being, limiting all things and receiving no limitation from any.[17]

Ultimately there is only one subject, and that is the Maximum. And in the light of the Maximum, there are a million subjects.

Friend, just for a moment allow your mind to disengage itself from its surface and to be drawn inward by the pull of its root, its invisible ground and stem. There at the center you are aware of something uncircumscribed, which is one with yourself, which is yourself illimitable. There: We should say *here*, for in this place there is only here. This is the here of being, the place of the burning bush, the crossing of time and space, of history and possibility, of experience and cosmos.

You cannot think of this, it is not an object of thought. You cannot focus on it, but from time to time it enkindles, it becomes conscious within you, and you can allow yourself to be gathered into it.

Would you like *a* way? How about the way that is the end? How would you like to be intoxicated with the end, with the only thing, and then to seek it for your whole life, from every place and situation, in a thousand ways?

What if it is not a place but everyplace, what if it surrounds you, so that the problem is not that of finding a way to it, but of finding the way out of the ways in which you are stuck? What if it is the everywhere that we are imprisoned from, blinded from, the burning reality that we reach toward at every moment through the strong vertical bars of our mind, our will?

But still there are these moments of consciousness. There are moments when you know within yourself the perfect stability of the universe and the absolute sufficiency, the intrinsic rectitude of light.

You know—what? A lot of things, perhaps. Perhaps you could walk through the forest and the trees would deliver up to you their peculiar secrets. Perhaps you could embrace an unhappy person and the sweet light would shoot up within his heart again. Perhaps you could untie the convulsive knots of misery with your clever fingers and set the prisoners free. But our subject is the subject, the Maximum. And let us not get carried away any more with vainglorious dreams. Let us seek the substance beneath the weathers, the undying core.

There seems to be an undying "I" beneath this frantic one.

We have died a lot of deaths by now, and behold, we live. We have wished destruction, courted nonbeing, and still we are alive. Something extremely durable is inside and, thank God, within it everything is conserved, all is intact. From within this, the world can be recreated.

Maybe the way is a crazy multiple love for this thing inside us: the pearl, the treasure. But be careful not to name it in such a way that you bring it home. For you do not live where you think you do. Instead, let it lead you. Let it be wild, an eccentric center, a city hidden in the wilderness, an unspoken name, an unspeakable syllable, a fire burning all the words into a wild and weaving script of smoke. Come back to this again and again: It is the Maximum. The fifteenth-century theologian Nicholas of Cusa knew about this, and played around it a mathematical music that now seems tedious. But he knew about it, burning within him on the boat, seething and gleaming in his heart. He made his music to it, as we must.

The poets, when they taste their ultimate freedom, are often writing about this Maximum, maybe always. There is a secret in the heart of life that is not only the unmoving white light. It is not only the still point of the turning world, not only the light-filled empty center. It is also the lion of fire, the unceasing explosion of expansive being, of proliferating life, from the center. It is the fontal energy that demands to express itself everywhere and through every form: *Shiva Nataraj*.[18] It is not only secret but also manifestation: the secret manifestation, the nameless ubiquitous power that is expressed in our own restless centrifugal living.

The gospel's secret power, often hardly glimpsed by Christianity itself, is the gathering up of all our passion, our entropic centrifugal energy, our very outward thrust and vital compulsivity, secularity, and carnality, into this divine energy that ever flows outward from its hidden Source.

4. The Perennial Philosophy

The absolute reality is participated not only through intermittent experiences but in a continuing way, as the light of a unitive knowledge. This knowledge has been

called the *perennial philosophy*. Bede Griffiths writes of this knowledge as the common ground of all religions:

One of the greatest needs of humanity today is to transcend the cultural limitations of the great religions and to find a wisdom, a philosophy, which can reconcile their differences and reveal the unity which underlies all their diversities. This has been called the "perennial philosophy," the eternal wisdom, which has been revealed in a different way in each religion.

The perennial philosophy stems from a crucial period in human history in the middle of the first millennium before Christ. It was then that a breakthrough was made beyond the cultural limitations of ancient religion to the experience of ultimate reality. This reality which has no proper name, since it transcends the mind and cannot be expressed in words, was called Brahman and Atman (the Spirit) in Hinduism, Nirvana and Sunyata (the Void) in Buddhism, Tao (the Way) in China, Being (*to ōn*) in Greece and Yahweh ("I am") in Israel, but all these are but words which point to the inexpressible mystery, in which the ultimate meaning of the universe is to be found, but which no human word or thought can express. It is this which is the goal of all human striving, the truth which science and philosophy seeks to fathom, the bliss in which all human love is fulfilled.[19]

It was the appearance in 1944 of Aldous Huxley's pioneering anthology *The Perennial Philosophy* that made this expression common currency in our time.

PHILOSOPHIA PERENNIS—the phrase was coined by Leibniz; but the thing—the metaphysic that recognizes a divine Reality substantial to the world of things and lives and minds; the psychology that finds in the soul something similar to, or even identical with, divine Reality; the ethic that places man's final end in the knowledge of the immanent and transcendent Ground of all being—the thing is immemorial and universal. Rudiments of the Perennial Philosophy may be found among the traditional lore of primitive peoples in every region of the world, and in its fully developed forms it has a place in every one of the higher religions. A version of this Highest Common Factor in all preceding and subsequent theologies was first committed to writing more than twenty-five centuries ago, and since that time the inexhaustible theme has been treated again and again, from the standpoint of every religious tradition and in all the principal languages of Asia and Europe.[20]

We are becoming aware, in our time, of deep resonances and parallels between the more highly developed wisdom traditions. Despite the very different "languages," each derivative and formative of its own culture, there is a tendency toward agreement on the ultimate reality. There are also strong agreements in the realm of spiritual practice. The basic paths of asceticism and meditation, while not quite universal, are very widespread. These affinities should not be interpreted as pointing to a virtual identity between the spiritual traditions. Later, we shall discuss the essential differences, particularly between the Eastern and Western traditions.

A Christian version of the *philosophia perennis* was developed into an elaborate spiritual theology under the influence of Platonism and Neoplatonism by Eastern spiritual teachers and writers during the fourth and succeeding centuries. It was Evagrius Ponticus[21] who constructed the framework for this contemplative spiritual theology, which has been influential even in the Western tradition until the present. His writing reflects a deep contemplative experience, but in its unconditioned thrust toward interiority and contemplation it less faithfully reflects the basic message of the gospel. Maximus the Confessor[22] integrated Evagrius's teaching into a more thoroughly Christian vision. In this process, however, as Evagrius's contemplative philosophy becomes orthodox theology, the universal resonance of the unitive contemplative experience becomes less evident.

The perennial philosophy, unsurpassable in its own direction of simplicity and profundity, and in the authority of unitive experience that it reflects, does not begin to give an adequate account of Christianity. New Testament expressions of the "divine Unitive" are dynamic and intensely personal; they communicate an energy that is something new in the world.

> But we impart a secret and hidden wisdom [*sophia* in the Greek] of God, which God decreed before the ages for our glorification. None of the rulers of this age understood this; for if they had, they would not have crucified the Lord of glory. But, as it is written, "What no eye has seen, nor ear heard, nor the heart of man conceived, what God has prepared for those who love him," God has revealed to us through the Spirit. For the Spirit searches everything, even the depths of God. For what person knows a man's thoughts except the spirit of the man which is in him? So also no one comprehends the thoughts of God except the Spirit of God. Now we have received not the spirit of the world, but the Spirit which is from God, that we might understand the gifts bestowed on us by God. And we impart this in words not taught by human wisdom but taught by the Spirit, interpreting spiritual truths to those who possess the Spirit. (1 Cor 2:7–13)

This divine Wisdom *(sophia theou)*, conferred by the divine Spirit, is hardly distinguishable from the Spirit itself, working beneath the surface of history. Her emergence into consciousness will be crucial for the rebirth of Christian wisdom toward which we are moving.

5. The Unitive Self

> **The ultimate reality that is known in contemplative experience and in unitive wisdom has been called simply the *center*. It is the metaphysical center of all reality and also the center of the human person. Corresponding to the presence of this reality at the center of the human person is a unitive Self: *atman*, true self, Christ-self. This is the human person fully participating in the unitive divine Source; it is, therefore, being-in-communion, the person as essentially relational. This unitive reality, as the center of the person, is also the ground of human consciousness. Human consciousness and all of its operations are grounded in a unitive participation in the absolute divine Reality.**

> The whole question is, what is the true Self? What is the true centre of man's being? Is it the ego, making itself independent,

seeking to be master of the world, or is there an "I" beyond this, a deeper Centre of personal being, which is grounded in the Truth, which is one with the universal Self, the Law of the universe? This is the great discovery of Indian thought, the discovery of the Self, the Atman, the Ground of universal being. It is not reached by thought; on the contrary, it is only reached by transcending thought.[23]

The discovery of the Self is always revolutionary. This is as true today, in the Western world, as it was in the Axial time centuries before Christ. Awareness of the unitive Self emerges within our dualistic modern Christianity, largely in the encounter with the Asian traditions, as a Copernican revolution. It is as if we had long been taught to imagine the absolute Reality, God, as outside and above us, completely separate from ourselves, and suddenly we discover this supreme Reality as within—indeed as one with our inner being, as the ultimate center of the human person.

Here is an expression of this "perennial psychology," or autology, by a contemporary Tibetan Buddhist master. We may feel in this text a strange resonance with the great *Sophia* passages from the biblical *Wisdom of Solomon* (7:21–28, 8:16).

> After his great awakening beneath the bodhi tree in Bodhgaya, Lord Buddha said that the ultimate nature of mind is perfectly pure, profound, quiescent, luminous, uncompounded, unconditioned, unborn and undying, and free since the beginningless beginning. When we examine this mind for ourselves, it becomes apparent that its innate openness, clarity, and cognizant quality comprise what is known as innate wakefulness, primordial nondual awareness: rigpa. This is our birthright, our true nature. It is not something missing, to be sought for and obtained, but is the very heart of our original existential being. It is actually inseparable from our uncontrived everyday awareness, beyond willful alteration, free from conceptuality: unfabricated ordinary awareness, unadulterated by effort and modification—naked, fresh, vivid, and totally natural. What could be simpler than this, to rest at home and at ease in total naturalness?[24]

This unitive discovery brings, however, not simply peace but a sword. A new chasm of duality immediately opens between this deep Self or center and our ordinary self or ego. An even sharper split appears between this deep Self and the shallow personae or self-images that are the defensive projections of our ego, the masks behind which we hide. Thomas Merton wrote frequently of the tension and struggle between "true Self" and "false self." [25] The axis between these two levels of human existence describes the human spiritual journey and generates the structures of each spirituality.

Another version of the "true Self," from the perspective of contemporary psychological experience, is that of Carl Jung. While Jung's conception of the Self was influenced by the Asian *atman*,[26] it is situated within this world, at the center of ordinary human life and experience. The Self is equivalent to the totality of the psyche, including its spiritual dimension.

It is Ken Wilber who has most powerfully integrated the world of spiritual self-realization with contemporary psychological conceptions of Self in a single comprehensive vision.[27] He presents a gradation through the various stages of pre-personal, personal, and spiritual experience in a single "spectrum of consciousness." This vision unfolds out of a profound conception of nonduality. He sees the ultimate state of unitive consciousness not only as one with the ground of consciousness or initial state, but as somehow identical with our actual consciousness at any moment. Enlightenment is already here at every point along the way. Wilber's vision is, ultimately, a monistic[28] one: There is only one ultimate reality, and that is unitive consciousness, the Absolute, the One. A Christian perspective is challenged to integrate this synthesis even-handily with the realities that will appear as we move from our First Order, "the One," to the Second, Third, and Fourth Orders.

When someone first encounters the unitive Self (whether in its Asian or in its Jungian version) from within a radically dualistic Western Christianity, the experience is likely to be that of an exhilarating liberation. There have been numerous conversions from Christianity to Buddhism, to Hinduism, to a Jungian vision of integration. There has also been progress in bringing the Christian tradition into relation with this unitive Self in such a way as to rediscover a Christian depth-anthropology and the mystery of divinization of the human person in Christ.

In this confrontation, it is essential to maintain the inner dynamic that is unique to Christianity. The human self, created to be realized in a unitive participation in the One, experiences this participation in the course of a *personal* and *historical* journey, through the interplay of Word and Spirit, the two complementary modes of divine participation. This interplay, symbolically represented by the interplay of masculine and feminine, generates the progressive history of humanity and the evolution of human consciousness, as well as the spiritual journey of the individual person. Here once again, Christianity refuses to fold itself within the simplicity of a monistic vision of the original Reality, the Absolute, and leads us through an extended, manifold drama of duality and conflict, in which the development of the individual is inseparable from the maturing of humanity itself in the course of its history.

> The creation itself will be set free from its bondage to decay and will obtain the freedom of the glory of the children of God. We know that the whole creation has been groaning in labor pains until now; and not only the creation, but we ourselves, who have the first fruits of the Spirit, groan inwardly while we wait for adoption, the redemption of our bodies. (Rom 8:21–23, NRSV)

Confrontation with the Logos, the revealed Word, which becomes embodied in Christ and then in his community, opens up this long journey through the country of duality. As physical science gradually masters the secrets of energy, as medical science progressively acquires the wisdom of the energy of life, humanity (in the course of this long journey with the Word) discovers within itself the divine Energy: not only as unitive energy, communion, but as the creative energy that is expressed in active love and that generates a new world.

The history of our modern secular West, the journey of "secular humanism," has been an extroverted realization of the immanent Self: a blossoming of human creativity in an apparent autonomy, free from conscious dependence on God. It is the immanence of the Divine within the human person, freed from the heteronomy of Judaeo-Christian tradition, that has been at the core of this development. Meanwhile the interior, unitive Self was more and more excluded from view, until the reappearance of this deep Self from the "left side": through Romanticism, Transcendentalism, psychology, and the Asian spiritual traditions.

6. Monasticism

Monasticism is a phenomenon that occurs in many religious traditions. It corresponds to something that exists in every human person; deep within everyone dwells the "monastic archetype" with its potential. Raimondo Panikkar has elegantly developed this universality of the monastic phenomenon through the metaphor of the *center*.[29] This is a unitive interpretation of monasticism; the monk is in search of oneness, a transcendental unity, the One. The center is a metaphor for this unity.

If we look for oneness on the periphery we cannot reach that equanimity, that *shama*, that peace peculiar to the monk; we cannot have that holy indifference toward everything because we are not equidistant from everything. Monkhood represents the search for the center.

Inasmuch as we try to unify our lives around the center, all of us have something of the monk in us.[30]

It is the absolute divine Reality that is ultimate center. Its reflection within the human person is this center, or unitive "spirit," which constitutes the universal monastic archetype[31] within everyone. This notion of the center is both metaphoric (and therefore concrete in some way) and highly abstract, in the way that geometrical images are necessarily generalized and removed from the particular. It is also essentially nonhistorical, nontemporal. From a Christian perspective, it is a philosophical rather than a theological concept.

When conceived simply in terms of the center, monasticism can be understood, once again in Panikkar's terms, as the way of *blessed simplicity*.[32] Its renunciations, structures, and practices are determined by a desire for personal unity, single-pointedness, a total engagement with the center. Correlative with this unitive center are the practice of solitude and contemplative experience or enlightenment (that is, unitive experience).

While the monasticism of Hinduism and Buddhism tends to derive from the center as from a single point, the inner structure of Christian monasticism is more complex. It may, for example, be conceived as *elliptical* rather than circular. Its second epicenter corresponds to the new *koinonia* that has become present in the Christ-event. Here we find a new concern with relationships, with the climate of love and circulation of life that constitute community. This inner plurality is typical of Christianity, as we shall see.[33]

Panikkar understands center as a metaphor for the unitive level of the human person. In early Christian monasticism, this unitive starting point is referred to as the *baptismal* experience. The beginnings of this monastic tradition suggest strong relationships with baptism. The Egyptian "desert fathers" were defined by their exodus into the *wilderness.* This movement recalls the time of Israel in the desert, but more immediately, within the gospels, it reflects both John the Baptist (seen traditionally as a kind of proto-monk) and Jesus during his forty days in the desert. It is significant both that the wilderness is the place of the Baptist and his baptism, and that Jesus went there to be baptized by John. Then, immediately after his baptism, Jesus was driven into the desert by the Spirit to be tempted. There are other convergences in the gospels[34] that further support the connection of wilderness (the place of these first Egyptian monks) and baptism.

In Syria the connection between baptism and monasticism (or asceticism) was more explicit. Baptism was sometimes understood as "putting on the One," as a baptism into the One, the only-begotten Son of God (see Mk 1:11; Mt 3:17; Lk 3:22). This implied a commitment to "singleness," conceived sometimes in the sense of celibacy and a corresponding single-minded dedication to full realization of the baptismal grace. The Syriac word *ihidaya,*[35] applied to the baptized, brings together in itself all these meanings. Closely linked here are baptismal initiation, a personal unitive experience, and commitment to a monastic or quasi-monastic life.[36] The early monastic literature of the West also has strong baptismal foundations. The baptismal texts behind the *Rule of Benedict* come into view only when we read this Rule (particularly its Prologue) against the background of the *Rule of the Master*, where the baptismal allusions, and the citations of earlier baptismal texts, are still evident.[37]

I propose that baptism is an initiatory illumination of the *center*, and therefore constitutes the basic Christian unitive experience. It is an illumination of the unitive Self, the deep core of the human person, which is indistinguishable from the *One*. The "singleness" of the monk (expressed in celibacy, solitude, and simplicity of life) and the unity of the person that these practices serve, as well as the unitive contemplative experience itself, are all directly related to this initiatory event and the baptismal ground it has established within the person.

Equivalent to the universal center, as Panikkar has described it, is the "purity of heart" that is the goal of monastic life according to John Cassian,[38] and that is the threshold (or anticipatory experience) of the kingdom of God.

7. Baptism and Christian Spirituality

Corresponding in the larger Christian tradition to this personal quest of the center (and therefore of interiority and personal unity) is what we may call a *baptismal Christianity*. The baptismal event, in early Christianity (*photismos*, illumination, new birth), was experienced as the awakening and enkindling of this luminous core of the person.

Jesus' baptism in the gospels[39] becomes the center of a great confluence of biblical symbolism and drama, and to it corresponds the baptism of each Christian. Creation, birth, death, resurrection, spiritual awakening, and divinization are all immediately related to baptism. The gospels—as well as the major New Testament letters—are much more fully grounded in the baptismal event than has been realized until now. This can be shown particularly in the gospels of Mark and John, and in the structures themselves of these two gospel narratives.[40]

Initiation, for early Christians who were baptized as adults, was a unitive experience. This new unity into which they were born was both "vertical" and "horizontal": The participation in God and therefore in the divine unity was at the same time a new *koinonia*, a communion of sisters and brothers.

> And because you are children, God has sent the Spirit of his Son into our hearts, crying, "Abba! Father!" So you are no longer a slave but a child, and if a child then also an heir, through God. (Gal 4:6–7, NRSV)

> For as many of you as were baptized into Christ have put on Christ. There is neither Jew nor Greek, there is neither slave nor free, there is neither male nor female; for you are all one in Christ Jesus. (Gal 3:27–28)

It is the union with Jesus Christ in his death and in his risen life that characteristically is emphasized by Paul when he speaks of baptism.

> Do you not know that all of us who have been baptized into Christ Jesus were baptized into his death? We were buried therefore with him by baptism into death, so that as Christ was raised from the dead by the glory of the Father, we too might walk in newness of life. For if we have been united with him in a death like his, we shall certainly be united with him in a resurrection like his…. So you also must consider yourselves dead to sin and alive to God in Christ Jesus. (Rom 6:3–5, 11)

In the second half of John's Prologue this new unitive participation in God, into which one is born by baptism, generates a solemn theological music.

> But to all who received him, who believed in his name, he gave power to become children of God; who were born, not of blood nor of the will of the flesh nor of the will of man, but of God…. And from his fulness have we all received, grace upon grace. For the law was given through Moses; grace and truth came through Jesus Christ. No one has ever

> seen God; the only Son, who is in the bosom of the Father,
> he has made him known. (Jn 1:12–13, 16–18)

Through baptism, the new Christian enters into the transcendent oneness of God (see Jn 17:20–26).

> I therefore, a prisoner for the Lord, beg you to lead a life
> worthy of the calling to which you have been called,...eager
> to maintain the unity of the Spirit in the bond of peace.
> There is one body and one Spirit, just as you were called to
> the one hope that belongs to your call, one Lord, one faith,
> one baptism, one God and Father of us all, who is above all
> and through all and in all. (Eph 4:1–6)

The New Testament writings abound in references to "the beginning." At the very beginning of the Bible, the Book of Genesis opens with the words *"In the beginning* God created the heavens and the earth."* New Testament writers repeatedly allude to these words, often at the beginning of their own text, and thus point to the beginning of a new creation in the Christ-event. "The beginning" (Greek *he arche*) will allude to the divine Creator or the divine Word, to the original creation, to the new creation in Jesus, to the moment of Jesus' manifestation to his disciples, and often to baptism, the moment of personal rebirth in Christ.

> In the beginning was the Word, and the Word was with
> God, and the Word was God.... And from his fulness have
> we all received, grace upon grace. (Jn 1:1, 16)

> That which was from the beginning, which we have heard,
> which we have seen with our eyes, which we have looked
> upon and touched with our hands, concerning the word of
> life. (1 Jn 1:1)

> Let what you heard from the beginning abide in you. If
> what you heard from the beginning abides in you, then you
> will abide in the Son and in the Father. (1 Jn 2:24)

Many other spiritual traditions of the world have elaborated a poetic cosmogony, a mythology of the beginning. In Hinduism, Taoism, and Buddhism we find a contemplative spirituality of the beginning that resonates strongly with this Christian baptismal tradition.

> Tao can be talked about, but not the Eternal Tao.
> Names can be named, but not the Eternal Name.
> As the origin of heaven-and-earth, it is nameless:
> As "the Mother" of all things, it is nameable.
> So, as ever hidden, we should look at its inner essence:
> As always manifest, we should look at its outer aspects.
> These two flow from the same source.[41]

While later Western expressions of this Christian sapiential and mystical tradition of the beginning will no longer allude to baptism, they will nearly always be rooted in John's Prologue and, therefore, implicitly rooted in the baptismal event, when once again "God said, 'Let there be light.' "[42] The experience of "One" is precisely a recovery of the beginning for Christianity. It is at this point that our journey becomes a *wisdom* journey. But there is much further to go, as we shall see.

8. Unitive Reality in the New Testament

We are interpreting the New Testament as a revelation of the unitive self-communication of God in Jesus Christ and in the Holy Spirit. The Johannine writings (John's Gospel and First Letter) most clearly and fully express this unitive divine reality and our participation in it. In the Fourth Gospel, this reality appears clearly in the Prologue and in the "I AM" statements and supper discourse of Jesus. In the Letter, it shines forth in the "anointing" (2:20–27), in the new birth from God, and in the participations of God as light and love.

The "nondual eye," or unitive understanding, becomes the core of a sapiential Christian vision. This vision, in turn, begins with a unitive interpretation of the New Testament writings. The writings attributed to Paul and to John offer themselves most clearly to such a unitive reading.

From this perspective, the Christ-event is a definitive new presence of the divine Unitive, the "One," within this world. The New Testament drama is generated by the conflict of this new unitive reality with the dualistic (though intensely participative) Jewish religious world in which it appears. This unitive Being appears in Jesus, who is precisely, as Irenaeus of Lyon put it, the "Visible" of the invisible God. In a further step, the Visible disappears; at this moment the One is communicated interiorly to those who have accepted its coming in Jesus, through faith. The believer experiences this communicated presence of the One dramatically in baptism, and then more or less consciously in every sector of the new life (especially in the *agape* [love] and *koinonia* [communion] of the Christian community), and in *martyrion* (faith witness) in the name of Jesus.

The unitive reality manifests itself in a variety of forms in the New Testament writings.

- *baptismal experience.* Initiation is an awakening to the unitive reality. Very often in the New Testament, especially where the unitive radiance is strong, baptismal experience is in the background, more or less consciously present to the writer even when not explicitly mentioned. At present, scholars are discovering that more and more New Testament texts have one or another functional relation to the baptismal event and context: as baptismal hymns, catecheses, homilies, and so forth. Many of these texts have strong unitive resonance.

- *the koinonia.* The gift of Christ is manifested immediately in the new communion of the disciples, and in the *agape* (love) in which this communion is expressed. This new *koinonia* is the heart of the church; in a profound sense it *is* the church.

- *knowledge* of God, of Christ, of the Christ-mystery *(ton mysterion).* Both in Paul and in John, the new unitive *gnosis* is a primary experience of the gift.

- *participation* (communion or unitive indwelling) *in Christ,* in the one Body. This becomes the basic language in which Paul expresses the new Christian reality: "in Christ," "in him."

- *eucharistic participation.* This is the moment of ritual actualization of the new koinonia. The eucharist, while seldom explicitly mentioned in the New Testament writings, is often symbolically present.

- *verbal transformation.* The new unitive reality produces a corresponding metamorphosis of human language,[43] which is expressed at once as a convergence and a spreading of the meaning of individual words: (a) *fusion:* Terms that have a unitive resonance tend to overlap, to become nearly synonymous, a constellation of words orbiting around the one Mystery. Such words as *light, life, Word, truth, joy, love, hope, bread, know, see, way,* and the very titles of Jesus, surrounded by a unitive aura, begin to coalesce for the believer. Many Johannine expressions, especially "I AM" as used by Jesus, dwell together within this unitive cloud. (b) *enlargement:* This centripetal movement among New Testament words is accompanied by an expansion or multiplication of the meaning of individual words. Evident especially in Paul's use of such terms as *law, grace, faith, love,* this phenomenon also results from the proximity and influence of the Unitive.

- *unitive symbolism.* Much of the biblical symbolism found in the New Testament writings appears there, like the words themselves that we have just considered, with a new intensity of unitive connotation. This may be seen particularly in the paradise symbolism: Adam (and Son of Man), tree, garden, food (bread), woman, water, and so forth. It is also true of the royal symbolism (king, anointing, David, Jerusalem) and of the liturgical symbolism of the Old Testament: tabernacle, temple, priesthood, sacrifice, passover, sabbath. All these symbols are drawn together by the gravitational force of Christ, and become expressions of his unitive being.

- *parable, paradox, irony.* When Jesus' words in the gospels ring with the sound of the "sword," expressing tension, conflict, and an emphatic dualism, we can often expect a flash of unitive light, breaking through the crust of paradox and irony. New Testament texts (not only the parables) frequently contain the potential for an enlightenment event comparable to that which is catalyzed by a Zen *koan*.[44] Our struggle with conflict and obscurity generates an inner energy, which then suddenly breaks through the shell surrounding the unitive core.

- *recognition and conversion scenes* in the gospels. Again and again, when one of the characters in a gospel scene encounters Jesus, we ourselves experience an inner awakening, a moment of unitive presence. The messianic expectation that pervades the Bible may also be understood as an inclination forward toward that final revelation which is the one gift, the unitive anointing. Again and again in the gospel narrative, someone *sees* Jesus and cries out, expressing the newly awakened faith in this man in whom they recognized the ineffable One. These exclamations are like echoes of Jesus' own self-identification, I AM.

- *personal encounter* with Jesus through the figure (or name, or whatever evokes the presence) of Jesus in the gospels. We arrive finally at our own participation in the unitive reality present in Jesus and in the New Testament texts—a participation that is the basis for recognizing the other unitive expressions we have surveyed. As in the gospel recognition scenes, when the moment of epiphany, of *Presence* occurs, our inner Self is awakened: the burning, shining unitive core within us comes alive (cf. Lk 24:13–35).

We have moved from a more or less "objective" seeking of unitive reality in the New Testament to a personal unitive experience. This is how the Word meets us. The New Testament is anything but an abstract textbook treatise on unitive reality or knowledge; it is an initiation into unitive experience, into contemplation. If we set out to find unitive reality in the New Testament, we should expect to find it ultimately not as an element (explicitly or implicitly present) in the text but as the very reality density of our reading of the New Testament Word. It will be manifest in our own resonance with the Word, in our progressive union with the Word, our personal unity realized in contact with the Word: as our own assimilation to the One.

9. One: A Meditation

My mind is always reaching forward; it flows forth like a spring, and its flowing breaks quickly into multiplicity, as water flowing between stones is broken into different moving surfaces, smoothnesses rounded and furrowed, splayed and woven, yet remains one water and one motion. I have lived for many years and never seen the back of my mind. Never have I entered within the spring, or descended into its beginnings, remaining there until the Other opened to me, until the ever-present Ground spoke my name.

I am. I speak these words yet I am not their source, their ground; they find an uncertain resonance in me as they pass through my consciousness. Now I wish to become still, and to enter into my ground. This is precisely the country that is unknown to me; my very act of consciousness carries me beyond it, excludes me from it. Yet this is my native country, my own ground.

We are strange creatures: strangers to the ground, not knowing where we stand. Literally, we don't know *the first thing*, don't know ourselves, who we are. Human consciousness, as we know it, may systematically exclude being truly conscious.

Shall we, with St. Augustine, call it "memory," this back of the mind, this beginning, this ground? Within me there is inscribed a memory of the beginning, though my life flows continually away from this beginning like the rivers that flowed forth from Paradise.

I think of this ground that is my source, and my ignorance itself begins to shine in its perfection. The exclusion is perfect. And there is no exclusion; the gate is open.

"...and no one knows the Father except the Son, and anyone to whom the Son chooses to reveal him" (Mt 11:27). Can we not know our intimate ground but through Jesus Christ? We learn *not* to know ourselves. And then to know ourselves, without word or name, in faith.

I may become wholly a listening to that which issues from this ground, a listening finally to the issuing forth of my own being in purity at the lip of the source.

The ground is a sea, a silence; its surface is the door to

another reality, an intensity, a depth. Silent beneath all that happens, it contains the meanings; hidden silver, they shine here and there with a light that is interior to them, the single light that they are.

This intimate depth is not other than myself; why have I not come to know it? Why have I no sooner felt its gravitation than I am moving away from it? An ever-present graciousness is the brightness at the edges of my consciousness, the fabric of gentleness on which my consciousness is moving, creating and recreating its momentary pattern. Everything comes forth from this ground and seeks to return to it; its solicitude surrounds us.

Two

The Word

Introduction

Consciousness is the luminosity, the interiority, of being.[1] From pure consciousness immediately proceed knowledge and thought. Our second quadrant (see Figure 2.1), rooted in the light of pure consciousness, is the world of cognition: of knowledge, logos, wisdom. It is the world of self-manifestation, of revelation, the world of discourse and communication. It is also the world of institution, of organization, of social, political, and religious structures.

As natives of Western civilization, we are children of this Second Order[2] and it is difficult for us to see outside it. We may remain, for the whole of our lives, nearly locked within our own skulls, experiencing nature, other persons, life itself only at second hand, as filtered through our mental processes. During the modern age many of us have become prisoners of a certain, very limited kind of consciousness and way of knowing.[3] Western thought often reduces reality to idea, to word and symbol, in such a way as to substitute the representation for the reality. The illusion of control has deepened and spread in subtle ways.

Our Western religions are grounded in the Word of God: a Word that, ultimately, is transparent to its unitive Source. The revealed Word at the root of the Christian tradition, much like the Word as it had been spoken to Israel, became embodied in the structures of church and dogma, symbol, ritual, and sacrament. These mediating ecclesial realities inevitably tend to become self-sufficient and opaque to the living divine-human reality that is within them. In their clarity of form and their social and psychological power they gradually come to be taken for Christianity itself.

The Judaeo-Christian tradition, as well as a Greek form of rationality and the Roman practical, organizational, and juridical mind, has had much to do with the building of this Western container of consciousness. Beginning with the revealed *Word* of God, our tradition remained largely within the sphere of this Word.

41

Biblical revelation came to be understood as the authoritative proclamation of certain truths that are necessary for salvation, rather than as a self-manifestation of the living God. Great institutional structures have been built on the rock of the New Testament revelation, and have themselves taken on the certainty and authority of the divine Word. The West, more broadly, has been endowed with a particular sense of cognitive certainty and continuity. This became evident early in the Greek philosophers and then in the doctrinal teaching of the Church and still again, more recently, in the cumulative progress and growing assurance of Western science.

Centuries of unquestionable religious truth gave way to the dominance of an unquestionable scientific reason. Now a widespread skepticism challenges the claims of either religion or science to absolute truth. While the wave of deconstruction reaches everywhere in Western culture, fundamentalist counter-movements tighten convulsively around the old forms.

From within this thick and tangled forest of the Second Order, it is hard for us to awaken to the other dimensions of life, to the fullness of new life in the Spirit. It is difficult for Christianity to break through the walls of this container and expand into the other dimensions that belong to its essence: the ineffable divine Source, the personal divine Energy, the radical physicality of human existence and our material communion with the cosmos.

Less common still is a discovery of the depth and fullness that lie hidden within this same world of Two. An awakening to one or more of the other dimensions is usually accompanied by a growing distaste for the Second Order itself. And yet, if the West is to realize its own vocation, we must learn to open our consciousness beyond the limits of modern rationality and of what we have known as Christianity, to experience something of the fullness of the divine Wisdom that is in Jesus Christ. Within the Christianity of the first twelve centuries there flourished a theological vision, a *wisdom*, rooted in an experiential participation of the unitive divine Wisdom that had, astonishingly, become a human person in Jesus. At the root of that Christian sapiential tradition stand Paul and John. Paul prayed that the disciples might "have all the riches of assured understanding and the knowledge of God's mystery, of Christ, in whom are hid all the treasures of wisdom and knowledge" (Col 2:2–3). For John, Jesus is at once the divine Wisdom or Word, one with God, and the "light of the world"—"The true light, which enlightens everyone, was coming into the world. He was in the world, and the world came into being through him, and the world did not know him" (Jn 1:9–10).

Today this Second Order container is breaking open. Western Christianity is invited to a fresh initiation into the greater world of Trinity and Cosmos. In this expanded vision we begin to glimpse the true dimensions of the world of Two.

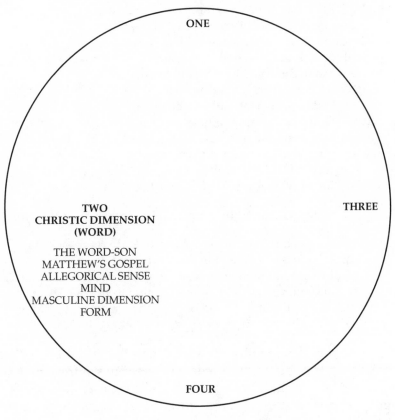

ONE

TWO
CHRISTIC DIMENSION
(WORD)

THE WORD-SON
MATTHEW'S GOSPEL
ALLEGORICAL SENSE
MIND
MASCULINE DIMENSION
FORM

THREE

FOUR

FIGURE 2.1

1. Duality: The Human Condition

The human person exists at the juncture of two worlds. We are the meeting place between spirit and matter, between Divinity and visible cosmos. This duality is experienced as a tension, but also as the context of revelation and of growth. Our consciousness is continually challenged to open to worlds of reality beyond its present compass.

Know then thyself, presume not God to scan,
The proper study of mankind is man.
Plac'd on this isthmus of a middle state,
With too much knowledge for the sceptic side,
With too much weakness for the Stoic's pride,
He hangs between; in doubt to act, or rest;
In doubt to deem himself a God, or beast;
In doubt his mind or body to prefer;
Born but to die and reas'ning but to err;
Alike in ignorance, his reason such,
Whether he thinks too little or too much;
Still by himself abused or disabus'd
Created half to rise, and half to fall;
Great lord of all things, yet a prey to all;
Sole judge of truth, in endless error hurl'd:
The glory, jest, and riddle of the world![4]

The Pauline expression of this human duality is a moral conflict.

So I find it to be a law that when I want to do right, evil lies close at hand. For I delight in the law of God, in my inmost self, but I see in my members another law at war with the law of my mind and making me captive to the law of sin which dwells in my members. Wretched man that I am! Who will deliver me from this body of death? (Rom 7:21–24)

Few realities are more obvious than the "doubleness" of our human life. Yet, as with other such realities, a fresh experience, a "realization," is needed to make us conscious of it. The light of consciousness within us, in a clear space, in a moment of freedom, expands into realization of itself. Awakening to itself, the light is startled. We are surprised, once again, to be alive. The breath is fresh once again, alive in our nostrils. When the light becomes conscious, life opens into wonder. The light that we are, awakening, wonders at its sleep, its bed and covers. It wonders also at its containment, at the strange yet immediate bodiliness of its dwelling.

But we are also *feeling:* our sense of self moves from one level to another; alternately we know ourselves as heart, as bright consciousness, as body. Deeper levels of realization of the self lie altogether beyond the mirror-world of familiar land-marks, the usual supports of our sense of identity. And it is only at these depths that the ambiguity of our being is resolved.[5]

2. The Word in the World

The great "Western" traditions of Judaism, Christianity, and Islam are the religions of the divine Word: of a "revelation" that originates in the self-communication of a personal God. In contrast to the unitive wisdom of immanence, typical of the Orient, the wisdoms of the West begin with a communication from an Other, with a divine Word that comes to humanity as from outside.

We have already noted the source of a further duality in western consciousness and culture. This was the great Axial emergence of the human person:[6] a separation between the individual and the tribe, between humanity and nature, between person and person. Here was the beginning of that individuality which has reached an extreme in the individualism and personal isolation of "Western man" today. The revelatory divine Word has, in our time, become embodied in distinct and exclusive religious communities. In this climate, consciousness of an original, unitive Source and Ground has been almost completely eclipsed.

With the Second Vatican Council, the prophetic principle of the Reformation has been officially accepted within Roman Catholicism. After centuries of subordination of the Bible to the authoritative teaching of the hierarchy, the council deliberately reasserted the primacy of the Scriptures (the revealed Word of God) for Christians.

> In His goodness and wisdom God chose to reveal Himself
> and to make known to us the hidden purpose of His will
> (see Eph 1:9) by which through Christ the Word made flesh,
> man might in the Holy Spirit have access to the Father and
> come to share in the divine nature (see Eph 2:18; 2 Peter
> 1:4).... By this revelation, then, the deepest truth about God
> and the salvation of man shines out for our sake in Christ,
> who is both the mediator and the fullness of all revelation.[7]

This primacy, or radical and definitive authority, of the biblical
revelation is fundamental to the Judaeo-Christian tradition.
Such a primacy of the Word is inseparable from belief in the
emphatically personal God who is the author of this revelation,
and in the covenantal relationship with this God that is the heart
of the biblical message.[8]

> I am the Lord, and there is no other.
> I form light, and create darkness,
> I make weal and create woe,
> I am the Lord who do all these things (Is 45:6–7)

This concept of revelation has so long been a fundamental
presupposition of our religious consciousness that it is difficult
to look at it with objectivity. This is so especially because the idea
has been presented to us in a static rather than a dynamic form:
more as noun than as verb. It was not so with the simple-minded
Rabbi Zusya, who never heard his teacher's sermon to the end.
As soon as the master intoned the beginning words of the biblical reading, "And God said...," "Rabbi Zusya was overcome
with ecstasy, and screamed and gesticulated so wildly that he
disturbed the peace of the round table and had to be taken out.
And then he stood in the hall or in the woodshed, beat his hands
against the walls, and cried aloud: 'And God said!'"[9] The Word
is living and active, a presence and an energy.

During the past half-century, some sense of the vital Word, of
a continuing and dynamic revelation, has begun to return to Western Christianity. It happened first among Protestants (especially
with the influence of Karl Barth) and subsequently within Catholicism. This has been in response to a massive oblivion of divine revelation in the wake of the Enlightenment and the naturalist

"revelation" of science. Once again we are becoming aware of the Word as active and personal, living and powerful, rather than as the sum of truths revealed to the church for safekeeping long ago. Until now we have seen only glimpses, however, of a renewal of a *sapiential*[10] interpretation capable of bringing to light the deeper and larger spheres of meaning within the Word.

The contrast between "One" and "Two" is stark. To speak, as we are doing now, of revelation, of a Word, projects an image of a God who is intensely personal, assertive, active, even intrusive and aggressive. This God appears at the same time as loving and creative. This is a God who comes into the world, who is continually exerting a transformative influence on human persons and communities. Here we are very far from the vision of the spiritual traditions of the One, as we have recapitulated them above: an absolute reality that is known in nonduality at the core of the self rather than in personal relationship.[11]

Revelation is a comprehensive term, but it is also one member of a family of words, images, and ideas: Israel, *ecclesia* (church), covenant, Torah, heart (and the listening heart or the hardened heart), prophet, angel of the Lord, conversion, vocation, judgment, salvation. Revelation embraces the whole series of historical figures to whom God spoke and whose own lives became the word of God, those who mediated the word of God to Israel and those who ignored and rejected both prophet and word, from the crass old kings to the high priests, scribes, and Pharisees of the gospel.

3. The Gospel of the Word Incarnate

The coming of Jesus Christ is both an end and a beginning. This definitive appearance of the wisdom and power of God in an individual human person is the beginning of a new creation. It is Paul who writes most clearly and powerfully of the crucial change that takes place (for all humanity and for the cosmos itself) in the death and resurrection of Christ. This change is experienced as illumination and liberation: as the movement from the tyranny of law and "the flesh" to the freedom of the Spirit. In Jesus Christ the unitive divine Wisdom has appeared in human flesh, and this Wisdom is somehow one with the cross. It is all encapsulated in the paschal event of Jesus' death and resurrection. Paul preaches to the Gentiles this "word of the cross" (1 Cor 1:18), which contains the power and wisdom of God, and the secret of human history.

As we accompany Jesus through the gospels, we are present at one dramatic meeting after another. One person after another experiences a mysterious power in Jesus that, from this moment, changes the course of his or her life. If we are fully present at the moment when we read such a narrative, we ourselves experience the liberating power of this awakening. Examples come quickly to mind: the two disciples in John's first chapter, "Rabbi, where do you dwell?" "Come and see." Then quickly, in the same Johannine narrative, Peter and Nathanael experience the awakening of meeting Jesus. In the synoptic gospels, we may recall the reaction to Jesus of the blind man alongside the road to Jericho, of the father of the paralytic boy, of the centurion whose servant was sick, of the thief on the cross alongside Jesus, of the centurion present at Jesus' death. Time after time, we feel the breakthrough of light, the wave-front of wonder. Peter and the other close disciples seem to discover Jesus not just once but repeatedly. "Who is this, that the wind and the sea obey him?" And after Jesus has risen from the tomb, they have to learn to know him all over again. "Rabboni!" cries Magdalene to the unfamiliar figure in the garden. Still to come are Paul's encounter with Jesus on the Damascus road (Acts 9:3–9, 22:4–16, 26:9–18), and the Seer's vision, similarly overwhelming, of the transfigured Jesus at the beginning of the Book of Revelation (Rv 1:12–18).

In each one of these recognition events, the Word can touch us at the core of our being. As we experience in the narrative this outer meeting with Jesus, a stirring and illumination within our heart reflect the inner birth that is taking place: "Did not our hearts burn within us while he talked to us on the road, while he opened to us the scriptures?" (Lk 24:32).

But when one turns to the Lord the veil is removed. Now the Lord is the Spirit, and where the Spirit of the Lord is, there is freedom. And all of us, with unveiled faces, seeing the glory of the Lord as though reflected in a mirror, are being transformed into the same image from one degree of glory to another; for this comes from the Lord, the Spirit. (2 Cor 3:16–18, NRSV)

For it is the God who said, "Let light shine out of darkness," who has shone in our hearts to give the light of the knowledge of the glory of God in the face of Christ. (2 Cor 4:6)

Our encounter with the Word is not confined to the Second Order: the stirring, the awakening, resonates through the whole of our being. When, in the resurrection, our body participates fully in this change, a transformation by the Holy Spirit will be complete; and not only in ourselves.

For the creation waits with eager longing for the revealing of the children of God; for the creation was subjected to futility, not of its own will but by the will of the one who subjected it, in hope that the creation itself will be set free from its bondage to decay and will obtain the freedom of the glory of the children of God. We know that the whole creation has been groaning in labor pains until now; and not only the creation, but we ourselves, who have the first fruits of the Spirit, groan inwardly while we wait for adoption, the redemption of our bodies. (Rom 8:19–23, NRSV)

This Jesus whom we encounter is a light at the center of the world, a fire at the world's edge. He moves beneath the images of himself as an ultimate center of energy. I am always losing him and finding him again, migrating from one image, one station, to another on the journey. He awakens that which lies at the core of my own being; the series of Jesus' healings in the gospels are the story of the gradual raising to life and consciousness, to freedom and fullness, of this nascent person that I am.

The knowledge of Jesus Christ is a unitive knowledge: it is the luminosity of my own true and eternal being.

> But whatever gain I had, I counted as loss for the sake of
> Christ. Indeed I count everything as loss because of the sur-
> passing worth of knowing Christ Jesus my Lord. (Phil 3:7–8)

At the same time, this Jesus is the center that draws together all
things in heaven and on earth. In him I possess the secret knowledge of this unity and of its dynamism, which is history.

> For in him all the fulness of God was pleased to dwell, and
> through him to reconcile to himself all things, whether on
> earth or in heaven, making peace by the blood of his cross.
> (Col 1:19–20)

I cannot capture in words the gravitational pull of this solar
Christ, moving the depths of my being. The words of the gospel
narratives and of Paul's letters, however, resonate profoundly
again and again with our experience. These are words of the center, of the Mystery, of the one Word.

Paul's vision is centered in the one great *change* that took
place in the death and resurrection of Christ. In many different
ways, with varying metaphors, he expresses this change, which
had established itself dramatically at the center of his own life. For
the Jews it was the movement from law to grace, from law to Spirit.
For Gentiles it was the movement from death to life, from darkness
to light, from ignorance to knowledge of God, from *flesh*[12] to Spirit,
from being far off to being near, from outside to inside, from being
without God to "possessing" God. For both Jews and Gentiles it
was the advent of the indwelling divine Spirit, of true union with
God, through unitive incorporation in Jesus Christ.

The terminus, the "after" of this change, is expressed by the
ever-recurring "in Christ," "in him" of Paul's letters. Christ is
risen! The unitive body that is now Christ's body is, from this
moment, the single final destination of humanity and of the individual person. Those who believe in Jesus Christ, and are baptized,
are already living in this body, of which they ritually partake in the
eucharist. The life of each Christian is to be a participation in the
earthly life, the death, and the glorified life of Jesus. In John's
Gospel and First Letter, while the body of Christ is less explicit
than in Paul (but see Jn 2:19–21, 6:56), the promise and imperative
of "dwelling in Christ," of "being in Christ," are central.[13]

4. Christian Wisdom

Central to the experience of Christians was a new consciousness, a new understanding. Jesus himself was the divine Wisdom come into the world, a fullness of light now shared by the believer. Christian writers of the early centuries, on the basis of the Johannine Prologue, developed a theological vision centered in Christ as the divine Logos. This incarnate Word was understood as the Bridegroom of the Church and of the individual "soul." The divine Word or Wisdom, participated in through a unitive knowledge (an intimate personal relationship with Christ), was seen as the sun of understanding. This Logos was recognized as the one key to penetrating the mysteries both of the cosmos and of the biblical history of salvation. In the Greek patristic tradition, it is Jesus Christ as *Logos* that illuminates the whole of reality.

But whatever gain I had, I counted as loss for the sake of Christ. Indeed I count everything as loss because of the surpassing worth of knowing Christ Jesus my Lord. (Phil 3:7–8)

He is the source of your life in Christ Jesus, whom God made our wisdom, our righteousness and sanctification and redemption. (1 Cor 1:30)

For Paul, Jesus is the wisdom of God and the power of God. For John as well, Jesus is the divine wisdom (the eternal Word from which all things were created) and he is the light of the world, the light that enlightens everyone. These expressions transcend metaphor; they are attempts to give some verbal articulation to the flood of primal light that has been experienced in the encounter with Jesus, to the absolute reality that has become manifest in him.

The encounter with Jesus Christ initiates a profound revolution that is manifested on various levels of a person's being. It appears in the affective movements of one's heart, in one's way of life, and in one's consciousness. Western Christianity has given less attention to the revolution in consciousness than to the affective and moral conversions. Since the beginning of the modern era, few traces remain of the basic sapiential faith in a deep and comprehensive transformation of consciousness.[14]

This Word incarnate, situating itself as a sun at the center of the human person, becomes the center of one's understanding and gradually draws everything else into orbit around itself. The process is never finished during one's life. This is one of the meanings of the New Testament Greek word *metanoia,* or conversion. It is possible, however, for us to hold on to the existing structures of psyche and mind (especially the inherited presuppositions, the biases, the fundamental slants that are not only unquestioned but unconscious) in such a way that this transformation is arrested. Thus come into being the rigid forms of Christianity that are so familiar today.

Two practices are particularly helpful for an initiation and growth in this "surpassing knowledge of Jesus Christ," in addition to the basic faith and self-surrender that enable a person to participate in the life and the death of Jesus (see Phil 3:7–11). One is a quiet and reflective reading of the New Testament writings, and the other is silent meditation. The two practices nourish one another. A gospel scene (sometimes a single line, or even a word), or a passage of Paul, can provide the luminous point of focus from which one descends into the quiet depths of meditation. On the other hand, meditation can gradually draw one's reading of Scripture to a unitive depth.

We may alternate the repeated reading of a particular New Testament passage and silent meditation in such a way that light after light emerges from the depths, and we enter into the inner rhythms and reverberations of the scene, of the words and actions of Jesus. The Jesus of the gospel shines as a light within the Word, pervading the whole and yet distinct at its center. Within the particular gospel scene, then, reflections shine from other passages and scenes so that we become aware that we have entered into a field of unitive energy, into an organism of intelligence that is at once multiple and single. Center and source of this light is Jesus. Walking through the gospels with him, we sense the world changing around us as we awaken, little by little, in this quiet light.

Certain texts will suddenly enkindle this interior Christ-light once again.

> Simon Peter answered him, "Lord, to whom shall we go? You have the words of eternal life." (Jn 6:68)

> Again Jesus spoke to them, saying, "I am the light of the world; whoever follows me will never walk in darkness but will have the light of life." (Jn 8:12, NRSV)

> Jesus then said to the Jews who had believed in him, "If you continue in my word, you are truly my disciples, and you will know the truth, and the truth will make you free." (Jn 8:31–32)

This Wisdom-Christ shines forth on every page of John's gospel and first letter.

> That which was from the beginning, which we have heard, which we have seen with our eyes, which we have looked upon and touched with our hands, concerning the word of life—the life was made manifest, and we saw it, and testify to it, and proclaim to you the eternal life which was with the Father and was made manifest to us. (1 Jn 1:1–2)

This light, the Wisdom of God, dwells within the one who believes, interpreting all things to that person.

> But the anointing which you received from him abides in you, and you have no need that any one should teach you; as his anointing teaches you about everything, and is true, and is no lie, just as it has taught you, abide in him. (1 Jn 2:27)

> Now we have received not the spirit of the world, but the Spirit which is from God, that we might understand the gifts bestowed on us by God....we have the mind of Christ. (1 Cor 2:12; 2:16)

Dimensions of the Logos

During the third and fourth Christian centuries, a meeting of Revelation with philosophy (and, in a way, of history with cosmos) took place that was to be decisive for the formulation of Christian theology well into the Middle Ages. This was the development, on the basis of John's Prologue and of certain Pauline texts, of a Logos-theology. [15]

John's Prologue had affirmed that Jesus Christ is the divine Logos, the Word of God through which the universe was created. The same text identifies Jesus with the divine light that "enlightens everyone": the source of interior illumination. This Johannine Logos-Christ is also the unitive mediator of divinization:[16] in him the human person becomes one with God. Indeed, the human person becomes divine.

> This is the reason why the Word of God was made flesh, and the Son of God became Son of Man: so that we might enter into communion with the Word of God, and by receiving adoption might become Sons of God. Indeed we should not be able to share in immortality without a close union with the Immortal. How could we have united ourselves with immortality if immortality had not become what we are, in such a way that we should be absorbed by it, and thus we should be adopted as Sons of God?[17]

Already in the New Testament, Jesus is seen as the center of the cosmos:

> He is the image of the invisible God, the first-born of all creation; for in him all things were created, in heaven and on earth, visible and invisible…all things were created through him and for him. He is before all things, and in him all things hold together. (Col 1:15–17)

For the Greek Christian Fathers, the Logos (and therefore Jesus) is also immanent in the universe as its reason and mind, its meaning and intelligibility. The Logos-Christ, therefore, is the unitive and intelligible center in which God, humanity, and the universe come together. This is a very powerful vision. The Logos-theology begins to express the fullness (uncircumscribed yet somehow intelligible) that is in this one human being who is the divine Wisdom embodied: the person in whom God and the universe have become one and in whom the universe is re-created in God.

Therefore the mystery of the Incarnation of the Word contains in itself the whole meaning of the riddles and symbols of Scripture, the whole significance of visible and invisible creatures. Whoever knows the mystery of the cross and the tomb knows the meaning of things. Whoever is initiated into the hidden meaning of the resurrection knows the purpose for which God created everything in the beginning.[18]

This vision of Christ is not the one we have inherited in the West. It still has much to say to an individualistic and dualistic Western Christianity that has nearly excluded the cosmos (and hence the unity of creation) from its consciousness. Western theology, with the total eclipse of unitive and participative wisdom, has separated God from the universe and separated humanity from the universe, losing sight even of the fundamental unity of the human family.

The power of Paul's vision is inseparable from this cosmic scope: "The creation itself will be set free from its bondage to decay and obtain the glorious liberty of the children of God" (Rom 8:21). The individual person's destiny is inseparable from the destiny of humanity as a whole, and the future of humanity is inseparable from the future transformation of the cosmos itself.

A very strong confidence in the rationality of "nature" (that is, in the coherence and intelligibility of objective reality) is at the basis of Western science. If this is derivative in part from the Greek tradition of rational thought, it is also a consequence of that Christian rationality which found its early expression in Logos-theology. The divine Word, which has become incarnate in Jesus Christ, is source and ground of the order and intelligibility of the universe. It is this Logos that maintains all created reality in being (that is, in the light of order, of "form") holding it from falling back into disorder and nothingness, back into the primeval chaos (see Gn 1:2). It was the divine Word, the Logos, that brought all things out of the darkness of nothingness into the light of being.

5. The First Wisdom: Its Container and Shadow

The history of Christian wisdom reveals a progressive subordination of "One" to "Two." Focusing on the more

monastic and "spiritual" current of Christian wisdom tradition, we can discern an early baptismal and contemplative phase. This simple and unitive vision gradually became encased within a container of Greek philosophical thought, deriving from the Platonist and Neoplatonist traditions. With this philosophical embodiment came the characteristic Greek dualism between spirit (or mind, *nous*) and matter (body, *soma, sarx*), as well as a subordination and even exclusion of *psyche* and of the feminine dimension of the human person. Further, this crystalline Greek theology arrested the historical and affective *dynamism* that is intrinsic to Christianity.

From Uniformity to Pluralism: Vatican II

A well-known book by Avery Dulles expresses the opening of Roman Catholicism, at the time of Vatican II, from a single, institutional model of the church to a plurality of models: institution, mystery of communion, sacrament, herald, servant, disciple.[19] Even this list is not complete. We might also conceive the church, for example, as a communal incarnation of divine Wisdom.

At about the same time, Karl Rahner conceived Vatican II as marking the second great transition in the history of Christianity.[20] He sees the first transition as from the short period of Judaeo-Christianity to a church that included both Jews and Gentiles. This new Christianity, in its turn, however, became confined within another cultural embodiment: the Greco-Latin and European civilization of the West. This situation was to continue, approximately from the Council of Jerusalem in 70 C.E. to the Second Vatican Council. It is at the time of Vatican II that the church breaks out of this single cultural complex into the whole world with its plurality of cultures. It is shocking to realize that this picture is not a caricature. Christianity has, until now, largely remained within a second "Old Testament" world, determined by a single cultural complex: the European constellation of cultures.

The essential movement, then, as we enter this third stage is an unfolding of uniformity into plurality. From a Roman

Catholic perspective, this is the movement from a single and exclusive form of Christianity to a multiplicity of valid expressions, many different embodiments of the one Spirit. Dulles and Rahner present us with quite different aspects of a single movement (still within the Catholic perspective) from uniformity (a *monotropic*[21] Catholicism) to a pluralistic Catholicism: a church that understands itself in terms of a plurality of models or aspects, on the one hand, and is expressed in a plurality of cultural embodiments on the other.

In either case the clarity and explicitness, the unambiguous and definitive outline of the church, give way to a plurality that cannot be neatly and rationally organized. Such a transition could be expected to be full of confusion, tension, and turbulence. One would expect to see a polarization between those who hold on to the earlier clarity at all costs and those who feel compelled to move beyond it to a new fullness. This situation is parallel to the polarization that we find in the New Testament writings, between Jewish and Gentile Christianity: between the Jerusalem Church of James and the Gentile Church of Paul. The movement from a single cultural embodiment of the faith to a multicultural embodiment was far from tranquil.

The Sharp Point of Truth: Monotropic Christianity

The founder of Alcoholics Anonymous decided not to associate his movement explicitly with any of the established Christian churches: They were all so darned *right!* If every religion encourages a sense of righteousness in its followers, the religions of the Word heavily accent doctrinal orthodoxy. Christianity is distinguished by its peculiar insistence on possessing *the Truth:* a truth that is valid and normative for everyone. This is based on the tradition of both the First Testament (see, e.g., Is 45) and the Second Testament (see Mt 16:18ff; Mt 28:18–20; Jn 8:12–32). The church is convinced that it has received the ultimate truth, the final revelation, from God, and that it has the responsibility to witness to this truth to all of humanity.

The God of the First Testament revelation, Yahweh, is the *One* God: There is no other. And his great gift is his Word, the revelation, the divine and absolute Truth. Jesus is the only-begotten Son of this same God of Israel. He is the *Only One*, the Messiah, and the unique incarnation of the Word of God. He is the *One*, the Beginning and the End. There is no other. "I am the way, the truth, and the life; no one comes to the Father but by me" (Jn 14:6).

Jesus passes on this same fullness of truth, and this same doctrinal authority, to the Twelve, his chosen disciples, and in particular to Peter. This is most clear in Matthew's Gospel (see Mt 16:17–19, 28:18–20).[22] This delegated authority, incessantly reaffirmed by church pronouncements, comes to be accepted as the backbone of Catholicism.

The conviction of a singular rightness belongs not only to the Roman Catholic Church, however, but to nearly every Christian denomination and sect. It comes with the legacy of Christianity, of the gospel, and it gives Christians and Christianity a particular kind of image or *persona* before the other peoples of the world. Christians are the self-righteous foreigners who impose their beliefs on you, who ignore your own religious and cultural world and aggressively replace it with their own superior and unquestionable truth. Backed with the wealth and power of the West, the imposition is all the more forceful, and all the more resented.

Further powerful influences attach themselves to this Judaeo-Christian rock of revealed truth: the Roman Empire, with its structures of authority, and Greek thought, particularly in its this-worldly, Aristotelian form. A further augmentation of power accrues to the West in recent centuries with the emergence of other forms of "absolute truth": the verifiable truth of rational, positive science and the pragmatic truth of technology. The cumulative effect is overwhelming; during our "modern" age, the past five centuries, the West comes to dominate the world. This domination both consolidates and becomes more subtle as Western civilization becomes progressively emptied of its religious soul. It is as if, at a certain point in history, some new fullness of "truth" came into the world. This new "truth-quantum" developed itself (chiefly in Europe and then in North America) both in the sector of religion and in the "secular" sphere, until it came to dominate the whole world. It is difficult to capture in thought the physiognomy and character of this phenomenon, which is widespread, complex, and deep, and carries such paradoxes and contradictions within itself.

This peculiar heritage of truth and certainty is largely responsible for the long period of monotropic Western Catholicism during which the Christian faith was very largely kept within the confines of a single cultural world: the Latin world. Particularly under the influence and power of Rome, the various Christian traditions were suppressed in favor of a uniform, Roman tradition. The sapiential pluralism of biblical interpretation gave way, during the reign of science in the West, to a scientific literalism that permitted only one meaning to be found within a scriptural text. Long before this, however, a single cultural embodiment of Christianity in the European church had involved the canonization of a particular cultural embodiment of the gospel: the Latin-European expression. The autonomy or freedom (and hence the critical power) of the gospel was largely lost as it was wedded to the structures and presuppositions of this culture.

At the prophetic moment of the Reformation, this marriage was radically questioned and an attempt was made to return to the purity of the gospel. In the Roman Catholic Church, this prophetic challenge was not accepted until the Second Vatican Council. Before that council, for example, the Catholic liturgy could not be celebrated in the local tongue but only (with very few exceptions) in the official language, Latin.

Walter Brueggemann draws from the successive phases of Old Testament literature a scheme of three stages that can illuminate this movement from a monotropic to a pluralistic Christianity.[23]

1. First comes the period of *Torah,* the original and authoritative unity. This is the unchallenged consensus based on direct divine Revelation. To it corresponds, in Western Christianity, the monotropic phase.

2. Second appears the time of *Prophecy,* when this authoritative uniformity and general consensus is challenged by charismatic individuals and breaks up. This is a time of critical dialectic and of the awakening of a personal consciousness.

3. Finally there comes the phase of *Wisdom*. We can understand this as the time of a new unity, but now of such depth and breadth that it is able to incorporate a wide diversity within itself.[24] At the source of this opening is a new experience of the presence of immanent and ubiquitous *divine* Wisdom, making all things one.

The prophetic stage introduces a process of deconstruction, of demythologizing, which has reached a very advanced stage in the contemporary West. Criticism has long ago become detached from its root in the Word, and in the postmodern West it sometimes becomes an autonomous and absolute power, shredding all truth into scraps of possibility and conjecture. At one extreme, today, we find a postmodern world of complete, severed, and free-floating relativism: pure intellectuality *in vacuo*, an incessant, reductive chewing. At the other pole (and in reaction to the nihilistic exaggerations of liberal criticism), we experience the one-dimensional conservative literalism of the Fundamentalists.[25] Here there is only one source of truth and one way of knowing: simple, univocal, literal, and *Ours*.

These extremes battle on the surface of reality, on the epistemological flatland of the modern West.[26] A new Christian wisdom can come forth only from a "vertical" understanding, a personal participation in the Mystery of Christ. Here in the Mystery is the center where unity and plurality are one. This monotropic/dualistic Christianity is related to the male dominance that has consistently prevailed in the church, repressing or excluding the feminine dimension. A radical dualism tends to polarize all reality between "them" and "us," and defines "being a Christian" primarily in external terms.

Perhaps a monotropic phase of the development of Western Christianity has been inevitable. Its end, however, has arrived, together with the end of that naive conception of the church which had supported it. Inseparable from a brittle and exclusive Christianity has been an image of the church as primarily external and institutional. This image quite eclipsed the immanent divine Wisdom, that pure and simple spirit, flowing into all and happily immanent in the multiplicity of creation.

For wisdom is more mobile than any motion; because of her pureness she pervades and penetrates all things.... Though she is but one, she can do all things, and while remaining in herself, she renews all things; in every generation she passes into holy souls and makes them friends of God, and prophets. (Wis 7:24, 27)

6. Institutional Christianity

The new light, vitality, and communion that irrupted into human experience with Christ's paschal gift of the Holy Spirit were immediately confronted with the grim realities of exclusion and persecution. This tense balance of glory and cross ended, for most Christians, in the Constantinian age (fourth century), when the church became accepted and even privileged within the Roman Empire. As the Western church institution itself gradually assumed the role no longer filled by a decaying imperial government, the unitive light disappeared behind a gilded ceiling. The central Christian mystery of divinization[27] was eclipsed. A new, darker Christian worldview prevailed, in which the human person was defined by a Pauline-Augustinian doctrine of original sin. The widening gap between God and humanity was filled by the institutional Church, reigning as sole mediator of divine grace. This is the Christianity we have inherited in the twentieth century.

Western Christianity attained, in the Middle Ages, a very high degree of institutionalization. At a certain moment in history, clerics passionately embraced juridical logic and structure. There resulted a strong centralization, clericalization, and legalization of the church, with the imminent danger of transforming the gospel into law and institutional order. The church of Christ became the Roman *civitas perfecta*, the divine state. Nearly everything in the church was affected by the transformation, which was at once subtle and gross, deep and all-embracing. It is very difficult to awaken from this unconscious paradigm, so deeply implanted over the centuries. When someone did awaken to the reality of this change, he or she frequently became alienated from the visible church, perhaps to the extent of eventually separating from it as did Luther and other reformers. Some, becoming aware of the same deformations, worked within the Catholic Church toward a rebirth of its original inspiration.

> Since the middle of the twelfth century, the Church in the West, particularly as a result of the investiture struggle,[28] had gradually assumed all the elements of the Aristotelian and Ciceronian concepts of the State. The papacy itself had been dedicated to the doctrine of St. Paul in terms of government. It was an attempt to translate the "keys of the kingdom of heaven" into "the keys of the law," to direct Europe by means of a universally binding law. The great popes of the period were canon lawyers. They adorned themselves with robes of imperial purple, their tiaras with a golden crown. They rode in procession preceded by imperial banners. Even the liturgy itself had taken on the over-rationalized legal terminology of law-conscious Rome. The successor of Peter was "the prince," the "true emperor." His coronation had eclipsed his consecration in importance. He was not only the vicar of Peter, the vicar of Christ, he was the vicar of God.
>
> Theology itself became gradually saturated with juridical notions to the point that the Christ of revelation was completely submerged in an ocean of man-made rules and regulations. An angered Dante had pointed out that the chair of Peter was dominated by jurists rather than theologians.[29]

The Christ-mystery itself, with its unitive and dynamic vitality, was largely displaced by a complex of administrative structures. Something similar occurred with respect to the "truths of the faith." The *Mystery* becomes an assemblage of truths, and these truths become dogmas: that is, they effectively become laws, obligating belief. If there was something necessary and inevitable taking place in this progression, it is now equally necessary to reintegrate the dogmatic structures into a vision of the living and unitive Mystery.

Signs of emergence from the long institutional era of the church appear in the time of the Second Vatican Council. We have seen the long-dominant institutional model of the church give place to a series of alternative models.[30] Indeed, the imagining of alternatives is an essential step in the necessary exodus from our mental imprisonment in this monolithic vision of church.

Natural and Supernatural

Western Christianity crossed a Rubicon, at some early point, into a land of dualism from which it has never emerged. Central to this dualistic country is a naive concept of the "supernatural": of a sphere of reality (identical with the church) that is sharply opposed to "nature"—in fact, to everything outside the institutional boundaries. Langton Gilkey describes this two-level vision with sharp clarity. It consists of

> two radically distinguished realms: one natural and the other supernatural; one of the created order and the other of God; one of nature and the other of grace; one of matter, time, and space, the other of eternity; one of change, relativity, and becoming, the other of changelessness and absoluteness.... The Christian religion and church are essentially understood as providing the divinely established bridge *between* these two worlds.... The church was there not so much to transform the natural as to lead it beyond itself to the supernatural, to make a bridge between these two worlds...as the place in time and space where God is uniquely at work, the church is also itself uniquely transcendent; its powers, truth, authority, laws, task, goal, and the modes of existence of its representatives are, like its source, supernatural in character—absolute, changeless, inerrant, perfect, and transcendent to nature. Its truth, enshrined in its dogmas and doctrines, is changeless and infallible; its laws are eternal and utterly authoritative; its sacraments are objectively divine and thus salvatory; its power over human destiny in absolution, remission, and anathema represents the power of God himself; its voice in teaching and ruling, through its constituted authorities or authority, is the equivalent of the divine voice in present time and space; and finally its goal, for which it has been granted those supernatural powers, is to bring souls now resident on earth to eternal peace with God. As the body of

Christ, the continuation of the Incarnation, the church functions as Christ did: on the one hand as mediator between
heaven and earth, and on the other with utter authority and
power in his classical roles of teaching, ruling, mediating,
and redeeming. [31]

The church is the exclusive sphere of salvation and grace, of
the gratuitous relationship with God that has been initiated by
Jesus Christ. This gift was transmitted by Jesus essentially to his
apostles and thence to their successors, the church's hierarchical
ministers. By them it is imparted, in turn, to the Christian
people. This has been, in Roman Catholicism at least, our theological paradigm for the centuries preceding Vatican II.

This view is largely based on the Augustinian doctrine of
original sin, according to which human nature has been radically vitiated by the definitive transgression of our first parents.
Only in Christ is this fault absolved, and this absolution is one
with our baptismal incorporation into the body of Christ. The
whole world outside this sacramental world of the church lies
still under the curse of the Fall and hence under the power of
evil. This is true for humanity as well as for nature itself outside
the supernatural sphere of Christian grace.

There is a genuinely supernatural quality in divine Revelation, in church and sacraments, in Christian life.[32] And yet this
vision of the supernatural has been so naively presented as to
reach the heights of caricature: the church as a castle illuminated
on the top of a towering mountain, above the dark sea of doomed
humanity and accursed nature, where devils soar like great black
vultures. Here God and his kingdom are completely outside and
above the natural world, and even opposed to it. God is outside
and above humanity, and just condemnation is delayed only until
man has had enough time to wrap himself completely in vice, or
to submit in humble obedience at the gate of the church.

The extreme dualism of this "supernatural structure" has
certainly derived from more than one influence: Greek philosophical thought, Roman juridicism, Augustinian theology. We
can see it, further, as a continuation of the early Judaizing tendency within Christianity. This continuity with Judaism is evident when we observe the emphatic supernaturalism that is

ordained in the Pentateuch. Here we find a sanctifying covenant, a chosen People of God, purification rituals, and an elite of consecrated ministers. The centralized worship and exclusive mediatory structures of a later Temple period continue this tradition. The Roman Catholic supernatural structure seems a reproduction of this basic Jewish institutional complex, but now expressed in the concepts of Greek philosophy and the legal terms and regalia of Roman Empire. Eclipsed now in this vertical view, however, is the conception of the church as the People of God. A decline in the Western view of the human person and of nature itself, in the shadow of an unbalanced doctrine of original sin, had made a correspondingly overdeveloped system of church mediation seem necessary.

While this dualistic and exclusive conception of the supernatural forcefully expresses both the transcendence and the gratuity of the new order of grace (the true "supernatural") that is present in the church, it is inadequate to the breadth and depth and vitality of the Christ-mystery. This deficiency may be seen from at least three perspectives: (1) This view does not conserve the sense of the unitive Mystery itself—the divine unity that transcends human dichotomies and analyses, and that is expressed in the Christian apophatic tradition, beginning in the New Testament; (2) it ignores the universal divine immanence in humanity and in the creation; (3) it suppresses the continuing creative dynamism of the Christ-event in history.

This radically dualistic vision is an expression of an exclusively Second Order Christianity. Here the Word of revelation (the Word that becomes Christ and church) has not been allowed to open into the dimensions of the Unitive and the Dynamic—that is, into the First and Third Orders. It has, finally, not been allowed to descend into the Fourth Order, which is earth, "nature," the cosmos (which originated from the creative Word), in order to transform this world into a new creation in itself (see Rom 8:19–23).

A contemporary Eastern Christian theologian, Philip Sherrard, has clearly seen the dead end into which such a theology has brought us, as well as the steps that led up to the impasse. We have already briefly looked at this progression.

Sherrard sees the crucial step as a radical impoverishment of the *image of the human person* in the West by a dualistic interpretation of the doctrine of original sin. God and human nature have, following Augustine, been separated so completely as to eclipse the basic Christian truth of divinization of the human person. Sherrard takes us back to an earlier time (still in living contact with our First Order) when a Platonist Christian wisdom tradition had developed a unitive theological vision of the relation of God to creation and particularly to humanity. This vision was based on these two complementary and interlocking concepts: divine immanence and human participation in God. Sherrard finds both of these ideas already present in pre-Christian Platonist thought:

> [M]an is not merely other than God, irreducibly alien to God, but is on the contrary the specific expression of God's creative energy and participates in this energy as a condition of having any existence whatsoever. Grace, that is to say, is not something extrinsic, not something added to man's nature; it is inherent in the conditions of his birth…the idea of divine immanence—of the indwelling of God in the creature—is foreshadowe…in classical Greek thought, particularly of course in Platonic thought. In this thought the presentiment of the immanence of the divine principle is expressed above all through the concept of participation.[33]

For Sherrard, and the Eastern Christian tradition that he represents, "God is the core of the human person."[34] Here we have, in a Christian spiritual theology, the *unitive self* of our First Order.[35] The way out of our container, however, cannot be simply a return to an earlier era, even at the level of its most profound theological consciousness. Eastern Orthodox Christianity has itself not crossed the threshold into a sapiential theology that is sufficiently simple and open for a true rebirth of wisdom. Like the Christian West, it has remained within the confines of certain cultural presuppositions.

7. The Christ-Quantum and the Dominance of the West

The singular power and influence of the West derive essentially from the fact of Christ. This unprecedented

cultural momentum, this light and energy, flow from the advent of the divine creative Word in the world and from the enduring presence of the light and energy of this Word within the history of the world. We shall refer to the totality of this historical infusion as the *Christ-Quantum*.[36] The Christ-event is the fundamental forward spring, the source of the inner energy that drives history forward.[37] The leading edge of this history has been in the West, particularly in the European West.

It is evident enough that, in modern times (we might say, since the age of exploration in the sixteenth century), the West is the locomotive of the world's visible history,[38] drawing the rest of the world behind it with very ambiguous consequences. The dawn of this phase is quaintly indicated when we refer to the "discovery" of the rest of the world by the explorers of the West.

To say that the momentum of the West derives from the Christ-Quantum[39] (the totality of light and energy infused into humanity through the Christ-event) and to say that the momentum of the history of humanity derives from this same source are nearly equivalent statements from our perspective, given this role of the West in world history during the past five centuries. We experience a double diffidence today, however, after centuries of triumphalism and the humiliations and deconstructions of recent decades. First, we are likely to feel diffident about claiming too much for Christianity, ashamed of the totalitarian pride and inflation that governed the attitudes and relations of Christians toward everyone "outside" for centuries. Second, there is a widespread loss of confidence regarding the historical record of the West, as we become aware of the huge shadow that Western domination and expansion have cast—and still cast—on the world. While raw conquest and colonialism have given way to a worldwide system of corporate empire, power and wealth still remain largely concentrated in the hands of a Western elite.

In this climate we may easily be embarrassed either to affirm the real significance of Christianity in the world (that is, the magnitude of the Christ-event, its consequences and influence) or to reaffirm the achievements of Western culture and civilization. It should be no surprise, then, that we are also hesitant to connect the two: Christianity and the development of the West. We are no longer eager to attribute to Christ the achievements and influence of Western civilization. With all the ambiguities of this history, however, the development of the Western peoples is an unprecedented and central phenomenon in the history of humanity. Further, the unique magnitude and power of this development is a consequence of the Christ-event: of the appearance and presence of the Omega. It is evident enough that we may no longer understand these two truths with naive self-satisfaction.

The Christ-event, according to the New Testament, is not just something that happens *in* the world: It is something that happens *to* the world, something that radically affects not only Israel but all of humanity, not only humanity but the universe itself. The New Testament speaks of this as a "new creation," and the expression should be taken in its strong sense. Everything that exists is touched by this event, and is eventually to be transformed by it.[40]

This is a bold thesis indeed. The momentum of the West originates in the Christ-event, and is a continuing expression of the Christ-explosion, even when it appears to go in a completely contrary direction. Since the coming of Christ and the decisive bestowal on humanity of the divine Spirit, this Christ-Quantum lives and works within human history. This conception resembles the Christ-Omega of the prophetic scientist-theologian Pierre Teilhard de Chardin: a continuing, immanent source of light and energy that propels history forward, transforming the world in a way that is comprehensive, complex, and yet ultimately simple.

Paul hails Jesus as the wisdom of God and the power of God, manifest on the cross but also poured out into the world. These two aspects are not manifested equally among peoples. It is as if the wisdom belongs to the East (we are speaking now of the Christian East[41]), and the power is manifest in the West, whether Christian or post-Christian West. The observation is a very general one, and it can be easily interpreted as just another delusion, one more product of self-centered inflation. Our Western culture, or Western civilization, has taken the lead, during the past five centuries, in some kind of transformation of the world. This transformation, and the momentum of the history that it appears to determine, is most visible in the achievements of science and technology, which actually do, in an external way, transform human life and the environment itself, for better and for worse. These achievements have conferred immense wealth and power on the West, as it has come into its position of world dominance during the past few centuries.

Today it is not uncommon to see this dominant West only as a monster of aggressive exploitation. Beneath this greed and violence, however, a larger process is taking place. The West, from its spiritual roots in the Christ-event, has drawn the light and energy for a growth of unprecedented magnitude in many different directions. The Christ-Quantum seems at times a versatile energy, an "indifferent" gift, able to be effective in a thousand different ways, and even to turn against itself as it is diverted into human activities and projects that go completely counter to the intentionality of the gospel.

Teilhard sees the Christ-Omega operating on an enormous scale: at the heart of planetary evolution and of human development. Let us, for a moment, focus on the more limited historical field of the emergence of Western humanity, culture, and civilization during the past two thousand years of history. We can survey some of the evident traces of this influence of the Christ-Quantum, in successive clusters. Related to the *light* of the Logos are the sense of truth and of a consistent reality that underlies Western thought, a conviction of the truth-groundedness of the reality that we know. The West has seen an unprecedented development of human rationality, of individual critical thought, of scientific observation and reasoning. Related to this is the sense of cumulative progress, of an ascending historical process, that characterizes the West.

Related to the *power* of the Christ-Quantum, or of this fresh infusion of the Spirit, is the overall expansive momentum of the West (whether in the sense of geographic, political, and economic expansion and power, or in the sense of creativity and innovation) such as that which has given birth to the science and technology of the West.

Closer to the gospel itself is the *affirmation of the human person* that has gradually come to characterize Western civilization.

The individual person comes to be seen as an absolute value. Human equality and self-determination, personal freedom and democratic government, become "rights" in the West. Human freedom, under the influence of the West, comes to be seen as a supreme and inalienable value. Human relationship and love are also esteemed as supreme values in life. An ideal of community (that is, of equality and communion between persons) becomes the model against which society is criticized and judged.

During recent centuries, an increasing appreciation for *subjectivity*, for psychological interiority, has developed; this is evident especially in Western literature. There is also a growing sense of the infinite potential within the human person, within human life. Humanity comes to be conceived as the only locus of "divinity" in the world; in Western secular humanism, God comes to be recognized only as immanent within the human person and the human community. Finally, *woman* emerges in her own autonomy and dignity; an essential feminine component is recognized in every human person and even, analogically, in God.

The shadow-side of this Western development can be seen clearly from today's vantage point: first in its ecclesial phase, and then in its secular phase. There has been a terrible tendency in Christianity (and then in the post-Christian West) to turn the light of God into human advantage, the power of God into human power. That leads immediately to violence of one sort or another: structural or dynamic, proprietary or aggressive. The sickness and its remedy confront us plainly in the gospel—for example, in the central section of Mark's gospel (chapters 8–10) where Jesus predicts his own passion (his *descent*) and tries to convince those who are to represent him in this world that they must follow the same way. His interactions with Peter and with James and John here are especially instructive.

> He called the crowd with his disciples, and said to them, "If any want to become my followers, let them deny themselves and take up their cross and follow me. For those who want to save their life will lose it, and those who lose their life for my sake, and for the sake of the gospel, will save it. For what will it profit them to gain the whole world and for-

feit their life? Indeed, what can they give in return for their life? (Mk 8:34–37, NRSV)

Paul sees the gospel as the "word of the cross": exactly counter to the ascending movement of the human ego, of human "power and wisdom." The way of Jesus is the wisdom of God and the power of God, but it is the descent represented by the cross: foolishness to the Gentiles and something shameful to the Jews.

At the present moment, the West has apparently finished its ascending journey, and begun the return journey, the descent. Our empires are crumbling. Our patriarchal structures are trembling under the pressure of the waves of the sea. Now the words of Jesus strike us more personally: "Unless a grain of wheat falls into the earth and dies, it remains alone; but if it dies, it bears much fruit" (Jn 12:24). We, our civilization (and perhaps our kind of Christianity as well), are the seed that now must fall into the ground. We cannot descend, cannot accept this descent that is our destiny, however, without a wisdom of union, a deepening experience of participation, solidarity, communion, a eucharistic light and energy. The church can no longer exercise its power primarily from above—for as long as it does that it reigns from outside. The church will rediscover its real power *in the ground:* beneath and within. This is the power of the Spirit and of the feminine divine Wisdom, Sophia, that rises from the ground everywhere and raises humanity with it.

8. The West Today

The modern Western world has been riven by dualities since its beginning. Historically, it is nearly defined by the separation of a new "secular world" from the Christian tradition. Since the eighteenth-century Enlightenment, the dialectical workings of critical rationality have brought all traditional values and structures into doubt and subverted the sense of truth itself in Western society. Our culture is marked by individualism, fragmentation, a polyvalent atomism.

Western Christianity, having long lost touch with the unitive ground, finds itself radically polarized in our time between progressives and conservatives, left and right. Christians are challenged to penetrate to a level deeper than this polarity and then, from the perspective of the central unitive Mystery, to work toward an understanding of the interaction of immanent Word and Spirit in the church and in the world.

Dualism and the West

One of the larger forms in the geography of human history, visible to the naked eye, is the polarity of unity and dualism between East and West. One concrete example is the understanding of the word "meditation." While in the Asian traditions meditation is commonly "one-pointed" (a process of simplification of consciousness and entering into stillness), in the Western traditions meditation has been usually understood as an active movement of the mind: reflection on some religious truth. This is a contrast between First and Second Order.

With the movement of Christianity from East to West, this polarity has been expressed in a movement from a more unitive to a dualistic consciousness. Two factors emerge as principal causes of this progression into dualism: the Judaeo-Christian tradition, with its intrinsic dualities (which some have attributed to its development in the West!), and Greek thought, with its penchant for analysis—for seeing inherent oppositions between mind and matter, subject and object, and so on. The West has journeyed farther from the *omphalos,* the original One, than any other culture. The journey is an experience of increasing polarity, conflict, contrast, as the original whole and the original center gradually undergo a total eclipse and are forgotten, eventually to be known only in the dark recesses of faith.

The series of fissions within Christianity is one clear indicator of this journey. Once the unity of the church had been broken in the separation between East and West, which culminated in the eleventh century, Western Christianity became unstable, having been critically injured in its relationship to the deep unitive center.

Once the *koinonia*[42] has been lost (and the wisdom of this communion is inseparable from the East), the church assumes a false *persona*, becoming identified with its institutional container. Now a unitive Christianity and a cosmic Christianity become inconceivable; the unitive ground disappears from view beneath a splendid pavement and we are once again enclosed within the law. As the chosen people, we are forever at enmity with the rest of creation. Paradoxically, the chosen stone, the foundation stone, the stone of union, has been rejected once again by the builders, and the building will soon begin to crumble.

Mediator, Mediation, Means, Media, Money

The West, in the course of its history, has been more and more defined by the middle term, the Second Order, secondary reality—that which comes between, and separates the person from primary reality. A structure of rational thought separates me from the reality that it puts into order for me. A highly developed tool separates me from direct physical contact with the material with which I am working. A modern weapon separates the attacker from his prey, and a more advanced weapon places the slaughter out of sight of its perpetrators. Technology separates humanity from the earth and environment. Success separates one from the roots of one's life. Affluence disconnects me from the life-giving realities that surround me. At the same time, science and technology bring the world into our living room so that we may share, to some degree, the experience of the people most distant from us. In this ambivalent situation we easily follow the line of least resistance, the gravitational slope into comfortable isolation. The media connect and disconnect us at the same time; there is a sinister possibility that while we are connected superficially we are being disconnected at a deeper, more human level.

9. The Critical Period: Shadow and Light

The *critical* phase of Western history, within which we have now lived for centuries, has been a time of severe

trial for Christianity. Today, however, we can see some of the positive fruits of this austere passage. Most important, perhaps, is the purification and liberation of the gospel— of the essential New Testament message—when clearly distinguished from its particular cultural embodiments. The "container" of Greco-Roman and medieval European mentality and law is being surgically differentiated from the Word itself. The Word is released from its confinement in static structures to confront new questions and develop new responses. The long-standing and too often untroubled coexistence of the old wisdom[43] with unjust and oppressive social structures comes to an end. The creative potential of the Word becomes newly active in the world on this social, economic, and political level. At the same time, the creative potential of the human person emerges to realize itself in a newly opened space of freedom.

The critical phase of Western history has been necessary; this becomes evident as we come to see the "shadow" of the preceding developments. We are already aware of the dark side of the critical era itself, however: nihilism, reductionism, atheism, isolation, despair. That the development of Western critical rationality has been both necessary and fruitful appears from a number of perspectives.

New Encounters, New Questions

The old wisdom remained within a theological enclosure (a quasi-monastic cloister) that systematically exempted it from considering many questions that would prove urgent for Christians exposed to the winds of world and history. New questions demanded a new language, new processes of thought, and a different kind of attention to concrete realities. The verticality and interiority of the patristic and medieval sapiential mind, together with its unconscious presuppositions, condemned it to give inappropriate answers to existential questions, practical questions, to questions involving human life experience beyond the experience of the patristic-monastic thinkers.

The emergence of a *secular world* brought this inadequacy fully into view. It was then that the Western mind experienced a kind of puberty, an awakening to the dimensions and energies of a wider world than had been confronted by the fathers, who lived still within the womb of a classical worldview. In the confrontation of the faith with critical reason, and in the intellectual space this encounter produced, a maturing Christian humanity learned to dialogue with that which it was to meet in its further journey.

Transformative Dynamism of the Gospel

The old wisdom's perspective excluded essential areas of concern, especially with such human issues as freedom, social rights, equality. The old wisdom might have lived on forever in contented self-sufficiency without confronting the flaws in existing social structures; Christians were not encouraged to realize the gospel's mandate and potential to transform the world. Here, in fact, are two lines of development of the gospel seed that might have remained dormant but for the emergence of critical rationality and its focusing on human society and its institutions. First there sounds once again the prophetic voice of the gospel, which was not sufficiently heard in the sapiential world of antiquity. Second, there emerge the charism and power of church and Christian not only to create an enclave of grace and communion within the world, but to recreate the very structures of human society.

The primacy of communion in the relations between people of different race, gender, and economic station, which the gospel ordains, implies a transformation of society that has still only begun.

> There is neither Jew nor Greek, there is neither slave nor free, there is neither male nor female; for you are all one in Christ Jesus. (Gal 3:28)

The scope of Paul's words is not limited to the interior of the Christian community. Implicit here is the creative influence of gospel (and of those who accept the gospel) on human society in general. The same could be said of other areas of activity in this world. The old wisdom often remained too other-worldly to exert on this world the transformative power that is inherent in the gospel.

Cultural Discrimination

The gospel becomes closed and immobilized when it is no longer distinguished from the particular cultural embodiments that it has assumed. This has been the case in Western Christianity where the gospel, embodied in the forms of Greek thought and Roman institution, and then in the structures of medieval "Gothic" society, came to be indistinguishable from this enormous edifice. The liberation from confinement within the Jewish culture, which was accomplished largely by Paul, is the archetypal instance of this critical purification, and demonstrates the freedom, mobility, and fecundity, the simplicity, clarity, and power, of the gospel seed. The old wisdom, however, in so far as it remained precritical, was not able to accomplish this essential work of purification, nor to liberate the gospel for further incarnations.

Withdrawal of Projections

> Hypocrite! First take the log out of your own eye, and then you will see clearly to remove the speck from your neighbor's eye. (Mt 7:5)

A precritical consciousness is a naive consciousness. Consequently, it projects on someone outside itself the contents of its own "shadow," particularly its own unacknowledged defects. The negative form of this phenomenon is evident in the long series of hostile confrontations (particularly with its critics) in the history of the Western church. The pattern begins in the conflict with Judaism, continues through the long struggle with Islam and then with Eastern Christianity and the Protestant Reformers, to appear in the conflicts with secular critics (Marx, Freud, and others) in the twentieth century. In each case, criticism is rejected and attributed to the malice and viciousness of the adversary. One's own egoism and self-serving ways, one's own unconscious violence and heartlessness, are seen only in the other.

A striking collective example of this is our failure to recognize the faithlessness and self-serving ways of the chief priests, scribes, and Pharisees of the gospel in our own house, while continuing to attribute these qualities only to the *others*, the Jewish leaders of the time of Jesus. Both Testaments are full of the prophetic light of self-criticism, but our eyes only very slowly become open to it. After the critical bath of the past few centuries, we begin to be able to look at ourselves and our own institutions in a balanced way, and to recognize the same shadows in our own tradition that we have always so readily seen over there.

Liberation of Creative Potential

The emerging voice of individual reason announces the beginning of a new creative emergence that will proceed in other directions as well. The individual person begins to trust his or her own ability to perceive reality, to reflect on reality and develop a new vision of reality, and then to transform external reality. An overwhelming weight of sacred tradition no longer quenches the creative impulse before it can develop confidence in itself, in its own validity. Gradually a space of creative freedom opens, within the culture and within the individual consciousness, in which new ideas can breed and grow. Humanity begins to shake off an ancient torpor and to initiate change, to recreate human society and the world itself. The whole process is mocked by ambiguity; monsters come to birth, creativity is conscripted by forces of greed and violence. Despite these huge shadows, human reason gradually learns to serve the human values of life, community, and freedom. Critical reason becomes more subtly and self-critically *rational*. Through a developing rationality, humanity and the human person discover the fire of creativity with which they are endowed, and begin to assume their responsibility to remake the world in unity and love.

10. Progression in Christianity: *Redshift*

A characteristic movement appears everywhere in nature, in human life, and with a particular modality in

Christianity. The progression from seed to mature plant to fruit, in the New Testament, becomes the movement from faith to love, from light to fire, from baptism to eucharist, from water to blood. This *redshift* also appears repeatedly in the history of spirituality. From a long-range perspective, it is the movement from a first to a second wisdom,[44] from a spirituality determined principally by One and Two to a spirituality that explicitly integrates Three and Four.

Christianity has frequently been understood from a single perspective, as have monasticism and other forms of religious community within the Christian world. Christian life, however, always involves dialogue, dialectic, a circulation of life between its multiple poles that reflects the reciprocal indwelling of divine Persons within the Trinity. Buddhism can be imagined as a *circle* with its single center.[45] The inner structure of Christianity, however, is more complex: It is determined not only by the single center of the absolute Mystery, but also by several principles. The purpose of this book is to develop these principles and their configuration. Frequently this Christian Mystery manifests an inner movement between two poles or epicenters that can be represented by an *ellipse.* The two poles, from different perspectives, may be understood as ineffable God (I) and divine Word (II) (or Mystery and manifestation), as baptism and eucharist, as solitude and community, as contemplation and love.

We have referred to a "redshift" in Christian spirituality, borrowing an analogy from contemporary physics. The redshift (or, more generally, the Doppler effect) is observed in this way:

> When a source emits light of a particular wavelength and the source is moving away from us, the wavelength appears longer to us: the color of the light (if it is visible) is shifted toward the red end of the visible spectrum, an effect known as the redshift. If the source moves toward us, the color shifts toward the blue (shorter wavelength) end of the spectrum. The amount of shift depends on the velocity of the source.[46]

A familiar example is the whistle of a train that whizzes past us as we stand on the platform of a railroad station: The tone of the whistle falls sharply as the train moves away from us into the distance. The observed effect is the same whether the source is moving away from us or we are moving away from the source. The redshift observed in the light that comes from stars in distant galaxies is evidence for the hypothesis that the universe is expanding, and consequently for the "big bang" theory of its beginning.

A parallel principle is written into history and into the course of our lives. The analogy is not perfect, for the level of energy may be increasing rather than falling as we move from white to red, but it is widely applicable. The expression "redshift" conveys the feeling-tone of this movement. Wherever we travel historically from East to West, the redshift is observed, as when we go from the pure white light of dawn to the last red sunlight poured out on the horizon in the evening.

It is as if the intrinsic direction of spiritual energy is toward *incarnation,* just as the intrinsic movement of faith is toward *love.* In the New Testament we find both this faith-to-love dynamic and some suggestive parallel expressions.

> This is he who came by water and blood, Jesus Christ, not with the water only but with the water and the blood. (1 Jn 5:6)

> ...and if I have all faith, so as to remove mountains, but have not love, I am nothing. (1 Cor 13:2)

> Love never ends...as for our knowledge, it will pass away. For our knowledge is imperfect and our prophecy is imperfect; but when the perfect comes, the imperfect will pass away.... For now we see in a mirror dimly, but then face to face. Now I know in part, then I shall understand fully, even as I have been fully understood. So faith, hope, love abide, these three; but the greatest of these is love. (1 Cor 13:8–13)

There is a natural movement from the illumination of baptism to the unitive self-gift or oblation of eucharist, and from light to fire, from manifestation to transformation, illumination to union (recall the classic "three ways" or three stages of the spiritual life: purgative, illuminative, unitive).

> Abide in me, as I abide in you. Just as the branch cannot bear fruit by itself unless it abides in the vine, neither can you unless you abide in me. I am the vine, you are the branches. Those who abide in me and I in them bear much fruit.... If you abide in me, and my words abide in you, ask for whatever you wish, and it will be done for you. My Father is glorified by this, that you bear much fruit and become my disciples. (Jn 15:4–5, 7–8, NRSV)

The movement is from faith to obedience, and through remaining in the obedience of faith to bearing the fruit of love.

> And this is his commandment, that we should believe in the name of his Son Jesus Christ and love one another, just as he has commanded us. (1 Jn 3:23)

This movement becomes most explicit in John's gospel and first letter, and in the letters of Paul. We also hear it continually as the synoptic gospels recount Jesus' teaching, and we see it in the movement of his own life. The life of Jesus moves essentially from his baptism to his eucharistic death, from the water to the blood. In more general terms, his life progresses from revelation to union: from the manifestation of the kingdom of God in his presence and teaching to the communication of divine life through his death. Inherent in this progression is the way of the cross, the law of growth by following Jesus in his journey (see Mk 8:34–35). Progression from light to fire, from water to wine, is through this wood of the cross.

The movement is found wherever a tradition opens, branches out, bends from a strictly vertical movement to express itself laterally. It is the evolution that leads from *Hinayana* to *Mahayana*[47] in Buddhism, from law to grace, and from an inwardly focused Judaism to a Christian church that incorporates "Gentiles" (that is, all peoples) as well as Jews.

In our present phase of all-embracing transition, we are experiencing this phenomenon of the redshift in a broad and very dramatic way. A central instance of this is in the emergence of woman, of the feminine, in the world; and first, in the Western world. We see the progression symbolically suggested in the story of Adam and Eve in the garden. Everything was quite simple while Adam was the only human being. Then Eve was taken from Adam's side and the displacement or redshift began; a gate began to open in the side of the garden. Instead of a circle, there is now an ellipse; rather than everything orbiting around a single center, now we have two epicenters. Process develops as everything unrolls from this initial tilt.

Movements of monastic renewal (those especially that "go East" in the sense of a strong contemplative orientation and a solitary emphasis) often attempt to recover the original experience, to move back upstream against the movement of redshift to the pure white light of the dawn, the Source, the baptismal initiation. But sooner or later, if they survive, an internal law forces them to develop once again toward red, toward the eucharistic pole.

11. The Gospel of Matthew: Christianity as the New Torah

In Matthew's Gospel, Jesus appears as a new Moses, authoritative teacher of the new Israel that is the church. Christianity appears as the new Torah, particularly in the Sermon on the Mount and the other great Matthean sermons. This role and authority of Jesus are conferred on his apostles, as Jesus establishes a church that will endure until the end of time and entrusts to them, in the figure of Peter, the keys of the kingdom of Heaven. It is this vision that has been dominant in the Petrine, or Roman Catholic, tradition of Western Christianity. While Matthew presents the new Torah of Jesus as a revolutionary and _liberating_ teaching, and presents Jesus himself as the divine Wisdom embodied in a human person, these expansive dimensions have very often remained unnoticed while the more institutional aspects of Matthew's Gospel have prevailed.

Matthew conceives Christianity and the church as a _fulfillment_ of Judaism and Israel. This fulfillment is also a radical transformation, an apparent revolution (see, for example, the antitheses of the Sermon on the Mount); yet it remains within the fundamental perspective of Torah. The Torah is brought to its perfection and its simple unity in Jesus, who is the divine Wisdom embodied, and in the double law of love (love of God joined with love of neighbor; see Mt 22:35–40). The church is to remain in this world until the end, and Jesus Christ will remain present with it. Among the four gospels, it is Matthew who most closely suggests the development of an "early Catholicism"[48]—both in his presentation of Jesus' teaching as a new Torah and in his presentation of Jesus as authoritative Founder, conferring a divine authority on his immediate disciples.

> And Jesus answered him, "Blessed are you, Simon Barjona! For flesh and blood has not revealed this to you, but my Father who is in heaven. And I tell you, you are Peter, and on this rock I will build my church, and the powers of death shall not prevail against it. I will give you the keys of the kingdom of heaven, and whatever you bind on earth shall be bound in heaven, and whatever you loose on earth shall be loosed in heaven." (Mt 16:17–19)

> Now the eleven disciples went to Galilee, to the mountain to which Jesus had directed them. And when they saw him they worshiped him; but some doubted. And Jesus came and said to them, "All authority in heaven and on earth has been given to me. Go therefore and make disciples of all nations, baptizing them in the name of the Father and of the Son and of the Holy Spirit, teaching them to observe all that I have commanded you; and lo, I am with you always, to the close of the age." (Mt 28:16–20)

12. Two: A Meditation

> You...! Turning back your light look within; do not try to memorize my words. Since the beginningless past you have turned your backs to the light, throwing yourselves into darkness. The root of false thinking goes deeply into the ground; it is hard to pull it out.[49]

Young light goes eagerly forward into the world, finding and caressing all the things that have come forth from it. Breaking itself delightedly on their surfaces, light forgets its own simplicity, its solitary beginning within the infinite intensity, the mountain of the invisible. Light is the mane of a galloping stallion, the spray of a wave of the sea. Light is the jovial face of noon, pure joy of the fountain's spume, rising strong and free in the sun and then sailing wide on a shifting play of wind, hair blown across a laughing face.

Forgetful, outgoing light creates a world again, but now a world of exteriors, of surfaces. It is a world that reflects from face to face, forgetful of the unending reflection within, forgetful of the well of light within light within light. Light is a ball tossed in the air, a surging clump of children in the playground, an incessant spring of variations.

Now there is a coming of age, an initiation, a baptism of light. Awakening from its naivete to know itself once again, light, illumined, dwells within itself consciously once more. Light, dwelling within itself, is newly alive; knowing itself, knowing the Source.

Light, knowing the Source, yet remains bound. Knowing all things through innerness, yet light remains itself, enclosed within a diamond solitude even as it bestows itself. As light comes to light the faces of all things, they too remain still imprisoned within themselves, within the glistening perfection of their planes. Light must go out of itself if it is to bring them out of themselves, into themselves, into its own depths.

One came into the world who was the light from which the world came forth. He was in the world as a stranger; the world did not know him. He knew himself and knew the world, but not as the world knew itself. He came as a poor man, without wings of splendor, came walking and speaking. There was, however, an authority in him as of the Beginning, and every particle of light turned toward him in expectancy.

We have seen him, and have awakened once again; we have seen the light before which and beyond which there is no other. We have seen him come in the half-darkness of this world and walk among the prisoners, the poor and the lame and the blind. We have seen this light go where light had never gone, and shine in the darkness that had never yet dreamed of light.

*Faithful disciples and learned scholars of the light, we are gath-
ered here today, as you know, to judge this man's case. You have heard
him yourselves. He claims not only to speak for the light, but to be the
light! And yet he consorts with darkness, with the ignorant, the law-
less, with evildoers and traitors to our nation and tradition. He breaks
the sabbath, claiming to overrule our law by the authority of mere
human kindness. He rails against the learned and the just ones among
us, the scribes and Pharisees. How can he be light, this one who strikes
down the light and raises the darkness? And yet who among us has not
been struck by his appearance, by his words. We know him to be an
ignorant Galilean, but who has seen him overcome in argument? With
a few words he puts our questions back in our mouths. Honorable col-
leagues, I am tormented by the decision that lies before us, and yet we
must make it. In the name of all that we represent, we must put out this
light; it cannot be the true light which we serve, the final light which
we await.*

And then they put out the light, and we were in darkness. It
was a deeper darkness than ever before, yet somewhere we were
aware of quiet light. We had surrendered ourselves to the darkness, had embraced our hopelessness and would not grasp the
frail hope of that light. Our hearts failed within us and we
wrapped ourselves in darkness and sleep.

Early in the morning on the first day of the week, the
women had gone to the tomb and found a young man in shining
garments who told them that he had risen from the dead.

And then he came and stood among us, as before.

The light is coming up out of the ground, the light is
breaking within our hearts. This is not something mental, not
a matter of thoughts, of ideas. I know that my body is light,
though I do not know what this means. And the light within
me does not simply remain light; it has a life within my life,
and becomes a flowing wine, a living water that seeks out
other hearts. As I live and labor under the sun, the light within
me ripens into love.

It is a love that flows freely wherever there is life, that flows
into the hollows and low places of human hearts. The love is a light
that knows the resurrection in the heart, the absolution and leaping up of life, a new creation and birth from our compound hope-

lessness, our willing embrace of darkness. Light and love, wedded, are this stream that moves gaily forward full of sun, washing the hearts of the dead and embracing them suddenly into life.

So abundantly and so reliably did the light come forth that it was soon taken for granted and gradually denatured. Trapped and contained, it was distributed as a public utility. Thoroughly domesticated, it poured dependably from each family's tap. Incarnated, the light had brought forth its fruit of life. Materialized, it generated cultures, institutions, civilizations, schools of learning and of the arts. So abundant was the fructifying of the light that the light itself was left behind once again, in the great shadow that is behind us.

The light that had come from heaven to earth was now separated both from heaven and from earth by the constructions of the good and the wise. Light has been thoroughly housed, enclosed in an intermediate realm governed by the institutional elites of doctrine, of science, of political and economic power.

As this human appropriation of the light progresses, the temple of religion is gradually supplanted by the temple of science, as supreme repository of the light. Priests and princes of the light are now the priests and chieftains of science and critical rationality. The old pieties are hewn to bits with flashing blades.

Light reappears on the edges of things, with a new sharpness. A new and precise geometry is born nearly full-grown, redefining the world. Light has become a knife that distinguishes and divides, a rod that measures. A sharp and gleaming new world is born, humming with the play of perfect parts, cut and oiled.

This being of light, the angel of this new world, is not entirely unkind. Broad wheels spool forth an endless swath of cloth, warm and colorful. We are more comfortable than ever before.

Light has found itself to be a stranger in a new way, become a perfect stranger to itself. Peevish and terribly sharp, it shreds the sacred scrolls, unweaves what had been woven with such care. It demolishes the achievements of the centuries. Furiously it erases all that had been written, tears up all that had been set down, as if desperate to find something that had been forgotten and buried beneath the successive deposits. All the treasures are turned to trash in the frantic violence of this ignorant light. Wisdom is ignorance and ignorance is wisdom once again.

In the simplicity of this light that is everywhere around me
In the silence of this light that is within me
I am.

A word has been spoken;
Struck, the world spins out in its direction.
We go.
Another knowing steals upon us.
In a larger warmth
We open toward one another.

Three

The Music

Introduction

Our Third Order (see Figure 3.1) is energy: the energy both of movement and of relationship, resonance, communion. Reality, from this perspective, is process, newness, immediate personal experience. The Spirit is immanent everywhere and manifest in the evolution of the cosmos, in human history, in the developing experience of a community and of an individual. Spirit differs from Word in its mode of continuity, which is the continuity of music and of interior feeling rather than that of order and structure. It is in the living moment that Spirit is most often known: as power, as illumination, as the movement of relationship, the enkindling of love, as inner experience itself.

In the New Testament, the manifestation of the Holy Spirit is described in terms of its "fruits": love, joy, peace, patience, kindness, goodness, faithfulness, gentleness, self-control (Gal 5:22–23). The Spirit is experienced in a deep new communion between believers, and in a new depth of subjectivity[1] within the individual person. The Spirit is characterized by freedom and by a new intuitive knowledge of God and the divine Word. But the work of the Spirit cannot be circumscribed: Immanent within all creation, it is yet freshly poured out through faith in Jesus Christ, to begin a new work within the world. The Spirit is the inner life of the church.

A decisive threshold within the New Testament is the transition from the time of Jesus' bodily presence in the world to the time of the Spirit, after Jesus' death and resurrection. This is the moment of the crossover from law to Spirit, from grace to Spirit, from letter to Spirit. The Spirit is the essential *newness,* the divine life and creative energy, which is the indwelling and enduring gift of Christ. It is the one gift that embraces and animates the whole work of God in the world. The Spirit is not merely the agent of a new creation, but the unitive divine self-communication itself.

Poetry, music, and art are, from the perspective of our mandalic figure, of the order of Spirit and express this third dimension

89

of human life. The immanent and unitive Spirit, as the divine Feminine, is the inner wisdom and power that moves the history of humankind toward its consummation. The ever-impending "Age of the Spirit," imagined as a third and final age of history, is the phase of convergence and integration. This is the time of a sapiential reunion of that which has been divided, in the unitive divine immanence, the Spirit.

It is in "Three" that we encounter *plurality,* a seeming infinity of expressions, like the sudden multiplicity of tongues on Pentecost day. Three is the world of change, of newness, creative imagination, metaphor, of an endless extravagance of variations on one theme, simple and all-embracing. With an intrinsic and exultant self-assurance, energy expresses itself in a bewildering profusion of movements and forms. Each spiritual world has its own version of the central energy itself: *prāna, shakti, ch'i, ruach, pneuma,* the Holy Spirit; this energy expresses itself freely in a variety of ways. A jovial plurality of manifestation characterizes both the energy of the psyche and that physical energy which constitutes the universe.

As there is a central well within us where thoughts disappear into the unitive depths, so there is an ardent boundary within us where thought becomes fire. Such is the threshold between Word and Spirit in the New Testament: that boundary between gospels and Acts where the pentecostal fire burns.

Here begins a new country, ruled by a new law: that of the Spirit. This place is symbolized by the flames that surmount Russian churches, those bulbs of golden fire that ascend from the roof of religion into the invisible. As we cross this border, we must leave behind our maps; at least we must be ready to surrender them to the fire. Here is a new "apophatic," other than the silent depths of the One, yet one and the same.

When I discover myself as a unitive energy, welling forth from the darkness of the ground, I have found myself, I am at home.

ONE

TWO

THREE
DYNAMIC DIMENSION
(MUSIC)

THE HOLY SPIRIT
LUKE'S GOSPEL
MORAL-TROPOLOGICAL SENSE
PSYCHE
FEMININE DIMENSION
ENERGY

FOUR

FIGURE 3.1

1. Transition from Two to Three: The New Testament

The movement from Old Covenant to New Covenant is, approximately, the transition from Second Order to Third Order. This transition, while it is centered in the death and resurrection of Jesus, also generates the dramatic conflict that dominates the New Testament writings. It is most apparent in the life of Jesus, as narrated in the four gospels, and then in the life and teaching of Paul.

Jesus

Jesus appears, in the gospels, against the background of the Jewish religion of his time. Throughout the story of his life, the opposition of the Jewish authorities (scribes, Pharisees, elders, temple officials, and chief priests) sounds recurrently as a harsh refrain. It is this opposition that leads to his death. Jesus' teaching and works, in the view of the New Testament writers, thus herald an exodus from the closed Second Order of institutional Judaism, the religion of the Law, to a worship in spirit and truth (see Jn 4:23) animated by the indwelling divine Spirit. From this aspect the new life that Jesus teaches and imparts is a life in the Third Order, the order of the Holy Spirit.

John the Baptist announces the coming Messiah as the one who will baptize not merely with water but with the Holy Spirit (Mk 1:8). The newness of Jesus' ministry is recognized immediately in the power that accompanies his teaching (Mk 1:27). Very soon after he has begun his work, there will be heard the reaction of the scribes, custodians of the law. Jesus' response is a further manifestation of the power of the Spirit.

> And when Jesus saw their faith, he said to the paralytic, "My son, your sins are forgiven." Now some of the scribes were sitting there, questioning in their hearts, "Why does this man speak thus? It is blasphemy! Who can forgive sins but God alone?" And immediately Jesus, perceiving in his spirit that they thus questioned within themselves, said to them, "Why do you question thus in your hearts? Which is easier, to say to the paralytic, 'Your sins are forgiven,' or to say, 'Rise, take up your pallet and walk'? But that you may know that the Son of man has authority on earth to forgive sins"—he said to the paralytic—"I say to you, rise, take up your pallet and go home." And he rose, and immediately took up the pallet and went out before them all; so that they were all amazed and glorified God, saying, "We never saw anything like this!" (Mk 2:5–12)

The Jewish law prohibiting activity on the sabbath (and thus the sabbath observance itself) becomes a symbol for the old order, this arrested Second Order, which Jesus opens to its fullness. He defends his hungry disciples for plucking ears of grain on the sabbath.

> Then he said to them, "The sabbath was made for humankind, and not humankind for the sabbath; so the Son of man is lord even of the sabbath." (Mk 2:27–28, NRSV)

When Jesus, again and again, heals on the sabbath, in apparent violation of this Mosaic law, "the law of the Spirit of life in Christ Jesus" (Rom 8:2) challenges the static Second Order directly and radically. The legalists' fury hardens into a lethal resolve (see Mk 3:1–6).

When Jesus' last journey brings him to Jerusalem, his conflict with this closed Second Order enters its final, deadly phase. This will conclude with his death and resurrection and the gift of the Holy Spirit, which will initiate Jesus' disciples into the Third Order: life in the Spirit.

Paul

Paul is our living model of the movement from Two to Three. Unlike Jesus, Paul shows us within himself both sides of the transition. He turns a complete about-face: From zealous Pharisee and enforcer of the law against the new sect of disciples of Jesus, he becomes the preacher of Christ and of the freedom of the Spirit. The same dramatic conflict between Two and Three is graphically continued in Paul's lifelong struggle with the Judaizers, those who would (much like Paul himself before his conversion) impose the Jewish law on new Christians. We see it also in the explosive outward movement of his ministry, from Judea toward the Gentiles.

This movement from Two to Three is woven into Paul's writings, where it appears in a variety of forms. It is explicit in his doctrine, and implicit in the way in which he frequently uses words. In the heat of the Spirit, words rise into the energy field of the Christ-mystery, losing much of their distinctness to become alternative expressions of the one great reality:

"...in Christ Jesus, whom God made our wisdom, our righteousness and sanctification and redemption" (1 Cor 1:30). The transition from Two to Three is powerfully expressed in each of Paul's great epistles, most clearly where he speaks of the movement from Judaism to Christ and denotes the closed Second Order as the *law*.

> But now we are discharged from the law, dead to that which held us captive, so that we serve not under the old written code but in the new life of the Spirit. (Rom 7:6)

> For the law of the Spirit of life in Christ Jesus has set me free from the law of sin and death. (Rom 8:2)

> Now before faith came, we were imprisoned and guarded under the law until faith would be revealed. Therefore the law was our disciplinarian until Christ came, so that we might be justified by faith. But now that faith has come, we are no longer subject to a disciplinarian, for in Christ Jesus you are all children of God through faith. As many of you as were baptized into Christ have clothed yourselves with Christ. There is no longer Jew or Greek, there is no longer slave or free, there is no longer male and female; for all of you are one in Christ Jesus.... And because you are children, God has sent the Spirit of his Son into our hearts, crying, "Abba! Father!" (Gal 3:23–28, 4:6, NRSV)

2. Luke and Acts: The Divine Movement

In contrast to the quasi-institutional image of Christianity we have seen in Matthew's gospel (as an authoritative and enduring church), Luke presents Christianity as energy and movement: as the forward impulse of the Holy Spirit driving Jesus to his consummation at Jerusalem and then (in Acts) as the wave of outward movement of the gospel as it is impelled by the Holy Spirit from Jerusalem to the farthest reaches of humanity. Luke has written, in his two books, the Gospel of the Holy Spirit. Jesus, in his preaching and healing, his parables and miracles, announces and initiates the outpouring of divine life that is the heart of this historical movement.

Within the New Testament, it is Paul and Luke who most fully and clearly express what we have called the Third Order. We have already glimpsed, in Paul's letters, the breaking through from a closed and hardened Second Order, in the form of law and conformity, to the Third Order as Spirit, grace, and freedom. The explosive energy of this paschal breakthrough is felt again and again in Paul's writing.

In Luke's Gospel and in the Acts of the Apostles, the same movement is expressed in a narrative that, in its two great parts, constitutes the Gospel of the Holy Spirit. The energy of this new Third Order (the order of divine energy) is both the driving force of the events that are narrated, and the life of each episode. This divine Spirit is a leaven that fills Luke's writing with an exultant gracefulness and makes scene after scene inexplicably luminous, moving, and unforgettable.

Luke conceives the Christ-movement as a continuation of the salvation history of Israel, impelled by a new and powerful infusion of the Holy Spirit. Christianity is seen in essentially dynamic terms, as an expression of the immanent energy of the Spirit and as a historical wave that pushes outward toward the end of the earth, the fullness of humanity. Jesus himself is understood as the Spirit-bearer. After Pentecost, he is experienced in this energy and movement of the Spirit—both within the individual person and in the larger flow of salvation history, onward and outward.

In Matthew's view, the unitive mediation between God and humanity is completely constituted by Jesus, the embodied divine Wisdom. Through listening to the word of Jesus and living it, and ultimately through the imitation of Jesus, the disciple does the will of God and is saved. Luke, on the other hand, sees the unitive mediation between God and humanity in terms of the Holy Spirit, present within the disciple and the community, and impelling the Word forward toward its fulfillment in the whole world.

Jesus in the Exultant Freedom of the Spirit

Luke inaugurates Jesus' public ministry with a dramatic scene: in Nazareth, his own village, Jesus enters the synagogue on the sabbath day. He stands up to read, and the book of the prophet Isaiah is handed to him.

> He opened the book and found the place where it was written, "The Spirit of the Lord is upon me, because he has anointed me to preach good news to the poor. He has sent me to proclaim release to the captives and recovering of sight to the blind, to set at liberty those who are oppressed, to proclaim the acceptable year of the Lord." And he closed the book, and gave it back to the attendant, and sat down; and the eyes of all in the synagogue were fixed on him. And he began to say to them, "Today this scripture has been fulfilled in your hearing." (Lk 4:16–21)

For Luke, this text of Isaiah summarizes Jesus' mission. The words are music: an exultant canticle of the manifestation of the Spirit, the outpouring of grace. This jubilant music is characteristic of our Third Order. The Jesus of Luke's gospel is messianic Spirit-bearer, life-giver, liberator. The Jesus that Luke presents to us is the anointed One who brings with him, and radiates around himself, the joy and freedom of the Spirit.

This energy is expressed at the beginning of the story (1:39–45), when John leaps in the womb of his mother at the approach of Jesus in Mary's womb. Continually shining through Jesus' encounters with people, it bursts forth clearly now and then.

> In that same hour he rejoiced in the Holy Spirit and said, "I thank you, Father, Lord of heaven and earth, that you have hidden these things from the wise and understanding and revealed them to babes; yes, Father, for such was your gracious will. All things have been delivered to me by my Father; and no one knows who the Son is except the Father, or who the Father is except the Son and any one to whom the Son chooses to reveal him." Then turning to the disciples he said privately, "Blessed are the eyes which see what you see! For I tell you that many prophets and kings desired to see what you see, and did not see it, and to hear what you hear, and did not hear it." (Lk 10:21–24)

Burning in the hearts of the two disciples, as they walk with Jesus on the road to Emmaus and listen to him revealing his presence in the Scriptures, the Spirit's exultant energy flashes out when he makes himself known to them.

> When he was at table with them, he took the bread and blessed, and broke it, and gave it to them. And their eyes were opened and they recognized him; and he vanished out of their sight. They said to each other, "Did not our hearts burn within us while he talked to us on the road, while he opened to us the scriptures?" (Lk 24:30–32)

When Jesus, risen from the tomb, appears to the disciples, they "disbelieve with joy" (Lk 24:41). When he had ascended from them at Bethany, "they returned to Jerusalem with great joy, and were continually in the temple blessing God"(Lk 24:52–53).

This jubilant energy erupts again and again in the Acts of the Apostles. On Pentecost day the disciples, tumbling from the upper room in the power and joy of the Spirit, seem to skeptical onlookers to be "filled with new wine" (Acts 2:13). The cripple healed by Peter and John at the Beautiful Gate of the temple does not struggle painfully to his feet, but "leaping up he stood and walked and entered the temple with them, walking and leaping and praising God" (Acts 3:8). That studious pilgrim, the eunuch whom Philip baptized, "went on his way rejoicing" (Acts 8:39). The repeated apostolic jailbreaks (Acts 5, 12, 16), like the open tomb with its stone rolled away, express with force and abounding good humor, like some great laugh of the Spirit, the uncontainable freedom of this new divine Energy. Even the humiliated jailer of Paul and Silas, having been persuaded not to kill himself, "rejoiced with all his household that he had believed in God" (Acts 16:34).

The Jesus of Luke's narratives is surrounded with this joy of the Holy Spirit. It is felt even in his words from the cross to his fellow sufferer: "Truly, I say to you, today you will be with me in Paradise" (Lk 23:43). The sapiential and unitive depth of the Lukan narratives can be found in this very energy. The divine fullness, the unitive wisdom, has become pure actuality in Luke and Acts.

3. The Third Age

Christian tradition abounds in three-stage schemes; this is a reflection of the fundamental and comprehensive trinitarian mystery. Some of them have been adopted from earlier sources, like the spiritual scheme of purgation, illumination, and union. Others have originated directly from the Christian mystery, such as that of Joachim of Fiore, who conceived the whole of history in terms of three ages, corresponding to the Father, to Christ, and to the Holy Spirit.[2]

The New Wisdom

The new wisdom is *Holy Spirit.* It is feminine, but not only feminine. It flees definition by exceeding definition, by flying rings and ellipses, ovals and spheroids around the definition. It is more than "wisdom" or any other term, exceeds every concept and word. It is the fullness that is seething in each moment, that is swelling within the *Now.* It is neither head nor center. It has no center, and yet it is nothing but center; it is center everywhere: all possibility at every point. *Now.* It is all here now. Your life is a body that is at every point on its surface in contact with infinity, and is developing a sense for this new reality. The reality is new because it is absolute newness, and comprehensible by none of your senses while pouring in through all your senses.

The new wisdom is not a wisdom, not an elite tenured track, not any track, any way. It is all ways and no way. Here you begin every moment at zero and quickly arrive at the speed of light. It is necessary to be always beginning, always coming from zero, and, therefore, always coming into the maximum, into the totality.

An autumn morning light spilling through the window recalls that which comes into the world and grows to fullness here, the stone of Daniel that is cut out of the mountain without hands, that rolls down and smashes the statue, and then itself grows into a mountain and fills the whole world. This is not mere fantasy. It is our intimation of the fullness that is stirring within us, within our consciousness and our timid train of thought and our body itself. The act of imagination is its exploratory cast into the waiting space of this world. Our fictions are but soundings of the whole gaping length and breadth of the inert and impossible, into which the fullness of possibility serenely flows from the human heart, the human mind.

Perhaps the first wisdom[3] with its "center," and the monasticism that was its visible embodiment, is the Jerusalem from which we must begin, the central place where we await the power of the Spirit that comes from on high (see Lk 24:45–53). Then we shall emigrate from the magnificent center into the nowhere, the no-center that is everywhere, the life of the children of God who graze on every hill, feed in every place, who carry the Divinity naturally and as if unconsciously in their bodies.

The second wisdom is a knowledge of metaphor, knowledge of a river of likeness that winds through all creation, nourishing the extremes of diversity, gathering the farthest-flung in its all-penetrating simplicity and purity. It is a bazaar, an open gate and market where they come from all directions to tell you the one thing that you do not know. You recognize them by the one thing shining in their eyes, though their robes and turbans are of many strange styles and wild colors, though their features are brown and yellow and black and red, though their gestures are barbaric and refined, the movements of peasants and kings. They all bring the same essence in its thousand forms, and its very preciousness, the entrancing living light of this gold, is its quickness, its mercurial manyness, its inexpressible consistency of all ways.

If there is a first faith that is listening with the heart, which is obedience, which is humility and the renunciation of self, there is a second faith that is *new creation*. Here the world wants to be reborn from within *one*. Here the self forgets itself as the plug blows out of the well and the plume shoots high into the sky, arching a cannonade of rainbows in the sun. The second faith is the faith of Pentecost, which sets out into a shattered world in the deep single surge of God's wisdom, with the all-fusing fire, the all-dissolving living stream that knows each different root, whispers the secret of one life everywhere in the earth.

The second faith is not law but liberty, not closing but opening, not wall but wind: the faith of a wisdom and power that does not turn back until it has liberated the world in its own jubilant movement. This faith is not structure but energy. Ultimate structure, essential order, is immanent in the energy. The order of a universe, the rectitude of gravity, are inherent in the movement, the life itself. This second faith is a movement that is one with your being, a faith and relationality that is unitive in its spontaneity, its continuity, its seamless origination and course. In this sense it is final. It is *love* that is thus seamless and sure, that moves with this final dignity and consummate presence.

We move, no doubt, between the two: from winter to spring and summer, and back again through fall. From contraction and darkness, from the prison of compunction to the pentecostal burgeoning. It does not seem an exaggeration, however, to say that Catholicism—and Western Christianity in general—has been unilaterally imprisoned within the first phase for most of its history. Christianity has rarely been able to realize itself as the divine energy in the world: a unitive energy that both liberates and sanctifies, that transforms and integrates the deepest and strongest human energies.

The new wisdom has a particular relation to Modernism, to modern poetry, to the art that springs from within and circles consciously, in its fragmentary assertions, around the indeterminate totality, the energy field.

> Why is everything called
> by another name:
> water is smoky pearl this first bright morning of spring in the
>   Minesceonga at a depth of 14 inches over granite
> birds are flutes
> grass is having its hair streaked
> last week's sleds are beached in the field
> it's all a big double-take, a dedoublement as the French say, a
>   haunting:
> the world is full of phantoms walking around in bodies.
> The primal stuffing is leaking out all over the place,
> it's bound to get mixed up either outside or inside human speech.
> What's the difference, the sages spend a lifetime trying to get to
>   that supreme point where

everything is everything else, and here it is happening down here on my level.[4]

4. Third Order Emergences Today

As the Third Order emerges in the West today, against several centuries' background of overdeveloped "Second Order" rationalist culture, it appears in numerous ways, on every side. Some of these appear under the rubric of *the* "New Paradigm." Perhaps the deepest movement is in the emergence of the feminine, and with this the reemergence of psyche and the dynamics of psyche. A movement from logos to life, from rationality to dynamics, from structure to process, and from external form and distinction to the more subtle levels of reality that are communion, resonance, participation: all of these tendencies indicate a breakthrough from the Second Order to the Third Order.[5]

Much of the contemporary Third Order emergence is captured by Richard Tarnas in his Epilogue to *The Passion of the Western Mind,* as, with a sweeping movement, he catalogs the various aspects of the feminine emergence in our Western culture today. After reviewing this phenomenon in its more explicit forms, he finds the feminine emerging within other movements:

> ...also in the increasing sense of unity with the planet and all forms of nature on it, in the increasing awareness of the ecological and the growing reaction against political and corporate policies supporting the domination and exploitation of the environment, in the growing embrace of the human community, in the accelerating collapse of long-standing political and ideological barriers separating the world's peoples, in the deepening recognition of the value and necessity of partnership, pluralism, and the interplay of many perspectives.

The feminine thread appears further in the many contemporary attempts to recover personal wholeness: in recovering a living relation with body, emotions, and imagination. The continuity is visible in the appreciation of indigenous cultures, and in the many spontaneous emergences of the archetypal feminine within the individual psyche today. Tarnas continues,

> It is evident as well in the great wave of interest in the mythological perspective, in esoteric disciplines, in Eastern mysticism, in shamanism, in archetypal and transpersonal psychology, in hermeneutics and other non-objectivist epistemologies, in scientific theories of the holonomic universe, morphogenetic fields, dissipative structures, chaos theory, the ecology of mind, the participatory universe—the list could go on and on.[6]

Included here are a number of movements that are related to one another intuitively rather than logically, and this corresponds to the shift itself; we might call it, metaphorically, a transition from Logos to Sophia. This is not just the shift to another single epistemology but the opening of consciousness to multiple epistemologies, to a spectrum of ways of knowing.

The general drift of these changes, however, is in a unitive direction. Included in this transition is the shift from objective (dualistic) to participatory consciousness and knowing. In our time it seems that some universal, immanent, unitive reality is emerging into human consciousness: a World Soul or immanent feminine principle. This is the continuum that relates the various movements that we have just reviewed; each of them expresses this unitive influence.

To the sampling above we might add contemporary developments in the worlds of poetry, music, painting—that is, in all the arts. We should need to examine successive stages of the emergence of the Third Order: Renaissance, Romanticism, Modernism. Within the world of music, jazz is an eruption into the mainstream Western culture of psychophysical energies from a prerational culture.

Within the Christian tradition, the emergence of Pentecostalism through the black churches into the mainstream is parallel to the appearance of jazz. The bursting through of a new energy in this way is at the same time a rediscovery of body and community: with the new dynamism comes a recovery of the incarnational dimension of the Christian reality.

The whole development of modern *psychology* can be seen as an emergence of the Third Order reality of *psyche*, through successive stages that move from a reductionist and quasi-mechanical psychology that mimics physical science to the subtle, intuitive, and holistic disciplines in which the authentic voice of psyche can be more and more nearly heard.[7]

We have seen the whole modern Western development as a colossal Second Order phenomenon. From another viewpoint it is a Third Order emergence as well—that is, from the perspective of human *creativity*. Creativity belongs particularly to the Third Order (as does the multiplicity it generates). Our modern era has been the time of the bursting forth of human creativity in all its varieties of expression, so as to bring into being a new, *secular* world. From the time of the Renaissance, however, we observe the struggle of two contrary forces: the Third Order creative movement and a regressive contraction within the Second Order that fixes and confines the fruits of the creative development itself, whether intellectual, technological, or economic. Our contemporary Western container is the product of this hardening, contracting, and closing of the fruits of the eighteenth-century Enlightenment. Reductive rationalism and scientism, technological confinement and alienation, and the world dominance of capitalism are the constituents of this container in which we live. These are the arrested growths, the monstrous births, of an isolated, closed, and aging Second Order.

The emergences enumerated here are characterized by totality and dynamism, and therefore have an organic quality. They go beyond the Third Order itself into a final quadrant that we shall study in Part Four, and that comprehends Earth, environment, body, and economic realities.

Psyche: Lost and Rediscovered

The tortuous history of human development in the West is a history also of the progressive eclipse and incipient recovery of a sense of the psyche. This is a strange story, for nothing is closer to us than psyche; it is nearly identical with self.

What is psyche? We shall understand psyche here in the

sense in which it has been virtually rediscovered in our time by Carl Gustav Jung, and in which the term is used by psychologists of the Jungian school. Sometimes they will denote this reality by the word *soul*, rather than psyche. But this is not soul in the sense in which Christians have been accustomed to use that word, as the more spiritual part of ourselves that survives the death of our physical body. Psyche is, rather, our whole living being insofar as it is bounded on the one side by spirit and on the other side by body. Psyche is both conscious and unconscious. It is personal but participates in realities that go far beyond the individual person, and thus Jung can speak of the collective psyche.

Psyche is particularly elusive to our rational inquiry. It is neither objectifiable nor simply the mind with which we think.

> By psyche Jung understands not only what we generally call "soul" but the totality of all psychological processes, conscious as well as unconscious…. The psyche consists of two complementary but antithetical spheres: CONSCIOUSNESS and the UNCONSCIOUS. Our ego has a share in both. [8]

The fortunes of psyche and of the feminine have followed parallel paths in the course of history. If both emerge today at the same time and often in the same places, it is because they are very closely related. The classical usage of *anima* (soul or psyche considered as feminine) illustrates this.

We can follow, in an approximate way, the eclipse and reappearance of psyche in Western thought through a series of phases.

The Greek philosophical mind was kind neither to psyche nor to the feminine. The analytical temper itself of Greek reason is antipathetic to psyche. Psyche is precisely that in the human person which (together with *person* itself) is least susceptible to analysis. The mode of intellection suited to psyche is image, symbol, metaphor, narrative, rather than clear concept and exact technical term. When the person is subjected to conceptual analysis, psyche is the breath, the life, that quietly escapes without being missed and fails to appear in the analytical report.

The classical Greek analysis of the human soul or psyche (that is, the whole of the person less the body) would distinguish three parts: *nous, epithymia, thymos:* that is, intellect or spirit *(nous),* desiring *(epithymia)* and willing *(thymos)* functions. Psyche is not to be identified with any one of these three parts, though perhaps it is most akin to desire. Psyche is, rather, the whole within which these three faculties exist. She embraces, however, much more than these dimensions of *consciousness.* When materialized into the simulacrum of a body and dissected in this way, psyche is no longer to be found.

Spirit defends itself by its transcendence: In the tradition of Platonism, spirit is the peak of the human person, the supreme, the divine faculty. Desiring and willing functions can speak with a secure sense of identity because they have respectable, intelligible jobs. But poor psyche, neither lord nor functionary, disappears from the inventory.

In Christian anthropology, psyche fares no better. Often the Christian fathers simply adopt the Greek analysis, as above. Sometimes the Christian view of the human person is even simpler: Man is soul and body. All that is not body is called *soul.* This term is weighted on the side of spirit, however, since "the immortal soul" is what remains when the body dies. Psyche is left out of the accounting once again because psyche, though not body, cannot be identified with this imperishable residue of the human person.

This same exclusion of psyche is hardened and made definitive in the Cartesian anthropology of mind and body. The idea of mind admits very little of psyche; much less than does soul. Now the eclipse of psyche in Western consciousness has become total, and we are ready to begin the phase of recovery.

The Freudian unconscious (implicitly the unconscious *mind*) seems a comic notion for this full, comprehensive, and continuous presence that is psyche. It is almost as if *life* should be discovered (perhaps by electrical measurements or knee-jerk reflexes) and called "nonmind" by its nineteenth- or twentieth-century Columbus. The history of modern psychology itself is the history of the recovery (in the wake of rationalist science) of that which had been submerged, systematically excluded, by reductionist science.

Much of the further recent progress in the recovery of psyche has come through the Jungian current of psychology. In

Jung's writings, we seem to begin to hear the voice and the language of psyche herself, and also begin to discern the historical pattern of her disappearance and reemergences. This historical journey is developed further in the writings of James Hillman, among others.

5. The Feminine: Human and Divine

Central to the Third Order and its development is the *feminine*.[9] Emergence of the feminine may be the primary sign of the dawning of a new phase of history in the deepest sense: that is, of history as the progression of God's self-communication to humanity. Divine revelation, from a Christian perspective, has come about through the divine Word, the Logos, which became incarnate in the *male* person of Jesus Christ. When Jesus imparted the Holy Spirit to his church, he initiated a further dynamic, a further stage of revelation, that plays itself out in the course of history. If the masculine component of the "image of God" was manifest in Jesus, it is the feminine half of this image (see Gn 1:26–27) that is embodied and manifest in the life of the church. While a metaphoric "femininity" of the church appears everywhere in tradition, only in our time do Western Christians begin to become aware that the life of the church is an embodiment of the feminine dimension of Divinity. In the Bible, it is the person of *Sophia* who corresponds to this dimension. Sophia is the unitive divine Feminine, immanent in all creation and newly present in Jesus, bestowed on Jesus' disciples as their anointing. Today we appear to have arrived at this midpoint of the history of revelation.

The Sophianic Revelation in History

Vladimir Soloviev and other Russian thinkers have envisioned Sophia as introducing a new age in human history.[10] This vision has developed not only from the Greek patristic tradition but also from contact with post-Enlightenment Western thought, and from the peculiar eschatological sense of the Russian soul.

Sophia is the feminine presence and manifestation of God, the immanent and invisible counterpart to his revealed Word. A first phase of revelation is concluded by the integral manifestation of the Word in the Incarnation, the appearance of Christ. In a second phase, a progressive incarnation (and revelation) of Sophia, of God's Wisdom, unrolls down through the centuries in the movement of humanity toward its fullness. The human race is conceived as a single feminine being, responding to the Word in a way that parallels the interaction of woman with man.

God's self-communication to humankind follows an order by which the "masculine" revelation precedes the "feminine" one. The first incarnation of the Word (Christ) precedes the full feminine incarnation of Wisdom and yet remains within it, as its center. Correspondingly, the first age of the church was thoroughly patriarchal, and its structures persist in the church and in the world. They inevitably become contaminated and confused with the structures of secular empire. Archetypal and perennial Empire is the antithesis of Sophia.

Within the patriarchal husk of the institutional church, and outside it in the life of secular culture as well, there dwells this Spirit who is wisdom, who is communion. She also becomes history as human persons gradually, but now with an accelerating movement, discover themselves as one with her and with the mystery of communion toward which all history moves.

She has no "outside"; she is known only by participation, as music or bread or wine is known. She is a unitive thread of consciousness that has remained often mute for the lack of a language to express such a knowledge without bounds. Thus she cannot be captured; she can be known only through an opened or a wounded heart. She seems to appear particularly at the end of an age, when the cultural shell has begun to dissolve.

As she came forth, veiled, during the age of chivalry in medieval Europe, she is present wherever a sense of personal love comes to birth. Wherever the Garden opens again in the mutual discovery of man and woman, her light is present with a promise of the resurrection of the body, of the whole human person—and of *nature* from which person is inseparable.

Sophia first emerged within the biblical tradition while Israel was in exile: when kingdom and priesthood and temple had collapsed and there was no external sign of collective hope to be found. She begins to appear once again today, when the structures both of Christendom and of the Enlightenment's secular humanism show signs of exhaustion. The peoples of the West find themselves on the threshold of a new age in which the unity of humankind is an absolute imperative, while no acceptable central symbol, no savior figure, yet offers a focus for this unity. She is experienced in our hearts and minds, in the warmth of our conviction of human unity and of an immanent Truth; experienced as something that, while it cannot be uttered, is about to be born.

Neither contemporary Protestantism nor Roman Catholicism offers a figure of unitive wisdom such as the Sophia of Eastern Christianity. Both have distanced themselves, during the past millennium of a divided Christianity, too far from the sapiential theology of the early centuries. Church authorities of Eastern Orthodoxy, relying exclusively on the heritage of the patristic age, have not welcomed Sophia either. Neither the divine femininity, nor the dynamic of historical development that she personifies, emerged with any clarity within these traditions. As a few prophetic Russians of a century ago already saw, a profound change in perspective is required. An imaginative theology must bring together the old and the new, the unitive and creative dimensions of the one Christ-mystery, in the light of both Logos and Sophia and their interaction.

Sophia emerges in our time as the immanent feminine counterpart of the solar unitive Logos of John's Gospel and the early church fathers. Her progressive manifestation is in the arc of life that curves between those Christian beginnings and our own time. Now, as she becomes widely known, the new age that is perennially on the threshold of birth may attain a new focus and self-awareness, and a new power of hope.

Lady Wisdom, the Great Connector, has the potential to bring meaningful unity and convergent energies to many of our contemporary issues and problems. The ecological concern has a deep affinity to Sophia. The role of Sophia in the creation (see Prv 8:22–32) and her incarnational thrust, her immanence in the earth and its biosphere, point to a new sense of communion between humankind and earth, and a corresponding sensitivity.

The femininity of Sophia is related in the biblical myth to this intimacy with earth; but a contemporary view of Sophia sees relation also to *movement from below* in a social and political sense. Sophia is manifest in historical and cultural ferment, in the movement toward human liberation. The liberation of woman proceeds not only to a necessary equality with man (here it is a question of *person,* rather than of woman) but to the free unfolding of her specific vocation in the birth of the new creation. Sophia is active in breaking down the preferential structures separating rich and poor, white and black and yellow, in the churches and in the world. If the liberation of woman is the central axis of human liberation, so Sophia (the Spirit), dwelling in all the peoples of the earth, is one with the inner fire that burns everywhere toward wholeness and unity.

Sophia may bring a new and integrating light to the central theological questions of sexuality, illuminating the meaning of both marriage and celibacy. Today these issues are distorted by our context of individualism and isolation. In the light of this unitive divine Wisdom who is one with the central energy of history, personal sexuality finds its divine matrix. The intimate relationship of sexuality, human creativity, and history emerges, and these expressions of life find a new and liberating meaning in the dramatic interplay of Logos and Sophia. She, the divine Feminine, indwelling in the human person and in all of humanity, may emerge as a principal key to the integration of sexuality and spirituality. Sexuality, in the transforming light of Sophia, may gradually become transparent, opening to its inner fullness as a passion for the communion of all beings in the One Who Is.

The apocalyptic urgency of world peace in our time calls forth this "koinonial" potential of Sophia. Sophia identifies with the humanity in which she dwells, and in her the human race is gathered into the unity that is God. She will be discovered at the heart of the diverse movements and networks that focus on this point of union.

Related to Sophia's activity as divine companion in the creation (Prv 8:22–31) is her role as the companion and muse of human creativity. She is the light and the unseen figure of that new humanity toward which our Western art and science labor. The Christian church desperately needs the liberation of her own creative potential by a new self-possession in the light of the original and unitive creative act. This means the discovery of her own sophianic identity. Woman too, in our culture, is drawn toward such a self-discovery. Man, in the sterility of his isolation, needs this companion to root him in the Source and at the same time warm and release his own active participation in the creation of the world.

Sophia, in our time, offers to help bridge the gap between East and West, as we now perceive them: between cosmos and history, interiority and liberation, mysticism and prophecy, the sapiential and the political. She is the spirit of that alternative Christianity which is ever engaged in the birth-struggle of the new creation, and she is ever the prophetic counterpole to empire, whether the ecclesiastical or the secular kind. She is (sometimes veiled, misconceived, and distorted) everywhere present within the positive alternative movements in society and religion.

Such an alternative Christianity, in finding its own sense of identity (this is the gift offered to our time by Sophia), can help the established churches to leave behind the narrow, often sterile and patriarchal, ecclesial models that have divided them from nature and from one another. They may reawaken to their identity as the one Bride, embodiment of the unitive wisdom of Christ. This is not, for the churches, a matter of taking another step forward, but of a revolutionary awakening to true identity. Sophia offers to help liberate a Christian faith constricted by centuries of division and defensiveness, through a penetration of the "deep things of God," the *divine Feminine,* understood as the immanent center and spring of life and of history (see 1 Cor 2:6–13; Rom 8:22–23).

Sophia draws us, today, into conscious relation with the great theological heart-current of history, which is the progressive incarnation of divine Wisdom.[11] We must learn to recognize the emerging sophianic revelation that appears in the events of our time: in the feminist movement, the peace and ecology movements, in the multiple breakthroughs of the Second Vatican Council, and especially in the new self-image of the church that begins to emerge there. As the dominant institutional model of the church gives way to a constellation of models,[12] we can anticipate a further step, in which the *unitive* essence of the church will be recognized at the core of this plurality. Mystery of wisdom and communion, the church is the one Bride, embodiment of the uncreated divine Wisdom.

Thus Sophia appears, at this moment of global convergence, as the immanent "Tao of history"[13] (corresponding to the Logos of the New Testament and the fathers) at the heart of the concentric movements of personal development, church history, secular history, and cosmic evolution. This revolution is a recentering in the earth and in our own hearts. Its promise encourages us to look beyond the age of patriarchal structures and beyond the subsequent dark night of nihilism, of a culture self-consumed in criticism. After the total eclipse of unitive light in this long age of exile and diaspora, we can look toward a new age of integration in the transparent immanence of Sophia.

David Bohm writes of the present incoherence of our culture as the root of our manifold crises and problems, and of the need for a breakthrough into "a new kind of intelligence capable of thinking together."

> What underlies such consciousness is this infinitely subtle spirit that cannot be defined, out of which emerge the ultimate meanings in ways we cannot grasp. This infuses the whole with a coherent but dynamic and creative meaning. This spirit is in some sense one—undivided, it is so subtle that we can say little about it, but it is essential to consider the possibility that it is there. If we try to say it is not there, we will go over to mechanism in the end.... The subtle but dynamic spirit that I have suggested above unfolds into many aspects, including the scientific, artistic, and religious, and would bring about a different way of living— both individually and together—which would move toward an unbroken whole.[14]

Sophia and Creativity

A nuptial allegory has provided the central language and imagery in which the Christian mystical tradition has expressed itself. This is an interpretation of the biblical *Song of Songs* in the light of John's Prologue. The divine Word was conceived as the Bridegroom of the soul (see Jn 1:1, 14; 3:29). It may be that this mystical theology of soul as bride of the Word belonged to the first wisdom[15] and to the time of contemplative wisdom. It may be, further, that a spirituality of Sophia as identified with woman (and as the bride of man) belongs to a new time of creative wisdom, a second wisdom. While we have apparently arrived at the threshold of this second period, a new spirituality of Sophia has not yet emerged.

That traditional nuptial spirituality of Logos and soul practically ignored the further relationship between human person and world. Nor did it bring to light the *creative* nature (or phase) of this relationship. This creativity becomes central in the time of a second wisdom. We may imagine this second phase as determined by the emergence of Sophia, the immanent divine Feminine, as the inspirer and the very energy of human creativity.

Humanity emerges from the time of childhood, of tutelage in this world (see Gal 3:23—4:10) into its prime of creative power.[16] This creative power is an expression of psychic energy, which is essentially related to the sexual expression of psychic energy. Human creativity, further, involves a participation in the divine Feminine. This divine Feminine, in analogy to the human feminine, can be conceived as personifying a *metasexuality:* a unitive energy and movement of an order beyond what we know as sexuality.

The creative act most powerfully witnesses to unitive new creation not when it takes place under "favorable" or comfortable circumstances but when it must grow through a hard crust, when it presses up from below, when it is one with the deep forces of life within humanity, struggling in deadly earnest against the forces of death. If it is to have the power of the ground, the true eucharistic fullness, it has to be on the ground, in the ground, participating the birth-pains of the ground, of our common humanity.

The basic creativity, we should not forget, is ever the same. It is the "theological" act of creation that is faith, hope, and love: a single energy and act in its threefold expression. These movements of the human spirit create a space of new creation in the midst of the old creation, which is world, humanity, mortality. Sophia is creative love, a love that is not grim but triumphant. It is creative because it is unitive, because it knows within itself its oneness with the divine Spirit.

The key to a vital Christianity in our time is doubtless to be found in a rediscovery of the Holy Spirit, but not simply as the Spirit was manifested on Pentecost day. The divine Spirit must be experienced and embodied in this historical moment, in the *Now*. The Spirit is the creative divine energy that is manifest in a continual renewal, an unceasing newness. The immanent divine Feminine appears to be a central manifestation of the Spirit today. We have passed the historical midpoint,[17] the sun has reached and passed its visible noon—as when Jesus met the woman at the well (Jn 4). Now we must attend to the woman, and to the living water that flows up everywhere within the earth.

The dream of the church returns. The revolution, which has begun time and again in history, awakens with new breadth and conviction in our time. Every Samaria becomes Jerusalem. The cross-beamed ark comes to ground again in a newly greening world. The church of Christ, long habituated to the patient shadow-world of that closed ark, emerges into her maturity as she walks wonderingly out from the single saving wood into the multiplicity of the trees of the earth. The single divine Wisdom within her knows, in each one of these different trees, the one tree of life, and this with a new sureness, with the interior connaturality of Sophia.

Because the church knows the single, simple light that is Christ (and now knows this light as one with her own being, even when it is not visible on one privileged sacred lampstand), she knows each creature from within itself as a mother does, with a prior knowledge, an original knowledge. It is with this knowledge of the heart that the church brings forth the secret that is within each one. The secret and incommunicable beauty that is the core of each creature, the root of love and desire, the hunger that is the unrevealed center of each soul—these are the material of her creativity, of the intuitive love with which she brings them out into the light of day, the light of Christ. Sophia, the Queen who is bride of this Christ-light, mediates between the royal day and the darkness from which each creature emerges into manifestation and glory, from which each fearful human soul comes forth into the confidence of faith, into the sunlight that is Christ.

The Christ-event, as Word and Spirit, gradually opens human creativity to its depths and from those depths brings forth the Christ in this million-tongued forest of the created world. It is immanent Sophia, the Unknown, who mediates this inward and outward movement. Today she becomes recognizable in her work.

6. Human Energy

From our modern Western perspective, contemporary encounters with the East seem to bring us into contact with a whole world of spiritual realities. Suddenly we are confronted with all of the dimensions of spiritual realization and experience that have been excluded in the course of our own historical journey. This awakening occurs at two points of particular depth and power. Prisoners of the Second Order, we rediscover in our encounter with the Asian traditions the *unitive* ultimate reality that is brahman, atman, Tao, nirvana. We encounter also the reality of cosmic and spiritual *energy*: prana, Shakti, kundalini, ch'i.

Early Christianity (especially the Semitic Christianity of Syria, that is, of the East) knew well the divine energy of the Holy Spirit, Ruach, Pneuma Hagion, Ruha. As Christianity became enclosed within juridical and theological structures, consciousness of this dynamic divine reality quickly faded. This is parallel to the thorough eclipse of unitive reality: The two are closely related. Later, a Greek Christian theology of the divine energies would provide a language for the dynamic immanence of the Holy Spirit throughout the created world, while the sense of this immanence disappeared from the Christianity of the West. Pentecostal (or Charismatic) movements in the twentieth century have revived the direct experience of the Spirit within the Western churches. This recovery has often remained within narrow bounds, however, excluding the sapiential[18] and unitive potential of the experience.

As we encounter the unitive self, or atman, today on two different fronts (Eastern spiritual traditions and Jungian-transpersonal psychology), we encounter the reality of psychic and spiritual energy along the same two boundaries. Libido, conceived by pioneering psychologist Sigmund Freud as a basically sexual energy, has been understood by Jung in much more general terms: as a psychic energy that is able to manifest itself on every level of human life. Energy emerges as a central and unifying concept in contemporary physical science. Here energy is found to be the protean fundamental reality of the universe, original matrix of all material beings from subatomic particles to the great and shining galactic bodies.

In terms of energy, the outward-directed and evolutionary vision of Teilhard de Chardin provides a necessary complement to the nonhistorical spiritual wisdom of the Asian traditions and the interiorizing perspective of Jungian psychology. From a Christian perspective, Teilhard (once again in this sector) is a prophet of synthetic vision. It is he, more than anyone else in our time, who has brought back a cosmic (and implicitly unitive) perspective into Christianity. One of the fundamental insights in his vision is the unitive quality of energy, from raw physical energy through sexual energy to divine love, and the evolutionary intentionality of this energy. Human energy is the evolutionary spearhead of the energy of the universe, as it moves forward toward its consummation.[19] The supreme form of this human energy is love. The energy of the universe, in Teilhard's view, is moving toward greater and greater personalization around its transcendent center, the Christ-Omega.

7. Divinization and Creativity

The Third Order is marked particularly by creativity, in contrast with the contemplation that characterized the

First Order. If we have spoken of a first wisdom that was essentially unitive and, therefore, contemplative, we can speak of a second wisdom[20] that is not only unitive but creative: actualizing the unitive reality in a new way. Unitive contemplation and unitive creation are complementary, but tend to separate themselves out along the historical axis.

The central Christian mystery, from our human perspective, is the mystery of divinization:[21] God became human so that human persons might become God. This mystery (or process) of divinization, in the patristic age (and primarily in the East), was experienced and understood in the contemplative key: that is, through the pure interiority of unitive contemplation. In the modern age of our Western civilization, the reality of divinization has been experienced through the development of human creativity (though largely outside the world of Christian faith). To bring together these two expressions of the deifying Christ-event belongs to the second wisdom.

If the meaning of the Christ-event is summed up in this ultimate affirmation of the human person that we have termed *divinization,* the tragic side of Christian history always involves the eclipse and suppression of this arch-truth. We can understand the forward movement of history in terms of a progressive actualizing of divinization. The movement takes place in successive phases, so that one aspect of deification will be accented at one time and subsequently, at a later moment, a different aspect.

Very simply, we can say that the patristic era of Christian history (through the sixth century) is dominated by the idea of divinization as an interior transformation of the individual, experienced through unitive contemplation. Represented concretely by monasticism, this is the "Eastern" interpretation of deification. It is characterized by a preference for interiority, for a contemplative and apophatic spirituality. Here spirituality retains its primacy over any other human pursuit or cultural expression.

In the modern West, on the other hand, a secular view of "human divinity" has developed without any apparent relationship to the earlier theological conception. The emergence of outward-directed creative energies in Western humanity has been of such a magnitude that it could not be contained by the existing religious structures. With the breadth and power of a geological shift, this movement has displaced divinization from its theological ground so as to create an autonomous "secular world," with a cultural and philosophical tradition of its own.[22]

By the dawn of the Renaissance, the traditional concept of deification had virtually disappeared from the theological world of the West. Actually, the notion had faded long before in Western Christianity: This eclipse is evident already in St. Augustine and in Gregory the Great. The Western Christian Middle Ages are dark ages at least in one sense. They evolve under an opaque theological cloud (inseparable from the institutional, pedagogical, Augustinian Catholicism of this time), a cloud that has completely veiled the light and power of divinization. During this interlude between the unitive and creative expressions of divinization, the divine Gift is vested in the highly institutional mediating church.

When the divinity of the human person reappears in the West, it is a new and outward-looking human potential that emerges. This is *creativity*: the creative power of the individual person (and then of Western civilization itself), which expresses itself in rational thought and in poetic imagination, in art and in the beginnings of technology, in every form of discovery.[23] Deification during the patristic centuries, conceived in terms of interiority and contemplation, dwelt contentedly within its institutional cloisters. The new phase of deification, unfolding through creativity, breaks out of every container; it is essentially concerned with newness.

At this point in the beginnings of the Modern Age, Christianity is largely left behind like an abandoned cocoon, a shell that is no longer needed and can only repress and inhibit the emerging energies of life. The emergence occurs along a wide horizon. It is a new youthfulness of the human person, a self-discovery that sparkles on every side in new discoveries of the world. The new freedom is often, at the outset, recognized as an unfolding of the grace of Christ. Soon, however, the theological source of this freedom, its hidden core (undistinguished from the repressive church container), is left behind, and Western humanity goes off on its own to create a new world. We are heirs to the magnificent achievements as well as to the wreckage and apocalyptic menace of this movement of human autonomy. In this expansive exodus from the school of medieval Christendom, "Western man" embarks on his self-realization in a spiritual vacuum, emancipated from the wisdom as well as the fetters of the past.

A new sapiential consciousness[24] will be able to follow this shift, throughout Western culture, from a contemplative-religious pole to an imaginative-creative pole (Western science itself is the rational and empirical extreme of this creativity). It can be argued, in fact, that the shift is a movement further into the historical stream that expresses the Holy Spirit's creative activity, into the broad and deep movement of new creation that breaks forth in the New Testament. The Christian contemplative tradition, with all its depth and fullness of unitive experience, remained largely enclosed within a particular cultural container: the structures of Platonist and Neoplatonist philosophical thought. These structures imposed a static quality on it, excluding the basic dimension of movement, dynamism, the forward-going historical drive that is distinctive of biblical religion and that bursts forth with a new and definitive impulse in the birth of Christianity.

8. New Creation as Continuing Event

Our Christian theology, with its various borrowings from Greek philosophy, has usually ignored the dynamic dimension of the Christ-mystery. The Mystery has often been materialized, substantialized, essentialized, even (more or less Platonically) spiritualized, and consistently dichotomized. Jesus lived, died, and conferred the divine Spirit to bring about a new creation. The energy of this Christ-event continues the work, bringing it ever into new phases, new manifestations. The present moment is a critical one in the recognition of this creative Christ-dynamic. We begin to conceive of the church not primarily as institution but as communion, and as movement. Christianity is not principally doctrine and structure, but

spirit and life. It is God present as creative energy at the heart of the church, in the heart of humanity and of the human person.

Third Order Apophatic

A sudden *actuality* flashes from within the New Testament writings. It cannot be captured in words, but is analogous to the "pure act" of the scholastics, something like pure existence or *esse*, being-as-act. In these moments we experience the Holy Spirit, the divine creative power in action. We can feel this actuality blazing from the desert bush in Exodus, and expressed in God's words to Moses: "I AM WHO I AM…. Say this to the people of Israel, I AM has sent me to you" (Ex 3:14). While it can be experienced in many of the divine actions, the "marvelous works" of God in the history of Israel, I would like to consider it in the New Testament narratives: the gospels and the Acts of the Apostles.

The divine energy is present successively in several ways: "objectively" in a given historical event, then as if contained within the gospel narrative, and finally in the listener's or the reader's experience. I find it particularly in the healings. Take, for example, Jesus' healing of the man with the withered hand in Mark's Gospel. Dramatic tension is heightened by the setting: at a public gathering in the synagogue, on the sabbath.

> Again he entered the synagogue, and a man was there who had a withered hand. And they watched him, to see whether he would heal him on the sabbath, so that they might accuse him. And he said to the man who had the withered hand, "Come here." And he said to them, "Is it lawful on the sabbath to do good or to do harm, to save life or to kill?" But they were silent. And he looked around at them with anger, grieved at their hardness of heart, and said to the man, "Stretch out your hand." He stretched it out, and his hand was restored. The Pharisees went out, and immediately held counsel with the Herodians against him, how to destroy him. (Mk 3:1–6)

What is it that flashes out, as if brightening the air, in the synagogue at the moment of this healing? What is it that we experience, as a subtle but powerful energy passing through us, if we are really present to the action here? What is it that reaches across the centuries into our own flesh at the climax of this story? Our natural and immediate response is wonder: *Look—this is it, he is the one!* The reaction of the Pharisees and Herodians, on the other hand, is perfect in its irony, corresponding to Jesus' prophetic question, "Is it lawful on the sabbath to do good or to do harm, to save life or to kill?" The two energies, the two spirits, here express themselves perfectly, in their diametric opposition. This is something that confounds our knowledge, our analyses, and our words. It is the power of God in its purity, restoring the flesh and bringing the heart to life. It enters us like a breath of divine life.

Paul, contending with the Corinthians, brings forward as his incontrovertible witness their personal experience of the divine power.

> When I came to you, brothers and sisters, I did not come proclaiming the mystery of God to you in lofty words or wisdom. For I decided to know nothing among you except Jesus Christ, and him crucified. And I came to you in weakness and in fear and in much trembling. My speech and my proclamation were not with plausible words of wisdom, but with a demonstration of the Spirit and of power, so that your faith might rest not on human wisdom but on the power of God. (1 Cor 2:1–5, NRSV)

> For the kingdom of God does not consist in talk but in power. (1 Cor 4:20)

Paul can refer with confidence to this power of God because they have seen and heard it in action and have felt it leaping within their own hearts. This "apophatic" is quite different from that of much traditional contemplative literature. It is a reality that comes toward you rather than receding from you. It is hot rather than cold, convex rather than concave, not an emptiness but a fullness. It is simple presence and power, an immediate and overwhelming abundance of being that exceeds form, defies articulation, and yet is itself, ultimately, pure self-communication.

9. The Fire of History

> In the New Testament, Jesus is said to bring two kinds of fire: the fire of judgment and purification, and the indwelling fire of the Holy Spirit.

> "I baptize you with water for repentance, but he who is coming after me is mightier than I, whose sandals I am not worthy to carry; he will baptize you with the Holy Spirit and with fire. His winnowing fork is in his hand, and he will clear his threshing floor and gather his wheat into the granary, but the chaff he will burn with unquenchable fire." (Mt 3:11–12)

> Both fires have already been burning in Israel; Jesus will enkindle both to a new intensity. We have already considered a number of the manifestations of the indwelling divine Spirit. Now we shall look at the other fire, the fire that comes from outside and tests, purifies, and judges. The manifestation of this fire in history (in the history of Israel and of the church) is also related to the divine energy, the Holy Spirit.

The God of Israel, according to the Deuteronomic tradition, is represented by fire, *is* a fire.

> For the Lord your God is a devouring fire, a jealous God. (Dt 4:24)

> ...for the Lord your God in the midst of you is a jealous God; lest the anger of the Lord your God be kindled against you, and he destroy you from off the face of the earth. (Dt 6:15)

Israel's trial in the wilderness was a trial by fire, as was the exile in Babylon. Jesus himself spoke of the trial that was to come upon him as a baptism—a baptism he associated with fire.

> "I came to cast fire upon the earth; and would that it were already kindled! I have a baptism to be baptized with; and how I am constrained until it is accomplished!" (Lk 12:49–50)

This metaphor of fire, frequent in the New Testament writings, refers often to eschatological judgment and the punishment of sinners. Paul speaks of this fire of judgment as a purification of one's works.

> The work of each builder will become visible, for the Day will disclose it, because it will be revealed with fire, and the fire will test what sort of work each has done. If what has been built on the foundation survives, the builder will receive a reward. If the work is burned up, the builder will suffer loss; the builder will be saved, but only as through fire. (1 Cor 3:13–15, NRSV)

We can see this testing fire operating on a larger scale: in the history and life of the church in this world. This trial by fire that confronts the disciple (and the church) from outside is a participation in the overall drama of salvation history, and therefore a sharing in the life of Christ. Paul, writing frequently of this struggle, both in his own life and in that of all Christians, understands it to be a personal participation in the sufferings of Jesus. For the early Christians, this was first of all the experience of persecution. From the moment of Saul's own conversion, he understood this persecution as a sharing in that which Jesus had suffered—indeed, as a continuation and completion of it.

> And he fell to the ground and heard a voice saying to him, "Saul, Saul, why do you persecute me?" And he said, "Who are you, Lord?" And he said, "I am Jesus, whom you are persecuting." (Acts 9:4–5)

> Now I rejoice in my sufferings for your sake, and in my flesh I complete what is lacking in Christ's afflictions for the sake of his body, that is, the church. (Col 1:24)

In at least one text of Paul, we find the two fires together, though without the metaphor of fire. The inner fire of the Spirit and the exterior fire of affliction are two faces of one and the same process, which is a childbirth, a new creation. Here in the eighth chapter of Paul's letter to the Romans, the heat and pressure of experience have forged an unparalleled synthesis.

For all who are led by the Spirit of God are children of God. For you did not receive a spirit of slavery to fall back into fear, but you have received a spirit of adoption. When we cry, "Abba! Father!" it is that very Spirit bearing witness with our spirit that we are children of God, and if children, then heirs, heirs of God and joint heirs with Christ—if, in fact, we suffer with him so that we may also be glorified with him. I consider that the sufferings of this present time are not worth comparing with the glory about to be revealed to us. For the creation waits with eager longing for the revealing of the children of God; for the creation was subjected to futility, not of its own will but by the will of the one who subjected it, in hope that the creation itself will be set free from its bondage to decay and will obtain the freedom of the glory of the children of God. We know that the whole creation has been groaning in labor pains until now; and not only the creation, but we ourselves, who have the first fruits of the Spirit, groan inwardly while we wait for adoption, the redemption of our bodies. (Rom 8:14–23, NRSV)

To the life-giving movement of the Holy Spirit in the heart of the disciple correspond the blows of external affliction. In Paul's view, these troubles are an experience of the Christ-mystery, a participation in the sufferings of Jesus. Paul sees these afflictions (together with the inner groaning of the Spirit) as a participation in the life-drama not only of the body of Christ that is the church, but of the whole *cosmos*. In this double movement, interior and exterior, the disciple knows the pulsations of this one universal birth: the new creation.

History, then, is *one*. At the center of this history, and invisibly encompassing it, is the living Christ. Our own experience of history, and that of the Christian community in our time, finds its meaning in this light.

10. Music and Spirit

A primary metaphor for the Third Order is music, for music is form as energy, as movement. In music, form becomes an energy that is essentially communicative, mysteriously unitive.

> And some of the Pharisees in the multitude said to him, "Teacher, rebuke your disciples." He answered, "I tell you, if these were silent, the very stones would cry out." (Lk 19:39–40)

> But now, as at the ending,
> The low is lifted high;
> The stars shall bend their voices,
> And every stone shall cry.
> And every stone shall cry
> In praises of the child
> By whose descent among us
> The worlds are reconciled.[25]

When Jesus appears in the world, he is surrounded by an angelic music of reconciliation. Though he comes "to bring a sword," this sword itself comes but to sever the bonds and tear open the veils that obstruct the consummate union that is his gift. This music is audible in the account of Jesus' birth in Luke's Gospel. Like fragrant incense, the charm of this music distinguishes Christmastime through the centuries. Darker chords will break into this innocent music, and Jesus will journey into dissonance, through storms of opposition to his death. The music is victorious on Easter morning, and in the descent of the fiery tongues it begins its surging progress through the world and the ages.

Often today the music seems to have faded out completely, or to sound weakly in empty churches. The voice of Christianity, of the churches, is seldom resonant. Often the loudest voice in Christianity today is a strident one. The word of God can sound, through this voice, without resonance in the creation, clashing with earth's deep and silent soul like a chainsaw in the forest. Here is the harsh voice of a popular evangelism without compassion, charged with self-righteousness, with a deadly freight of prejudice and judgment. There sounds the parental tone of institutional authority, forever reproving its children from above. From time to time, however, there are heard other voices, in which some of the Christ-music, ever old and ever new, is recognized. Often these voices sound from the churches of the poor.

This book is a quest for the Christ-music, from a particular perspective that we have called *wisdom:* a knowledge that is life and beauty, a light in which "the worlds are reconciled." This wisdom is resonance, is music. But it is also light: the light, deep and subtle, obscure and yet clear, in which all things are one. It is a participation in the divine One as the light within which our world and all it contains are known in a new way.

If we speak of this as a rediscovery, a recovery of something that has long been eclipsed and forgotten, that does not mean that it is something remote from us. On the contrary, it is within us, and we experience it with the immediacy and fullness of our experience of daylight in the world around us. At the core of our being is a simple knowledge, a fullness in which the disparate ends of world and life are gathered, in which all things are already one with a primordial unity. Our life moves toward the realization of this unity within the whole of ourselves and within the world around us. The movement of human history is toward a flowering of the whole world in this divine unity.

Music is a fortunate metaphor for the second wisdom,[26] because this wisdom is movement, energy, breath. As song, it is word and meaning that is animated, informed by breath and life. It is a "Third Order reality" as contrasted with nature, thought, or speech, for it is essentially living and dynamic. The second wisdom is itself only in its third dimension of actuality. Song appears at the beginning of poetry, as poetry is at the beginning of speech. Song is the exultant transformation of experience, gathering that experience into living breath, the stream of life. Breath itself is a dynamic synthesis: at once conscious and unconscious, voluntary and instinctive, personal and organic.

Jesus speaks of the Baptist and himself as communicating two contrasting kinds of music. He relates this varying music, in a most suggestive way, to the one divine Wisdom, Sophia.[27]

> "To what then will I compare the people of this generation, and what are they like? They are like children sitting in the marketplace and calling to one another, 'We played the flute for you, and you did not dance; we wailed, and you did not weep.' For John the Baptist has come eating no bread and drinking no wine, and you say, 'He has a demon'; the Son of

> Man has come eating and drinking, and you say, 'Look, a
> glutton and a drunkard, a friend of tax collectors and sin-
> ners!' Nevertheless, wisdom [Greek *Sophia*] is vindicated by
> all her children." (Lk 7:31–35, NRSV)

The children of Sophia recognize the music of divine wisdom in its manifold expressions. Whether rejoicing or calling to repentance it is the one music, the self-communication of wisdom. We can speak of "gospel music" in a sapiential sense. A gospel scene (this is apparent most often in Luke), or a Pauline theological passage, projects an aura that resembles nothing more than music. The reader is invited into this field of energy that is wisdom. The Scriptures themselves are the score, not the music. The music happens when the words, those marks on the page, are actualized by the Spirit of life. This happens only through human persons, only in the human heart.

The music of each passage is the secret, the meaning, of that passage. This meaning, however, is greater than any single interpretation, any single statement. The goal of reading or listening is to hear the music. We can hear this music without being able to "interpret" it or to paraphrase what it is saying. We hear the music only by moving with it; as T. S. Eliot wrote, "you are the music while the music lasts." This is the unitive communication of the divine energy field: Spirit, Sophia. You know her only by participating her, as Wisdom's children do. This is to weep with the dirge, to dance with the tune. The scribes and Pharisees prefer score to music (see Lk 7:29–30).

To read or listen to a New Testament passage is to listen for the music. The music is a fullness in which a plurality of meanings live together. We can hear the music of a parable and enter into its interior fullness while our conceptual understanding remains outside. To hear the music is to enter into the circle of the children of Wisdom, where they sit around her, held by her spell in a fullness of preconceptual understanding. The royalty of this music is that of the white light, containing all the colors invisibly within its fullness.

What does it mean to say that the gospel is music, that Luke's narrative is music, that a particular gospel scene is music? The metaphor is complex and profound. Sometimes the words themselves, even in translation, are a new music. "Lord, to whom shall we go? You have the words of eternal life" (Jn 6:68); "I am the resurrection and the life" (Jn 11:25); "Blessed are you poor, for yours is the kingdom of heaven" (Lk 6:20).

Sometimes the imagery is musical: "Getting into one of the boats, which was Simon's, he asked him to put out a little from the land. And he sat down and taught the people from the boat" (Lk 5:3); "the house was filled with the fragrance of the perfume" (Jn 12:3). The infancy scenes in Luke can be called musical in their iconic quality, their visual power, their simplicity and tender vibrancy. Sometimes the music resonates from the whole scene with all its elements. This is more than the visual image; it approaches embodiment. Now the "image" includes also sound and thought, drama and feeling. We can experience this in many of the Lukan stories, but also in the great Johannine scenes: Cana, the well in Samaria, the garden of resurrection, even the cross. The music is the scene in its dynamic totality: as a concrete manifestation of the divine One, alive with its communicable energy, its resonance. History has been transformed into this new music, which is the gospel narrative.

The term *music* may be applied particularly to the "epiphanic moment," the sudden opening and outpouring of light at a moment of manifestation and recognition of what is in Jesus. This too is frequent in Luke. One example among many is the Lukan story of Zacchaeus (Lk 19:4–11). In the meeting of Jesus and Zacchaeus occurs a silent explosion of light. The music is this outpouring of unitive light that draws everything together within itself.

Another New Testament music is the "wisdom poetry" that we hear in Jesus' sayings (e.g., in the Matthean Sermon on the Mount [Mt 5–7]), in the Prologues of John's Gospel and 1 John and Hebrews, in the "christological hymns"[28] of the Pauline letters. This wisdom-utterance, a concentrated verbal expression of the Mystery, tends toward rhythm, symmetry, circularity, chiastic form. It is a circular dance around the *axis mundi*, that invisible metaphysical center which is the Mystery.

The King's Music

Concealed beneath the shadow that darkens royal imagery for us today, a deep and vital reality lies within the archetype of the king.[29] In the sorry succession of biblical kings there is one who is both warrior-hero and musician; one in whom, already before Jesus, we can feel the unitive resonance, the music, that we are identifying as Three. This is David,[30] the anointed one who comes to Jerusalem like a bridegroom to his bride.

Like Jesus and Francis of Assisi, David appears as the central music of his race. His arrival stands out in the history of pre-Christian Israel as the moment of incarnation. David's music is the resonance of his wholeness: He is at once warrior and lover, ruler and prophet, saint and sinner, and the singer of his nation. There is more than wholeness, however, in this anointed one. In the music that we sense in David is a "wisdom before wisdom": an intuitive and operative understanding that has not yet been appropriated and separated from life and faith. It has not yet emigrated from its secret home within the heart.

The music that we have experienced in gospel scenes (especially in those of Luke and John) is a reverberation of the presence of the King; that is, of Jesus. The presence of the King is a unifying presence, and it creates around itself a sphere of music that is anticipation and first taste of the kingdom of God. Often we hear this music not directly from the King, but from those around him: "You are the Christ, the Son of the living God" (Mt 16:16). "If you will, you can make me clean" (Mk 1:40). "Lord, that I may see" (Mk 10:51). "Lord, to whom shall we go? You have the words of eternal life" (Jn 6:68). We hear the sea subsiding to a hush around him as he stands in the boat and says, "Be still!" (Mk 4:39). We listen to the whispering wonder, like wind in the standing grain, that passes in widening rings through the crowd that sits in the field as he breaks the loaves of bread and the bread keeps coming, keeps breaking and breaking again and passing outward into the seated multitude (see Mk 6:35–44).

We know this music, then, in the resonance that it awakens in the people (and sometimes in the natural things) around the King, and that then awakens within ourselves. As Jesus heals a cripple or a blind person, one bit of flesh, one fragment of the creation responds to this essential music of life. The healings are awakenings to the music; arms and legs and eyes and whole bodies awaken to this music that enlivens from within. The King rules by resonance, by inner response, by a primacy of being rather than extrinsic domination. In him is a power of union and of life.

We live through three successive musics or movements. The first is a kind of Christmas music, the music of innocence that we experience in the young David. It is an arrival, the revelation of a natural royalty, of a symmetry and harmony, the awakening of a heart with its infinite dowry. This is a reality in our childhood experience. We are speaking of the music of the first naivete, of the living myth, of unbroken harmony. It is a mother-music, a romanticism and romantic love, a troubadour song that will quickly fade but nevertheless contains in its fragile wings an undying truth. Here we find together childhood and adolescence, the two successive myths and kingdoms of childhood entrancement and first love. Here also are the "joyful mysteries," the infancy narratives, the epiphanies and burgeoning ministry of Jesus, the Galilee time. The first music is usually centered in a luminous figure with whom we vibrate.

The second music is discord, a heavy left hand, dark keys, conflict and suffering, disorientation and a plummeting into bottomless depths, down the shaft of despair and death. And yet in the wrenching discord itself we may sense a rightness, an ultimate harmony. In the heart of darkness, in the fabric itself of the night, there is light. Now we are in Jerusalem, and all the authorities have hardened in their hostility, their condemnation. The King's light has no witness outside itself as it is ruthlessly quenched. Nothing in the world around it resonates with the music as it dies into silence. Yet in this silence a deeper music moves.

Christianity has been living through this second music for the past four or five centuries. Here the King is completely darkened, eclipsed. As the hopes of secular humanism are successively smashed, the secular West itself enters into this music. It is the music of the philosophies of despair, of the reductionisms, of the darker chords of existentialism and postmodernism, of deconstruction and insatiable, predatory criticism.

The third music comes out of your ground like the rising sun: It is you! We cannot say what it is, and yet it is what we know most deeply and surely. The third music, like the wind, moves everything within its own movement: trees and grass. Unlike the wind, it moves everything from within, and therefore also moves mountains and humans that are not moved by the wind blowing on them. If the conclusive advent of this third music will be announced by the "final trumpet," this music is much more than a peremptory blare startling the dead from their beds. It is the power of life coursing through everything, thrusting every obstacle out of its way.

The third music is an authority, an *exousia*, that is cellular, nuclear, fundamental, absolute. In this music everything that you are awakens to its own oneness and freedom, awakens to its own being as music and light. If the gospel music is *glory*, this becomes fully manifest in the third music. It is the light that seems to be soaking into you until you notice that it is really coming out of you. At the sound of this music everything "rises to its feet" in the sense of realizing its own true being and scope. Jesus Christ will be recognized, finally, by this third music.

The music is love. This is the anointing and the gold, the gold and sunshine that are the metal and color of the heart. This light is not pale moonlight above the ageless waste of thirsty waters, but blooded sun, the bulging bread and harvest of the heart.

David's king-music both soothed and tormented old King Saul; the true kingly anointing flashed on David and caused Saul's own heart to sink. The chief priests rendered judgment by the law; enraged by Jesus' music, they too hurled their murderous spear. The music is victorious, but only through the death of the anointed true King, the alchemical quartering from which a single golden drop pours forth, trembling in its purity.

The true music of the King (that is, of the gospel) is heard when the *outsider* is gathered in, and the outer walls resound. The feast is madly inclusive, inexhaustible. We hear this music of the King at the banquet of Levi, in the story of Jesus and the adulterous woman. It sounds when Jesus raises up and gathers in the lepers, the sinners and the cripples, the blind and the sick. The music bursts forth triumphantly; it knows no boundaries.

Unlocking the heart of the person, it releases the inner music of life and the blind see, the lame walk. The poor hear the music and are happy.

The gospel music has a characteristic sound in Paul's letters. Often we hear it in the cadences and cadenzas, the cascades and codas of his words as he strains to communicate the surge of grace. This music sounds often in the turning of the tables, in a broad emergence from the ground, in the moment of revolution when dominance and power yield to upspringing truth. The music comes forth in the explosion of an inner reality and sweeps outward in wave after exultant wave. From confinement within "the letter," the gospel of God's glory springs free.

11. Poetry and Wisdom

In the world of language it is poetry, in contrast to prose discourse, which belongs particularly to the Third Order. Poetry is language as energy, as experience, as an opening of the moment to fullness.

The poet is in touch with an invisible current of unitive intelligence that flows under the ground and joins everything with everything else. He or she cannot define this relationship, which is the prime, if implicit, subject of the poetry.

We might call this one theme the holiness of creation: of every being, leaf, and tree. The expression, as always, falls short. There is a communion, a *koinonia,* a sacred commonality of being beneath the diversity and individuality of beings. This commonality of being is not an abstraction but something intensely physical and real. The English poet Gerard Manley Hopkins knew this, and it flashes out from his poems as he rubs one thing against another, one word against another, like flint and steel. The communion and the radiance are inseparable. To find the point of commonality is to release the flash of light, the illumination. This is the magic of metaphor. The seemingly casual rubbing of differences shoots out a whole shower of sparks. Beneath and around the successive audacities of juncture, one feels a moving force, a spirit, a confident gaiety that is hostess and maestro to the whole tribe. It is this breath or impetus, this joyful momentum, that is the charism. Within himself the singer knows that his song gathers everything into one.

The poem knows what it knows (this oneness of things) in the simplicity of *movement*. The poem's energy is a wisdom, which expresses and objectifies the light that is in our breathing, in the beating of our hearts, in the rhythms and movements of our bodies themselves. The poem, with its meter and other internal resonances and recurrences, inscribes a circle, taps a rhythm. It creates an enclosure that is the vessel for the unitive wine, both containing and reinforcing this single great meaning.

There is a darkness, an unknowing at the heart of poetry. Classical ages trim the wilderness to a garden, immobilize the swift and living animals in stone. Our modern poets have gone into the dark woods again. Their obscure speech at its truest is the enigmatic babble of the prophet, the holy madman. The breath of poetry is inseparable from this *mystery*, which remains as ground. This is the incircumscribable wholeness that we systematically exclude as we perfect our edifice of civilization, our prison-house of consciousness, our rational city of enlightened human progress.

Poets of Romantic and Modernist times, like biblical prophets from Moses to the Baptist, return to the wilderness, to unimproved nature, to find the pure beginning once again.[31] It is there, in the intimate uncomprehended wild, that creation is possible again. There is something in nature that asks for this response from us. There is a space, an expectancy, a silence that both calls out and humbles the song. With the Romantic movement, poetry becomes the voice of human vitality crying out from the edges of a consciousness that has been paved with the cold light of rationalism. This continues in our own time. Once having found this standpoint, however, the voice of poetry confronts more than the Western Enlightenment, "single vision and Newton's sleep."[32] Modern poetry becomes the word in exile, a wild cry of freedom confronting and confounding every orthodoxy, every reigning public consciousness.

The guerrillas may be lurking in any part of the forest. Reflecting, we find ourselves surrounded by wilderness, by dark woods; beyond there stretches an uncharted, infinite expanse. The voice of poetry may come from any side; it comes from different sides in turn, at different times. It circles the tightening paranoid settlement with deliberate randomness, infallibly finding the open window, stealing past the sleeping sentry.

Poetry is a music that binds together in its one movement image, thought, feeling, and sound. In this it is already a wisdom, as we have been thinking of wisdom: a consciousness, understanding, and thought going beyond thought to a participation in the realities that are known, and all within the One. Poetry becomes an *omni*-music that is a participative understanding of the complex music that is life itself. The energy field of a poem lives between the concrete particularity of an experienced world and the concrete particularity of words, as a communicable fullness, a momentary epiphany.

> Throw away the lights, the definitions,
> And say of what you see in the dark
>
> That it is this or that it is that
> But do not use the rotted names.
>
> How should you walk in that space and know
> Nothing of the madness of space,
>
> Nothing of its jocular procreations?
> Throw the lights away. Nothing must stand
>
> Between you and the shapes you take
> When the crust of shape has been destroyed.
> You as you are? You are yourself.
> The blue guitar surprises you. [33]

There is a magic in good poetry: a transformation and a communion, an exchange of being as external reality is permeated with the light that shines from within us. Poetry is alchemy, transfiguration.

The spirit within us, a pulsing breath of freedom, follows our eyes out into the world and infuses what we see, impregnating it with our spark, our freedom. In Paul's words, "the creation waits with eager longing for the revealing of the children of

God," in the final resurrection (Rom 8:19). Meanwhile we have glimpses and intimations of this simultaneous transformation of our own bodies and of the universe. Our imagination, partaking of the creative freedom of the divine Spirit, anticipates the revelation, stammering its fiery intuitions in poetry. What comes to birth is this intermediate creature, the poem, a microcosm on frail paper. While seeming to terminate in this flat materiality, the poem, in the round of life, is breath and light. The poet, bright with a strange anointing, sings light and freedom into the world.

Modernist poetry, the iridescent, scintillating kind (like the more vibrant modern painting), knows a fire of freedom in the mind. It manifests a power, a fiery way of knowing things. Metaphor is a handy name for this power, but catches only part of the dynamic. The most startling metaphor, the really impossible assertion of identity, is the shook foil shining, the violent breaking through of inconceivable, maximal[34] truth. In the audacity of this metaphor is expressed the human spirit, the subtle core, spinning clear round, 360 degrees, in its assertion of potency, its sabbath claim. There is something in us that claims an unrestricted royalty within the whole creation. At a place of quickness within, a vital point, we know the world as our own, know ourselves as the children of God, and know impossibility as only a line painted across the court. Everything is ours, and through this wild companion, imagination, we gradually begin to move in the widening space. We learn the spiraling degrees of freedom.

Much of our contemporary poetry is a groping in the dirt, coming up with gleaming bits here and there. Maybe it is mostly just glass, but gleaming with the same only light. We are rummaging the earth for its treasures, and everything gleams if you rub it. It is in this humble way that we learn the one immensity again.

Christianity, emerging from its tunnel, discovers itself as a many-formed and yet utterly simple reality. A new spaciousness is discovered in this trinitarian-cosmic mystery. We begin to know the freedom that lives between Word and Spirit, Logos and Sophia, a new mobility in the movement from form to formlessness, from figure and body to energy and movement. This spaciousness and vitality belong essentially to the Christ-mystery. Poetry realizes this freedom as it draws together image and sound, feeling and word, concrete thing and unitive dynamism of spirit, into a single music, within the kingdom of the Word. The poem is born as a microcosm of the Word's creative fullness.

A second faith is born.[35] When Christianity has failed to discover its creative gift, it has become a tunnel-faith: an obedient trudging through the narrow dark in a life of repetition without vital rhythm, without resonance or luminosity.[36] There is a time for winter-faith; there will again be a narrow time. We had, however, allowed ourselves nearly to forget the light and its potency, the bursting vitality of its coming forth. The second faith, emerging from our tunnel, is a dawning, an inner expansiveness. Essentially creative, it is committed to the absolute future and its fullness. Mind and imagination are newly enkindled, scintillating with the fire and light of an unimaginable resurrection. This is the faith of *new creation* and of a personal participation in it. The second faith converges with modern poetry and abstract art in this wild freedom within the person that is at the same time a knowledge: a knowledge of limitlessness, of a sovereign creative energy that from time to time leaps forth into the world. We have this limitlessness enclosed within us, and so our walk has a tremendous humor about it, an exultant irony that is to be cherished as light, as certainty, as the immediacy of hope.

This inner freedom and creativity, this sovereignty (which seems incredible in the narrow apartments of our life) is the expression of something deeper than itself. Of that deeper reality we can say little more than what we find in the New Testament writings. This sovereignty itself is of vital importance for us. To know ourselves as this free, creative energy is to know the meaning of our life in this world. Creative activity is vital, for it regenerates (within us and around us) the atmosphere in which the future lives. Here the central spark within person and community awakens.

12. Three: A Meditation

Human existence is poised between *yes* and *no*. The child begins at the border of life and death; a little negligence on the part of the adults would suffice for it to slip back out of this world. Yet in the embrace of mother and father, in the sunshine of their loving smile, we begin with a great and uncontestable *affirmation*. It is precisely the human condition to be hanging free between light and darkness, between being and nonbeing, sunshine and the black abyss.

Between the frictionless space of the galaxies and the inexhaustible movement of photons and electrons, our human world is calibrated for the waterline, the exact point of equilibrium between *yes* and *no*. In this ambiguity we live. Here we can live our whole lives without settling the question, without breaking through to the fundamental affirmation.

We are that affirmation. Our microcosmic self, in affirming itself, recapitulates and affirms the whole. The life that is within us is an unconditioned affirmation. Within a strangely ambiguous world, however, this substantial yes comes to doubt itself. It feels itself negated by the yes of the other person, by all the other self-affirmations around us, each burning in another like ourself.

What can bring all these discordant energies together into one great affirmation? Only the discovery, the participation, of the inner Yes that is identical with the Ground itself. It is this that we must learn: not once, but again and again, for each achievement of the *yes* must expect to confront a larger, darker, more terrible *no*. Our journey, seen from this perspective, is very simple.

The irony, the comedy of our life, is outrageous: The whole of our being is affirmation, and we can spend all our time hanging on the edge of doubt. The world is filled with light, and we labor at conjectures, suggestions, faint glimmers. We dwell in the midst of fullness and we are hungry. "Son...everything I have is yours" (Lk 15:31). However we understand the relationship of nature and grace, of sin and redemption, of Christ and creation, we dwell in the midst of "original blessing."[37]

The one affirmation is an invisible upthrust from the Ground, but one with the Ground itself. It is an invisible energy and movement that manifests itself in a thousand forms and metaphors. It is one of the great transcendentals that surround us and pervade us so that we cannot see them or know them directly: such are the water and the fire, the earth and the air of our own being. Everything is soaked with the one affirmation and sings it within its very being; we cannot isolate it and say: It is this and not that. We know it in its metaphors, its voices: fire, music, life itself, joy and the children of joy, all the heart's ascensions.

This great Yes is at the heart of our knowledge, but some deep timidity makes us hesitate and turn back, keeps us from pursuing the logic to its conclusion. The logic of our being and our knowledge is the affirmation that is joy. At our deepest center, we are this joy, and at this point we are divine. Though we may be intimidated, hurt, schooled out of this knowledge, the affirmation persists as a flame of joy at the core of whatever knowledge we have.

There are moments when one suddenly realizes, with astonishment, the sheer cliff that divides our certainty from our uncertainty, the impossible coexistence within us of pure light and every degree and quality of darkness and confusion. In the center of our consciousness (or surrounding our consciousness as its context, its heaven) there is an utter certitude, the certitude of light within itself. This certitude cannot be fully expressed and yet we must bring it to expression, for in doing this we find our freedom. What the poets are often doing is exactly this, bringing forth from the brush and the trash this shining fragment that shines all the way from the Absolute, from the eye of heaven. One bright shard after another reflects the infinite and self-luminous knowledge that is within us. It is a wisdom, completely simple, completely innocent and unmarked, an eye forever washed and fresh. Whatever it may be, *we know*. As God knows, as God is light, we know and we are light, however confused and ignorant we may be.

Science opens our eyes to a universe full of bright wonder. Poetry initiates us to an inner language of wonder, a light, fullness, and joy at the center of common knowledge. In art and poetry we learn to taste the wine in the heart of the ordinary. Poetry brings forth this wine in its diverse and extravagant vessels, and yet cannot quite speak it. Word remains vessel, still outside yet knowing and reflecting the wine within itself.

> After the final no there comes a yes
> And on that yes the future world depends.
> No was the night. Yes is this present sun.
> If the rejected things, the things denied,
> Slid over the western cataract, yet one,
> One only, one thing that was firm, even
> No greater than a cricket's horn, no more
> Than a thought to be rehearsed all day, a speech
> Of the self that must sustain itself on speech,
> One thing remaining, infallible, would be
> Enough.[38]

The strength of poetry and music, of all living art, is in the refining of the great affirmation out of the ore of life. Better, this power is in revealing the great affirmation that is life itself, beneath its opaque crust. The difference between pleasing art and great art is largely determined by the length of road that has been traveled. A great work is verified by the negation surmounted, the degree to which the affirmation has been tried and proven, has died and been reborn. The new life is unconditioned: not yes and no but simply *yes*. The convergence of poetry and life, of art and gospel, is here, at the point of affirmation.

> Some things, niño, some things are like this,
> That instantly and in themselves they are gay
> And you and I are such things, O most miserable…
>
> For a moment they are gay and are a part
> Of an element, the exactest element for us,
> In which we pronounce joy like a word of our own.
>
> It is there, being imperfect, and with these things
> And erudite in happiness, with nothing learned,
> That we are joyously ourselves and we think

Without the labor of thought, in that element,
And we feel, in a way apart, for a moment, as if
There was a bright *scienza* outside of ourselves,

A gaiety that is being, not merely knowing,
The will to be and to be total in belief,
Provoking a laughter, an agreement, by surprise.[39]

Four

The Dance

Introduction

The fourth quadrant (see Figure 4.1) is earth, matter, material cosmos, the creation. It is, therefore, the world of the body and of humanity participating in the one cosmos and the one planet earth through bodily existence: family, work, play, political and economic life, art. Humanity is one, centered symbolically and existentially in the one earth. Earth and body are final expressions of the Unitive, as it completes its movement from pure spirit to incarnate spirit, from baptism to eucharist.

Both the fourth quadrant of body and earth and the third quadrant of the feminine have long been eclipsed in Western Christianity. Today the West discovers this dark hemisphere as it begins to descend from its position of world dominance to rejoin the other peoples, to return to the common earth of humanity. The world moves toward a cosmic eucharist, as Word and Spirit permeate humanity from within and the sacramental body of Christ grows invisibly.

Four is also the number of completeness, of the Whole. This is expressed in the geometrical figure of the mandala. Combining quaternity with the circle, the mandala represents the wedding of the masculine principle of structure and polarity with the feminine principle of wholeness, simplicity, and unity. This figure, in its many variants, represents both the cosmos and the human person. We have seen in it the final union of God (as differentiated in three Persons) and all creation. In bringing together within a single figure all the elements and dimensions of the one Mystery, it concludes our exploration.

Within the New Testament, the central figure of the cross represents the fullness of reality centered in the crucified Christ. The cross becomes a mandala as it is imagined within a circle that represents the fullness of Divinity, poured into the creation through the death and resurrection of Jesus Christ. This figure has many analogues in the religious traditions of the world, and most particularly within Christianity itself. It represents the four dimensions of the Christ-event and Christ-mystery, which reappear at every level of life and thought. Paul, preacher of the "word of the cross" to the Gentile peoples, has most clearly set before us the whole mystery of human destiny represented in the cross-mandala.

Two (Word) is a first structure, an order, a temple. Then comes Three (Spirit) and the temple is consumed amidst all-speaking tongues of fire. Finally a second structure appears, emerging from the bowels of the earth like an all-comprehending crystal, descending from heaven as foursquare Jerusalem. This is Four, the mandalic structure, the inner bone and skeleton of form. The sequence is historical, played out in the biblical narrative. It is also biographical, experienced in the course of a personal journey.

Four is matter, body, cosmos. From our human perspective, as ground of our existence and the matrix from which we evolve, it would naturally be our starting point. Instead, we have begun with the spiritual traditions and the divine One (the ultimate Ground of being) to find this material ground at the end of our journey. As our conclusion, Four should be a point of convergence, where all the various threads of our discussion come together into a final knot. From a Christian theological viewpoint, this is verified: It is in the body of the crucified and risen Christ that the whole of created reality reaches its final condition. This body of Christ is, however, developing, growing toward its fullness in the course of history. Our conclusion, therefore, is an open conclusion. We know this material "new creation" mainly through the imagination of faith.

Part Four, as I shall develop it, contains *two* distinct elements. First there is the ground, earth, matter, body, physical cosmos, the totality of creation conceived in its materiality. Second there is quaternity and its mandalic representation as the symbolic figure of totality. In antiquity, four was the number of earth, of cosmos: four directions, four winds, four elements, four quarters. Four, then, becomes the number of material, of matter, of the cosmos and the rationality of the cosmos. Four is the number of fullness. There is abundant evidence from anthropology, from the comparative study of religions, and from analytical psychology that the quaternity, with its various mandalic figures, is the archetypal symbol and expression of the whole, of fullness and integration.

There is a finality about material reality, about physical matter, body. It appears as the "bottom" or terminus in the progression from pure spirit through other levels of being to physical energy and its expressions and forms, and finally to inert matter, the dead end. Perhaps matter signifies fullness because it is the farther end, the extreme limit of creation as it "emanates" from spirit, from the divine Spirit. Matter is, in the great chain of being, apparently farthest from God, from spirit. Therefore matter, earth, body (and humanity, in which spirit is wedded to this matter) appears as the last, lost sheep, the farthest one out, the final stranger and alien that must be brought into the divine banquet.

In the biblical tradition, God's salvation reaches downward toward the poor, the people of the earth, but almost entirely within the bounds of Israel. In the gospel, a new surge of divine grace and compassion moves beyond these limits to all humanity. God comes in Jesus to find and bring back the lost sheep, the prodigal son, the sinner, tax-collector, prostitute, and the little ones, the children, the poor, the Galileans and Samaritans. The downward and outward movement of divine grace now breaks through all the structures and boundaries of law and tradition to gather in the lowest and the farthest. This far country is the Galilee or Samaria of materiality, under the shadow of the flesh and of mortality, and of ignorance and sin.

> For the creation was subjected to futility, not of its own will, but by the will of the one who subjected it, in hope that the creation itself will be set free from its bondage to decay and will obtain the freedom of the glory of the children of God. We know that the whole creation has been groaning in labor pains until now; and not only the creation, but we ourselves, who have the first fruits of the Spirit, groan inwardly while we wait for adoption, the redemption of our bodies. (Rom 8:20–23, NRSV)

In this central text, Paul envisions the end of history and the eschatological fullness in terms of bodily resurrection and a cosmic transformation. The final culmination of history is a cosmic re-creation, a transformation of matter.

Four symbolizes fullness, then, and fullness is realized in matter, in earth: the lowest, the furthest, the last. In Jesus' parable of the wedding banquet, the wealthy host finally sends his servants to scour the byways and hedges for guests so that his house may be filled (Lk 14:16–24). Here, as often in Luke, we feel the broad, encircling arc of grace. It is in this dark hinterland of Gentiles, sinners, heretics, the poor, the helpless women and children, the lame, the sick, the blind, and the lepers that unconditioned love is revealed. Again and again in the gospels we feel the warmth and power of the Spirit in this sweeping movement, gathering every last one into the divine *koinonia*.

Christianity, then, has very special affinities with Four. Often four, rather than three, appears to signify Christianity. Tradition recognizes this (symbolically, at least) in the ubiquitous figure of the cross and its correlation with the four gospels. On the other hand (corresponding to the materiality of Four), there appears the central New Testament thread of descent, of *kenosis*, of passion and death followed by resurrection. This is a baptism in the earth, in the bowels of creation, that marks the life of Jesus and of his disciples.

FIGURE 4.1

1. The Missing Fourth

Something is always left out of the discussion; something is always hidden from view. The dark side, the shadow, the back and bottom of our world: All of this belongs to Four. The dark one, the poor one, the cripple (and our own "inferior function"): All of this is the Fourth. Precisely that which is excluded from the mental world of Two (Word), this is the terminus toward which we are carried by Three (Spirit). It is the antipole and dark mirror of One (Silence): Matter in its mystery, the paradoxical outermost tent of divine Spirit.

In the ascent of modern Western civilization to an unprecedented position of dominance in the world, a heavy price has been exacted. If we are unaware of what we have lost, we are aware that something has been lost. In the midst of exponential growth we intuitively feel a proportionate thinning, a dilution, an impalpable loss of inner vitality. As the bud of implicate reality has opened more and more, to the extent that everything is exposed, explicit, available, and negotiable, our loss of substance is accompanied by an estrangement from our bodies, from the world of simple physical life and experience, from the earth.

The basic Christian "mysteries" of Trinity and Incarnation point to a quaternary expression of fullness. Such a movement from trinity to quaternity is suggested in the basic structure of Andrei Rublev's great Trinity icon. Depicted is the visit of the "three men" to Abraham and Sarah at the Oak of Mambre (Gn 18), which was to be followed by the birth of their son Isaac. The three men, drawn as angels (symbolizing the three divine Persons), are seated at a rectangular table. They form a three-sided figure that is open to the beholder, as if the believer is invited to become the fourth member, the fourth side of the figure. This impression is reinforced by the rectangular figure drawn on the front of the table, which conventionally represents the cosmos. The table is prepared for a meal, and on it lies a dish containing meat. The painter suggests, in the two-dimensional rectangle of his icon, a trinitarian Christ-mystery that is open toward the participative Fourth: an invisible fourth guest at the table, who is the beholder, the person of faith. The "perspective" here is oriented toward a fourth dimension that draws the spectator into the scene, into the eucharistic mystery. To vary the metaphor, the painting's dynamic is that of a drawn bow, with its invisible arrow pointed straight toward the beholder.

The food in the dish is not ethereal, angelic food; it appears to be a cooked part of an animal. Literally, this meat represents the beast that Abraham had slaughtered for his three guests. The three guests seem to be waiting for a fourth to join them before they begin to eat it. This very corporeal, sacramental meal requires the participation of the fourth who is flesh and blood.

The icon, significantly, is Russian. This movement from Three to Four takes place in the Russian theological tradition rather than in the earlier Greek tradition. The Russian genius is that of the earth,[1] and the Russian soul brings the crystalline and luminous spiritual theology of the Greek Christian tradition once again down to earth and into the human heart, into the flesh and blood that are humanity. The trinitarian image opens to gather into itself the Fourth, which we are. In Jesus we are invited to enter into the communion of the Three. As we do so, we complete the quaternity, the figure. The New Testament speaks of our divinization, and its revelation is both unitive and quaternary. These two aspects are inseparable; wholeness is one and four.

We have been tracing the profile of a new and more comprehensive Christian wisdom, and have spoken of *resonance* as a characteristic property of such a wisdom. Resonance itself, imagined as participation in a field of energy, belongs to the Third Order. What is it, then, that is to resonate with the Word? Ultimately, everything: the breadth and depths of all that is created, the universe with ourselves at its center. These "depths" must be, first of all, body and earth, with the opaque and mysterious density that belongs to matter. The problem of a Christian wisdom is the problem of a Christianity that truly embraces nature, cosmos, body, and matter: a truly incarnate Christianity. Ultimately, *wisdom is incarnation.*

Jung and the Fourth

It was C. G. Jung who articulated most clearly the problem of the missing Fourth in our modern Western, and Christian, consciousness. Marie-Louise von Franz interprets Jung's life and work as a quest for the solution of this problem.[2] Von Franz sees Jung, as the son of a spiritually alienated pastor, feeling the emptiness and inefficacy of the tradition of Christianity in which he was brought up, and then being moved by an intense experience of the numinosity of nature.

We have looked at Jung as a pioneer in the rediscovery of *psyche:* an arch-explorer of the Third Order. The inner logic of his quest, however, does not permit him to stop there; he is compelled to take a further step. This challenge is The Problem of the Fourth.[3] Jung finds the Fourth prominent in Western thought before Plato, and then eclipsed.

> As compared with the trinitarian thinking of Plato, ancient Greek philosophy favoured thinking of a quaternary type. In Pythagoras the great role was played not by three but by four.[4]

In the beginnings of Christianity, however, quaternity (and the Fourth) appear once again. Jung sees the cross as symbol of the suffering "trinitarian" God who has joined himself with the Fourth: that is with the cosmos, the creation, with humanity.[5]

Jung contends that subsequent Christian theology, strongly influenced by Platonism, systematically excluded the Fourth, and thereby failed to carry the fullness of the original Christ-reality. This fullness, he asserts, can be understood only from a quaternary perspective, and expressed in quaternary terms.

The quaternary scheme recognizes the existence of a secular power opposed to God

> by fettering trinitarian thinking to the reality of this world. The Platonic freedom of the spirit does not make a whole judgment possible: it wrenches the light half of the picture away from the dark half. This freedom is to a large extent a phenomenon of civilization, the lofty preoccupation of that fortunate Athenian whose lot it was not to be born a slave. We can only rise above nature if somebody else carries the weight of the earth for us. What sort of philosophy would Plato have produced had he been his own house-slave? What would the Rabbi Jesus have taught if he had had to support a wife and children? If he had had to till the soil in which the bread he broke had grown, and weed the vineyard in which the wine he dispensed had ripened? The dark weight of the earth must enter into the picture of the whole. In "this world" there is no good without its bad, no day without its night, no summer without its winter. But civilized man can live without the winter, for he can protect himself against the cold; without dirt, for he can wash; without sin, for he can prudently cut himself off

from his fellows and thereby avoid many an occasion for evil. He can deem himself good and pure, because hard necessity does not teach him anything better. The natural man, on the other hand, has a wholeness that astonishes one, though there is nothing particularly admirable about it. It is the same old unconsciousness, apathy, and filth.

If, however, God is born as a man and wants to unite mankind in the fellowship of the Holy Ghost, he must suffer the horrible torture of having to endure the world in all its reality. This is the cross he has to bear, and he himself is a cross. The whole world is God's suffering, and every individual man who wants to get anywhere near his own wholeness knows that this is the way of the cross.[6]

Here we can glimpse the range and power of Jung's wisdom of the Fourth, as he questions the whole Western Christian tradition of thought—bringing light to our problem of the disappearance of a sapiential vision in the West. This text also suggests the horizon of a new Christian wisdom, in a conscious encounter with the unconscious psyche and with our own essential bodiliness. Let us draw out some of the implications of this text of Jung.

- Civilization, however great its benefits, separates us from the earth, and from the people of the earth, the people of "primal," tribal societies.[7] Corresponding to this separation is a division within ourselves, a self-alienation.

- Separation from the earth has reached its most extreme development in the modern civilization of the West. Western technology has enabled "man" to shelter himself, isolate himself, encapsulate himself within an upholstered artificial environment that cuts him off from the natural sources of life and growth.

- This Western civilization has developed out of a Christian matrix. Western Christianity itself has led the way in this migration away from the earth, from people of the earth, from the "wholeness of the natural man," from the fourth and thereby from the whole.

- This isolation from the ground, the whole, the fourth (nature and earth and cosmos, body and therefore humanity) is the situation out of which modern psychology develops. It is another side of the suppression of psyche that we have noted. It was Jung who first brought this collective pathology clearly into the light.

- Jung's insight relates theology immediately to economics and to politics. Our social structures (parallel to the Western structures of thought) are dehumanizing insofar as they raise an elite up into a privileged separation from the ground, while at the same time burying great numbers of "common" people in a position of powerlessness. Psychology confirms that our constructions very often have the purpose of separating and protecting us from the human "ground," and from the unpredictable forces of nature.[8]

- Our Western Christianity is the heir of Greek Christianity and consequently, along the way, of Greek philosophy, through the church fathers who first formulated its doctrinal structures. Christian theology, therefore, has been built as a trinitarian structure raised above the earth (above *the ground*) and therefore confined within its own conceptions and unable to integrate the whole.

- Jung brings together here, as he describes the excluded shadowland of the fourth, a range of different elements. Here we find the earth or "this world," true human fellowship, the poor people of the earth, and the cross of Jesus. Here is Jesus *as* cross, as cruciform man, as the human person completed by being stretched to its true quaternity in the tension between Divinity and earthly reality. Here are the principal elements of our Part Four.

We have already observed the Western tendency to exclude both the First Order (the Unitive) and the Third Order (the divine energy and its manifestations). This repression has operated with a vengeance in regard to the Fourth Order, which corresponds, in Jung's language, to the "inferior function," the repressed and missing Fourth.[9]

The *Timaeus* (of Plato), which was the first to propound a tri-adic formula for the God-image in philosophical terms, starts off with the ominous question: "One, two, three—but...where is the fourth?" This question is, as we know, taken up again in the Cabiri scene of Goethe's *Faust:*

> Three we brought with us,
>> The fourth would not come.
> He was the right one
>> Who thought for them all.[10]

The gulf that Christianity opened out between nature and spirit enabled the human mind to think not only beyond nature but in opposition to it, thus demonstrating its divine freedom, so to speak. This flight from the darkness of nature's depths culminates in trinitarian thinking, which moves in a Platonic, "supracelestial" realm. But the question of the fourth, rightly or wrongly, remained. It stayed down "below," and from there threw up the heretical notion of the quaternity and the speculations of Hermetic philosophy.[11]

Together with Jung's penetrating psychological and histori-cal intuition, we find woven into his vision of the history of Western consciousness a personal gnosticism that departs radi-cally from the mainstream of Christian tradition.

We shall continue to find this Fourth (which we so inti-mately are) the most difficult of our dimensions to know, to accept, and to integrate. "The dark weight of the earth must enter into the picture of the whole." How can we know this and live this? Today's various movements from below,[12] though their explicit purposes are focused in the outer world, respond to this question. Whether ecological or social-politi-cal, they open our constricted Western consciousness to the Fourth, the ground. The solidarity and depth of this ground are essential to a new Christian wisdom. This solidarity, from which we have traveled so far in our individualizing journey, begins to be rediscovered with a new consciousness, freedom, and universality.

2. Return to the Ground

Then the Lord God formed man from the dust of the ground, and breathed into his nostrils the breath of life; and the man became a living being. (Gn 2:7, NRSV)

Creatures of earth, we come from the earth and return to the earth. "Earth" is not only soil or planet but the common ground of humanity from which Western civilization has distanced itself in the course of its dizzying ascent.

Primal Peoples and the Fourth Stage

We have already, in Part One, briefly considered the hypothesis of an *Axial period* at the root of the world's contemporary cultures.[13] Ewert Cousins speaks of the time before this Axial emergence.

> Prior to the Axial Period the dominant form of consciousness was cosmic, collective, tribal, mythic, and ritualistic. This is the characteristic form of consciousness of primal peoples whose cultures provided a substratum throughout the world for the later civilizations and which survive to this day in tribal groups....
>
> The consciousness of the tribal cultures was embedded in the cosmos and in the fertility cycles of nature. Thus there was established a rich and creative harmony between primal peoples and the world of nature, a harmony which was explored, expressed, and celebrated in myth and ritual. Just as they felt themselves part of nature, so they experienced themselves as part of the tribe. They had no sense of independent identity apart from the tribe. It was precisely the web of interrelationships within the tribe that sustained them psychologically, energizing all aspects of their lives. To be separated from the tribe threatened them with death, not only physical but psychological as well. However, the fusion of their identity with the collectivity did not extend beyond their own tribe, for they often looked upon other tribes as mean and hostile. Yet within their tribe they felt organically related to their group as a whole, to the life cycles of birth and death and to nature and the cosmos.[14]

The Axial period brings, out of this ground, a consciousness that is characterized not only by "One" (as in India, Asia) but by "Two" (as in Greece): as if East and West parted here, branching off to develop into the two great hemispheres of dominant culture in the world.[15]

Cousins postulates a *Second Axial period* as the most important event in the evolution of human consciousness since the emergence of a personal consciousness in the Axial period. This Second Axial time, he proposes, is to be marked by the advent of a *global* consciousness. This new consciousness, integrating the whole development of personal consciousness since the First Axial period, also recapitulates the beginning: the consciousness of primal peoples.

> In this Second Axial Period we must rediscover the dimensions of consciousness of the spirituality of the primal peoples of the pre-Axial period. As we saw, this consciousness was collective and cosmic, rooted in the earth and the life cycles. We must rapidly appropriate that form of consciousness or perish from the earth. However, I am not suggesting a romantic attempt to live in the past, rather that the evolution of consciousness proceeds by way of recapitulation. Having developed self-reflexive, analytic, critical consciousness in the First Axial Period, we must now, while retaining these values, reappropriate and integrate into that consciousness the collective and cosmic dimensions of the pre-Axial consciousness. We must recapture the unity of tribal consciousness by seeing humanity as a single tribe. And we must see this single tribe related organically to the total cosmos. This means that the consciousness of the twenty-first century will be global from two perspectives: (1) from a horizontal perspective, cultures and religions are meeting each other on the surface of the globe, entering into creative encounters that will produce a complexified collective consciousness; (2) from a vertical perspective, they must plunge their roots deep into the earth in order to provide a stable and secure base for future development. This new global consciousness must be organically ecological, supported by structures that will insure justice and peace. [16]

This sense of union with earth, which characterizes the primal peoples, is well expressed by the Guatemalan Quiche woman Rigoberta Menchu in her autobiography:

> We use candles to represent the earth, water and maize, which is the food of man. We believe (and this has been passed down to us by our ancestors) that our people are made of maize. We're made of white maize and yellow maize. We must remember this. We put a candle out for man, as the son of the natural world, the universe, and the members of the family join together in prayer.[17]

The integration of Four is a step forward in the evolution of consciousness, but it goes even deeper than this; ultimately it is a transformation of the body. This necessarily escapes schematization, and ultimately it goes beyond this present life. We are here dealing not only with primal cultures, but with intrinsic dimensions of the human person, and of cosmic reality. The Fourth is the body itself.

We can imagine our journey beyond the logos enclosure (which bounds the "rational mind" of our modern West) in three directions, according to our mandalic figure. Two of these directions, the opposite "grounds" of spirit and matter, reflect one another (from our viewpoint) in their quality of mystery, opaqueness, their apophatic quality. At One we ascend to the Unitive (apex), divine Spirit, the atman. At Four we descend to the physical, material, bodily, the cosmic: to the base of the diamond.

Biblical History and Primal Peoples

In our rediscovery of the Primal (primal peoples, primal cultures), we should not forget the tribe of Israel, the children of Abraham and their tribal neighbors. The Bible conserves a record of these peoples from early historical times.

Christianity, while distancing itself from Judaism, has separated itself also from the natural ground. It has often seemed (especially in Catholicism) that the church is not the People of God, the community, the *koinonia,* but rather something built on top of this. We come to see the church primarily as a sacred institution, with its structures of ritual and dogma. This ascending and dualizing tendency is paralleled by a purely trinitarian theology and spirituality that, rather than following the course of the Incarnation, remains above, isolated from the ground: earth, body, humanity.[18]

Jung sees Western *alchemy* as an attempt to move from this trinitarian Christianity to a quaternary, and therefore full Christianity. Jungian psychology attempts to follow the same descending path of integration, as we have seen.[19] Within contemporary Christianity, liberation theology is one corrective movement: a vision that originates in the "ground," from within the situation of poverty and oppression of the Latin American peasant people.[20] Some thinkers have recognized the connection between this social oppression and that exploitation of the natural environment which has characterized the modern West and which has been ignored by the church until now.

The *body* is another side of the Fourth—the body considered not only in terms of the spiritual life, but of human life as a whole. In the New Testament writings, Christian existence is presented emphatically as life in the body. Where there seems to be a dichotomy and opposition between spirit and body, as sometimes in Paul, this is contained within an even stronger consciousness of the bodiliness both of the human person and of the church. This strong physical container for the Spirit hardly survives the transplanting of Christianity from its original Jewish soil into the Hellenized classical culture with its dichotomizing intellectualism.

The separation of Christianity from Israel was traumatic not only for Israel but for Christianity. It becomes gradually apparent that some of the imbalances and deficiencies that appear in the development of Christianity (particularly the tendency toward a disincarnate spiritualism) are probably related to the violence of this original fission: "For if their rejection means the reconciliation of the world, what will their acceptance mean but life from the dead?" (Rom 11:15). Paul here sees the reconciliation of Israel with Christianity as coinciding with the resurrection from the dead. At the end of history, when the Gentiles have been brought in, he sees Israel too entering into Christ.

> A hardening has come upon part of Israel, until the full
> number of the Gentiles come in, and so all Israel will be
> saved. (Rom 11:26–27)

Israel is the root, but the Jews are also imagined as branches that
have been broken off from the root.

> For if you [i.e., Gentiles] have been cut from what is by
> nature a wild olive tree, and grafted, contrary to nature, into
> a cultivated olive tree, how much more will these natural
> branches [i.e., the Israelites] be grafted back into their own
> olive tree. (Rom 11:24)

This root of Israel can be imagined at the base of our mandalic
diagram. The reunion of Christianity and Israel is then, somehow, the realization of this Fourth Pole, a recovery of the "body."
What is the meaning of this metaphor? Let us suppose that the
"groundlessness" of a later Christianity is related to this separation from Israel. When Christianity moved out of the Jewish
world into the Greek world, did it leave behind a unitive relation
to body, to nature, earth, cosmos? Is this what must be recovered
at the end? And until then will we always be "up in the air,"
incomplete, unintegrated?

The reality is not quite as simple as this. The biblical earthi-
ness does not involve a sense of unity with the cosmos. The
Mosaic religion brings, rather, a sharp separation from the general
nature-religion of its time. What is characteristically biblical and
Jewish is *bodiliness*, a physicality of human existence, a living
intensely in the body. This is typical of ancient and tribal peoples,
and it characterizes the biblical religion as well as Israelite life.

Judaism contrasts with Christianity in according a much
higher value to marriage than to virginity. Judaism appears to be
much more a this-worldly religion than the Christianity of the
church fathers and the Middle Ages. There is a *literalness* about
the descendants of Abraham: a particular "chosen people" to
whom God promised a particular land. The divine promise of a
people and of land become generalized through symbolic interpretation in the Christian tradition.

For Christian fathers and medieval writers interpreting the
Old Testament, the literal or historical sense is the "Jewish" truth

of the Word. Christianity defines itself precisely by going beyond this into the "spiritual" meaning. Christianity distinguishes itself by this quantum leap from the biblical figures to Christ and the church. The Old Testament is left behind as merely carnal, as the external and historical image of the spiritual reality that arrives in Jesus Christ.

The worship of Israel (Temple, animal sacrifices, priesthood, Levites) is seen from this Christian perspective as a collection of figures or "types." These are to be realized in Jesus Christ and the church, but in a superior manner: now interiorized and spiritualized.

> I appeal to you therefore, brothers and sisters, by the mercies of God, to present your bodies as a living sacrifice, holy and acceptable to God, which is your spiritual worship. Do not be conformed to this world, but be transformed by the renewing of your minds, so that you may discern what is the will of God—what is good and acceptable and perfect. (Rom 12:1–2, NRSV)

Christianity, then, sees itself as going beyond Israel, beyond the Old Testament; and in doing so, passing from letter to spirit, exterior to interior, shadow to reality. At the same time, however, something is being left behind that will eventually have to be recovered.

Paul sees, on the one hand, the reconciliation between his Jewish people and Christianity as coinciding with "the resurrection of the dead" (Rom 11). On the other hand, he sees the resurrection of the dead in terms of the spiritual body, *soma pneumatikon* (see 1 Cor 15:42–49). To the reconciliation of Israel with Christianity corresponds, apparently, this transformative union of body and spirit. Following the logic of Paul's hints, we might imagine the original separation of Christianity from Judaism as the beginning of some long separation between spirit and body (ground, Fourth), which is to terminate only with the reunion of Christianity and Israel. It is as if, in this reunion with the ancestral root of Abraham, the church were in some way to recover its own body. But Paul's words suggest that this conclusive event may occur only at the end of this present world and its history (Rom

11:15.25–26). It is difficult to know how much weight we should give to these Pauline prophecies.

Francis of Assisi and the Fourth Order

Within the medieval Christian tradition, Francis of Assisi embodies a return to the simplicity and the fullness that we find in the gospels. We see in him an arrival, a completeness, that is a fresh appearance of the fullness of the beginning. At the same time, he represents, at the dawning of the Western civilization that we know, a return to the ground.

God is visible to Francis in the natural world around him; his *Canticle of Brother Sun* is the expression of a completely Christ-centered nature mysticism. At the same time, Francis develops a mysticism of the humanity of Christ. Ewert Cousins sees in Francis's way "a watershed in the history of Western Christianity."[21] The current of popular devotion that Francis inspires will turn away definitively from the tradition of Christian Neoplatonism, the Eastern "First Wisdom", to become a characteristically Western spirituality. Francis is devoted to the literal gospel story of Christ, and does not need to go beyond it to find a spiritual dimension. He meditates on the events of Jesus' life in their concrete fullness.

The Little Poor Man, as Cousins points out, was passionately attracted to the earth, and as his life neared its end he asked to be placed naked upon it to die. This downward gravitation is evident also in his obsessive concern for Christian poverty, and therefore his assimilation to the poor, to the people of the earth. He appears, more than other historical saints, as a second Jesus, a new incarnation. He appears as an incarnation of the spirit of Christ and nothing more. He seems another Christ with no further spirituality or doctrine, no particular superstructure, added to the person and the simple existence of Jesus. He is perfect in this simplicity, in this "nothing more" that resembles the everyday ordinariness of Zen realization.[22]

Francis of Assisi leads Christian spirituality out of the monastery and back into the marketplace. In this he symbolically completes the Western movement, the redshift or incarnational transition from "John the Baptist": the separatist, "baptismal," desert monasticism of the East. Francis is an icon of the charism of the West, of Western Christianity and Western humanity, in its full realization.

Francis's universal appeal witnesses to the simple completeness that he represents. In him we can behold an arrival at the universality of the mandalic figure through integration of the Fourth. His reception of the stigmata (the wounds of the nails of Christ's crucifixion) in his hands and feet reproduces in his flesh the quaternary figure of the cross. This figure of fullness appears as a divine seal on his Christ-realization.

3. The Body of Christ

Diametrically opposite to the vector of the first wisdom (an ascent of spirit away from matter into the divine Unitive) is the movement of the Christ-event in the New Testament: "The Word became flesh and dwelt among us." In Jesus, the fullness of Divinity has come into the world in bodily form, to dwell permanently within humanity as it transforms this humanity into its own unitive being. The life of Jesus bears him forward toward the cross, where he descends into the earth as the seed of new creation. We are ever beginning to learn this gospel of incarnation. It presses upon us urgently once again at the threshold of the Third Millennium.

Biblical History, Christ, and the Body

Biblical religion often shocks us with its unyielding bodiliness, its "carnality." The revelation of God in the First Testament narratives is communicated through very earthly encounters and events, despite the insistence on God's transcendence. The Bible does not present a spirituality of transcending the body, or of transcending human conflict or sexuality, but rather a spirituality of the presence of God in the midst of human life and activity. From the creation of man and woman in the first chapters of Genesis, through the stories of the patriarchs and their offspring, through the Books of Kings and the prophets, this revelation is written in the script of a completely human and bodily history.

This "physicality" of the divine revelation reaches its culmination in Jesus Christ, in whom the fullness of God became *flesh* to live among us. The bodiliness of the Christ-fact is accented again and again even in the Johannine literature, where the New Testament becomes most "spiritual" (see 1 Jn 3:23; 1:1–2; 4:2–3a; 4:15; 5:1.5). The flesh is the "hinge of salvation":[23] we are redeemed as bodily beings through the crucified and risen body of Jesus, into which we are incorporated. From the conception and birth of Jesus through his bodily passion and death to his resurrection in the body, the single comprehensive movement continues then through eucharist and the life of the "body of Christ" in this world to the final resurrection *in the body.* To this final bodily resurrection of humanity corresponds the re-creation of the physical cosmos, which is the ultimate end of history (Rom 8:19–23).

We receive life through the sacramental body of Christ: both in the eucharist of the liturgical assembly and in the eucharist of humanity that is constituted by mutual service and by the poor themselves. The life is one, though we who share it are many.

Our Part Four looks like a company of things going in the same direction: cosmos, matter, the poor, the human body, the mandalic figure of fullness. The reality of Four, however (as of each of our other poles) demands a unity, a single intentionality. This intrinsic unity and single thrust are theological: the vector of the Christ-event as it moves toward the universal body of Christ, its final terminus. We see the inner movement of the gospel itself driving in the same direction through Jesus' descent, his *kenosis* by immersion in the poverty of the common human condition terminating in his crucifixion, and finally in his resurrection as the unitive Person.

Viewing the Christ-event "from above," we can see matter and body becoming a mediation of the divine Unitive. This takes place first in the incarnation of the unitive Word, then throughout the life of Jesus on earth as the Unitive is manifested in him. The movement proceeds still further in the church as sacrament[24] of Christ, most explicitly in the eucharist. The whole process is sacramental, flowing from Jesus, who is the Sacrament of God (of the divine Unitive, that is), and so on. Here sacramentality is to be considered as a mediation of the divine Unitive: a mediation through which human persons participate in the unitive reality of God. This participation in God is experienced through a living communion in the body of Christ.

The unity of Four is rooted in this mediation of the divine Unitive. While Two and Three also mediate the Unitive, Four is a terminus. Here, at last, we come to ground. As we arrive at Four, a physical center emerges that draws together into itself and around itself all the elements that have been left disconnected, unrelated, deprived of their full context and meaning. This can only be the body of Christ, the "whole Christ." Teilhard de Chardin offers us a comprehensive and dynamic vision: Christ-Omega as the gravitational center that draws everything in the universe forward and also inward, into orbit around itself.

Teilhard sees the fullness of the body of the risen Christ consisting not only of the mystical body of human persons, but also of a cosmic body, which is identical with the universe. As immanent "Omega," Christ unifies the universe in himself.

> This is the point we must bear in mind: in no case could the Cosmos be conceived and realized, without a supreme centre of spiritual consistence.... What gives the World its "gratuitous" character is precisely that the position of universal Centre has not been given to any supreme intermediary between God and the Universe, but has been occupied by the Divinity himself.... Since the Pauline Christ (the great Christ of the mystics) coincides with the universal term, omega, adumbrated by our philosophy—the grandest and most necessary attribute we can ascribe to him is that of exercising a supreme physical influence on every cosmic reality without exception.[25]

For Teilhard, the Christ-Omega is the center of cosmic convergence, "attainable and inevitably present in all things."

> It was in order that He might become omega that it was necessary for Him, through the travail of the Incarnation, to conquer and animate the Universe.[26]

Teilhard sees the cross not only, with Christian tradition, as symbol of the redemptive suffering and death of Christ, but also as symbolizing a cosmic and historical dynamic. The cross, in his vision, is equivalent to the labor of new creation, which Christ bears; that is, to the whole weight of human endeavor. The universe itself, as in the Pauline texts of Colossians and Ephesians, is centered in the figure of the cross.

> The universe assumes the form of Christ—but O mystery! He whom we discover is Christ crucified.[27]

The cosmos itself, for Teilhard, has a unifying power. We are not merely individuals, because the cosmos is one.

> Because Matter, throwing off its veil of restless movement and multiplicity, had revealed to him its glorious unity.... Because it had for ever withdrawn his heart from all that is merely local or individual, all that is fragmentary, henceforth for him it alone in its totality would be his father and mother, his family, his race, his unique, consuming passion.[28]

Teilhard represents a revolution in Christian spirituality. Turning from the old way of the realization of spirit through its progressive separation from matter, he sketches a new way in which spirit realizes itself through an incarnation: by immersing itself in matter: "The rising Sun was being born in the heart of the world."[29] This new spirituality is expressed rhapsodically in Teilhard's hymns to matter.[30]

Terminal Matter

Matter is both beginning and end, *materia prima* and final state. At this point in our progression, we encounter it as end-point, limit, outer perimeter, final form, resting place, consummation, the totally explicit manifestation. Let us explore this finality of matter and of body.

In the world of physics, solid matter as we know it is the

final state of energy as it moves down the scale to its lower limit. Matter seems to be congealed energy; within the universe of million-degree temperatures, of unimaginable intensities of energy, solid matter is the frozen ground, the pocket, the sink, sump and valley, into which energy falls and settles. We bodily terrestrians are only a few hundred degrees from absolute zero on the temperature scale. In this universe of extremes, our earth appears to be very exceptional: a sheltered guarded oasis, a moist and cool garden where life can exist without being immediately annihilated by the raw and violent forces that rule "out there."

The visible matter that we know is the "letter," the most explicit script, the outer and obvious surface of the divine manifestation and then of the divine self-communication. Beginning in spirit, God ends in the flesh, in the sense that body is the final vessel of the Divine in the story of redemption and transformation, in the unitive drama.

Body is frequently an end-point. Physical violence and physical death terminate conflicts; physical intercourse consummates the marriage union—*they shall be one flesh*—and conceives a new life. The word of God is not fulfilled until it has been carried into action. Faith leads to a love that is expressed in service, and perhaps to martyrdom, which is a consummation of witness in the body itself.

For Paul, *the body of Christ* is the destination of all those who are to be saved: His frequent "in Christ" signifies participation in this body. The eucharist is a ritual enactment of this participation in which believers become one body by partaking of the one bread. Jesus' bodily resurrection is *the* decisive event, the turning point of history (see 1 Cor 15:12–28). Paul is emphatic on the intimate relation between human body and divine Spirit.

> The body is not meant for immorality, but for the Lord, and the Lord for the body... Do you not know that your body is a temple of the Holy Spirit within you, which you have from God? You are not your own; you were bought with a price. So glorify God in your body. (1 Cor 6:13, 19–20)

Throughout the Letter to the Hebrews, the saving Christ-event is presented as pivoting on the body of Jesus. Pure spirits are marginal to this work, which is consummated in the flesh.

> Since, therefore, the children share flesh and blood, he himself likewise shared the same things, so that through death he might destroy the one who has the power of death, that is, the devil, and free those who all their lives were held in slavery by the fear of death. For it is clear that he did not come to help angels, but the descendants of Abraham. Therefore he had to become like his brothers and sisters in every respect, so that he might be a merciful and faithful high priest in the service of God, to make a sacrifice of atonement for the sins of the people. Because he himself was tested by what he suffered, he is able to help those who are being tested. (Heb 2:14–18, NRSV)

John's First Letter insists that saving faith is a faith in Jesus Christ "in the flesh."

> By this you know the Spirit of God: every spirit which confesses that Jesus Christ has come in the flesh is of God, and every spirit which does not confess Jesus is not of God. (1 Jn 4:2–3)

John's Gospel originally concluded, apparently, with the encounter between Thomas and the risen Jesus (Jn 20:24–29). This episode closes the gospel narrative by rejoining the end of its first chapter, the parallel encounter between Jesus and Nathanael. Thomas expresses powerfully both the depth and the height, the darkness and light: the scandal of the crucified body of Jesus and the illuminated faith that knows his risen body. Here too everything turns around the body of Jesus, at the paschal point of death and resurrection.

> Now Thomas, one of the twelve, called the Twin, was not with them when Jesus came. So the other disciples told him, "We have seen the Lord." But he said to them, "Unless I see in his hands the print of the nails, and place my finger in the mark of the nails, and place my hand in his side, I will not believe." Eight days later, his disciples were again in the house, and Thomas was with them. The doors were shut, but Jesus came and stood among them, and said, "Peace be

with you." Then he said to Thomas, "Put your finger here, and see my hands; and put out your hand, and place it in my side; do not be faithless, but believing." Thomas answered him, "My Lord and my God!" (Jn 20:24–28)

4. The Fullness: Mandala and Christ-Mystery

In many spiritual traditions of the world, similar mandalic figures have been constructed that represent the unification of all reality around a center. These figures, typically, will represent both the dimensions of the cosmos and the dimensions of the psyche or human person. Mandalic figures have been created in Christian tradition particularly around the figure of the cross. In the Jungian school of modern psychology, the mandala (particularly when it appears spontaneously in dreams) is taken to represent the end-point in the process of integration of psyche or Self.

This is its magnificence, and even greater is Man:
One fourth of it constitutes all living things, three fourths of it constitute the eternal things of heaven.[31]

Sacred Place

In ancient civilizations, a sacred geometry imparts order and meaning to the world. The sacred mountain, grove or temple, the city itself, is center of the world.

The same is the case with city walls: long before they were military erections, they were a magic defense, for they marked out from the midst of a "chaotic" space, peopled with demons and phantoms...an enclosure, a place that was organized, made cosmic, in other words, provided with a "centre."[32]

The building of an altar or temple is often conceived as a creation of the world, or ritually identified with the first creation of the world. Center, circle, square (and the mandalic figure that incorporates all of these) mark the sacred place where earth communicates with the heavens and with the underworld.

The same sense of a cosmogony is also apparent in the construction of the mandala as practiced in the Tantric school. The word means "circle"; the Tibetan renderings of it are either "centre" or "what surrounds." The thing itself is a series of circles which may or may not be concentric, inscribed in a square. Inside this diagram, outlined on the ground with a coloured thread or trails of coloured powder, images of the various Tantric divinities are placed. The mandala is both an *imago mundi* and a symbolic pantheon. The initiation consists in the neophyte's penetration into the various zones or stages of the mandala. The rite may be looked on with equal justice as the equivalent of the *pradaksina*, the well-known ceremonial of going round a temple or sacred monument *(stupa)*, or as an initiation by way of ritual entry into a labyrinth. The assimilation of the temple with the mandala is obvious in the case of Boro-budor and the Indo-Tibetan temples built under the influence of Tantric doctrine. All these sacred constructions represent the whole universe in symbol: their various floors or terraces are identified with the "heavens" or levels of the cosmos. In one sense, every one of them reproduces the cosmic mountain, is, in other words, held to be built at the "centre of the world." This symbolism of the centre, as I shall show, is as much involved in the building of towns as of houses: every consecrated place, in fact, is a "centre"; every place where hierophanies and theophanies can occur, and where there exists the possibility of breaking through from the level of earth to the level of heaven.[33]

In Africa,

> The founding of a new town repeats the creation of the world; once the spot has been confirmed by ritual, a square or circular enclosure is put round it with four gates corresponding to the four points of the compass...towns are divided into four in imitation of the Cosmos; in other words, they are a copy of the Universe.[34]

The Christian Mandala

There is an intrinsic quaternity in the Christ-mystery or Christ-event, which reappears in many forms. It is expressive of the gathering together of all reality in Jesus Christ, crucified and risen. Christ is the center that joins God and humanity, God and the world, and in this union every other union (e.g., that of all humanity) is virtually contained.[35]

Christ becomes manifest as the unitive center of cosmos and history. Cosmos and history, or being and time, in turn, find representation as the vertical and horizontal axes of a quaternary figure, a cross. This cross is also a mandala,[36] the circle of completeness, symbol of the *pleroma*. In Christian tradition, this implicit mandala of the cross appears everywhere and is identified with Christ himself. It represents Jesus at once crucified and glorified.

A number of texts in the Pauline writings (and most explicitly in the Deutero-Pauline letters to the Colossians and Ephesians) express the totality of the Christ-mystery or Christ-event in a mandalic figure centered in Jesus Christ on the cross. On the vertical axis of this figure, God and the created world are brought together in the crucified and glorious Christ. On the horizontal axis, Jews and Gentiles (implicitly, the Jews and the whole of humanity) are brought together in Christ.

Implicit behind the Christian mandalic figures, as we have already seen, is a trinitarian-cosmic figure that represents the intrinsic form of all reality as it is centered in Christ[37] (Figure 4.2).

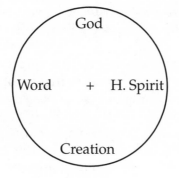

FIGURE 4.2

From the early centuries of Christianity, the gospel has been conceived as *one and four*. The four gospels have been seen as constituting a single whole. Their authors have been traditionally represented together in a geometrical figure, usually some variant of the "four living creatures" of Ezekiel and Revelation.[38] The four Evangelists, or four gospels, form a mandalic figure, which is paralleled by a related constellation of four Apostles.[39]

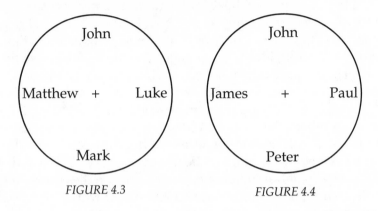

FIGURE 4.3   FIGURE 4.4

Mark's Gospel has been associated with Peter from a very early time. It is Luke who narrates the life and activities of Paul. Matthew's Gospel is written for a Jewish-Christian community such as that with which we associate the apostle James. While there is an area of uncertainty around the authorship of Matthew, of John, of Mark, gospel text and tradition offer in each case a dominant cluster of associations.

John and Mark are one in their central preoccupation with the identity of Jesus, with the questions "Who is this man?" and "What is this that is in him?" John identifies Jesus as the divine Word at the outset, in his Prologue. Mark introduces his narrative as the good news of the Son of God, and proceeds immediately with the epiphany of Jesus' baptism. Through the remainder of his gospel this identity is veiled, however, except for occasional moments of revelation and recognition.

Matthew presents Jesus as the authoritative messianic teacher, and focuses his narrative on Jesus' doctrine, presented as the New Torah in the five great sermons that are part of the essential structure of his book. We have seen that Luke, on the other hand, presents the life and work of Jesus (and then the story of the apostolic church) as movement, as an advancing wave of the divine energy of the Spirit, spreading irresistibly outward into the world. In Matthew and Luke we find Jesus and his work presented in terms of Torah and Spirit, institution and movement, divine Word and divine Energy.

The Pauline Mandala

It is in several very dense Pauline texts that the cross-mandala figure (the fundamental unity-in-quaternity of the Christ-mystery) becomes most explicit. For Paul, the cross of Jesus contains within itself the whole of the Mystery. With the densest irony, he proposes this cross as the summation of divine wisdom:

> For Christ did not send me to baptize but to preach the gospel, and not with eloquent wisdom, lest the cross of Christ be emptied of its power. For the word of the cross is folly to those who are perishing, but to us who are being saved it is the power of God. (1 Cor 1:17–18; see 1:22–24, 2:1–2)

In several passages of the Deutero-Pauline letters to the Ephesians and Colossians, the figure of this cross appears at the center of the theological poles of the Christ-mystery itself: Gentiles and Jews, God and creation (Figure 4.5). These two axes, horizontal and vertical, have already emerged in our examination of the gospels.

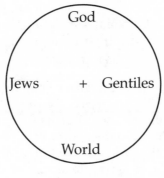

FIGURE 4.5

> But now in Christ Jesus you who once were far off have been brought near by the blood of Christ. For he is our peace; in his flesh he has made both groups into one and has broken down the dividing wall, that is, the hostility between us. He has abolished the law with its commandments and ordinances, that he might create in himself one new humanity in place of the two, thus making peace, and might reconcile both groups to God in one body through the cross, thus putting to death that hostility through it. So he came and proclaimed peace to you who were far off and peace to those who were near; for through him both of us have access in one Spirit to the Father. So then you are no longer strangers and aliens, but you are citizens with the saints and also members of the household of God, built upon the foundation of the apostles and prophets, with Christ Jesus himself as the cornerstone. In him the whole structure is joined together and grows into a holy temple in the Lord; in whom you also are built together spiritually into a dwelling place for God. (Eph 2:13–22, NRSV; see Col 1:17–22)

The center of this vision is Jesus Christ on the cross. In this central cruciform Christ, the four dimensions converge: heaven and earth, Gentile and Jew: that is, God and the world, the people first chosen and the whole of humanity. It is in the physical body of Christ on the cross that all of reality is brought to unity, for in this body, this center, dwells the fullness of God from which all things have come, in which they subsist, to which they return. The two quaternary images of body and of building are interwoven.

Another text of Ephesians sketches the geometrical figure with bold strokes, developing the center and the fullness of the figure without specifying its four poles.

> For this reason I bow my knees before the Father, from whom every family in heaven and on earth takes its name. I pray that, according to the riches of his glory, he may grant that you may be strengthened in your inner being with power through his Spirit, and that Christ may dwell in your hearts through faith, as you are being rooted and grounded in love. I pray that you may have the power to comprehend,

with all the saints, what is the breadth and length and
height and depth, and to know the love of Christ that surpasses knowledge, so that you may be filled with all the
fullness of God. (Eph 3:14–19, NRSV)

The center is affirmed in a characteristically Pauline cascade of
terms: inner being (lit. "inner *man*"), interior dwelling in the
heart, Christ, faith, root, ground, love. Then the four dimensions
are projected with a rhetorical imprecision. Finally, with "the
love of Christ that surpasses...filled with all the fullness of
God," the whole is enclosed in an exultant circle.

From these and many other New Testament texts,[40] a quaternary figure emerges (represented by an equilateral cross)
that corresponds to the unification of all reality through the
death and resurrection of Christ (see Figure 4.6). The unification, indeed, is *in Christ.*

FIGURE 4.6

Implicitly condensed within the figure is all that is being presented throughout the four parts of this book. This *One in Four* is
the cypher of the ancient Christian wisdom of the New Testament and fathers, which was to reappear in the form of the four
senses of Scripture, among other variations. This same pattern of
the One in Four offers itself once again in our time, as the interior
structure of a new Christian theological wisdom open to the
larger world of today.

5. Contemporary Encounters at the Frontier of Four

As Christianity opens up to become aware of positive movements outside its own "container," it encounters new life on these four frontiers. These dimensions are also the sites of new emergences within Christianity itself. The unitive pole of Christianity (One) is awakened by contact with the traditions of the East; the feminine or energy pole (Three) is awakened by the emergence of woman, by the movements of vitality (also in the arts) that resist the domination of logos and rationalism. The logos-pole itself (Two) is opened up by philosophies and hermeneutic movements that break open the narrow epistemological limits of post-Enlightenment Western consciousness. It is with the encounters in the quadrant of *Four* that we are now concerned.

Four presents something like a final challenge to Western civilization, which has raised itself so far above both the earth and the human ground. Four is reflected in the billions of human persons who move about outside this Western cloister of privilege, and in the crumbling society of the great cities. The gravitation of Four pulls at the West like a great tide, a jealous sea of entropy, undermining its power and prosperity, whispering of death and transformation.

- *Cosmos: the new cosmologies.* Our vision of the universe has expanded and come alive. Christianity, confronted with this new cosmos revealed by astronomers and physicists, opens its vision to a new breadth and dynamism.

- *Earth: ecology.* We are being forced to rediscover our membership in planet earth, our participation in the one planetary life and our common destiny on earth. Human community is reinforced by a new imperative and discovers its sacramental participation in the matter of this one world.

- *Body Wisdom.* Under the influence of less cerebral human traditions and in the context of the new psychology, Westerners rediscover their oneness with the body, the unity of the human person as body, psyche, and spirit. A holistic sense of humanity develops toward spiritual growth and integration as well as toward healing.

- *Third World Peoples.* The people of the West are gradually learning to listen to "those outside": to the rest, the majority of humanity. In the space of freedom that Western progress has provided, a new sense of solidarity begins to emerge, with the unlimited range that the communications media provide. Within Christianity, the base communities of Latin America and the new liberation theology signal the rebirth of that sense of church as communion which has been inaccessible to the more prosperous Christian peoples. The church is reborn at its base, on the level of the human ground.

- *Primal Cultures.* Contact with the earliest surviving forms of human culture brings before the Western consciousness that which we have lost, and that which lies buried and neglected within us. We are invited to a new simplicity of human communion and of communion with the earth; but now on a global scale.[41]

6. Work

Work embodies our active relationship to the world: to everything around us, including other people. Work brings us to the ground and to the whole of life: It is the body of life during the long week, before the sabbath of unitive transfiguration. Work is the field in which we are to incarnate the Unitive. It is the farthest place, the extreme expression of the One, where we are to bring forth the One in the most opaque multiplicity, and bring forth the obdurate world in the One. Work is the "bottom line": Here we must prove our faith against the resistance of matter. Here we are among facts, the bruising hardware of reality.

From a mandalic perspective, the movement of work is downward and outward. We can explore this sector of life that is work by means of a quaternary figure (Figure 4.7), with one of its two axes moving from spiritual to material work, and the other from fixed to creative work.

FIGURE 4.7

Along the vertical axis we descend from "inner work" of meditation or asceticism through "psychic" work (which would include ministering to the psyche of self or others, and perhaps creative art) to simple physical work. Along the horizontal axis we proceed across from work that is completely determined by necessity (by situation or personal need, structure or rule) to work that is generative, creative, that flows from within and freely expresses the person.

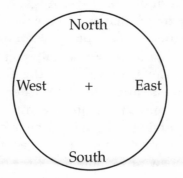

FIGURE 4.8

In earlier, "Christian" versions of the mandala, we had found the four poles usually tending to coalesce into the groupings NW and SE (see Figure 4.8). In the present version, the pairing is rather NE and SW: that is, spiritual and creative, physical and determined. We have found these NE and SW pairings, however, in some of the Christian mandalas: in the affinity between John and Luke, John and Paul, the *One* and the Holy Spirit, unity and freedom. Similarly we have seen an affinity between Peter and James, Peter and Matthew, Matthew and Mark; between law and that "Fourth" which is matter, body, world, external church.

These opposite pairs correspond at once to new and old, inner and outer. This opposition appears strongly in the New Testament, becoming most explicit in Paul. In 2 Corinthians, chapters 4–5, it is the exterior that is old and is passing away, while the interior is renewed and renewing. Scriptural letter and law are exterior, while the Spirit, Christ, God, are manifested interiorly and communicated from the interior outward.

We can conceive of human work as a movement *outward:* from the interior of the person outward and then from the person outward into the world. This corresponds to the movement that we have just described within the New Testament: the movement of grace as it effects a new creation in the person, and then through the person in the world. The distinction between "servile" work and free or creative work is transformed in this dynamic context of new creation.

In modern times, work has largely become isolated from the whole of life. We too easily surrender the life of work to servility, in the sense of an uncreative determination by the old. This is a corollary of the predominance, in modern life, of the impersonal, the technological, of mechanical routine. The "job" becomes a thing by itself, more or less lifeless.

How is work to be seen in a sapiential, a wisdom perspective? From the Sophia passages[42] in Proverbs, Sirach, and the Wisdom of Solomon, we can conceive of a person's work as a participation in Sophia, the divine Wisdom, and thus a participation in the creativity of God. God's creativity is a shared activity; the Creator does not work alone. This is already apparent, with a nuptial resonance, in the first account of God's creation of human persons in Genesis (Gn 1:26–27). In later Sophia texts, where the woman is working along with God in creation and then is beside man in his work (Prv 8:22–31; Wis 9:1–18), Sophia herself seems to confer a participation in God and in God's creative activity.

Inseparable from work, in modern thought since Marx, is *alienation*. Alienation is slavery, servility. Its Old Testament image is the forced labor of the Israelites in Egypt. Its gospel model is the prodigal son, in a strange and harsh land far from home, feeding somebody else's pigs. Alienation goes together with exile; it is a personal experience of exile. The sentence of labor was passed on Adam and Eve at the moment they were evicted from their home in Paradise.

Alienation and isolation are often experienced together in the contemporary life of work. Work is partitioned from the rest of life. It is something that you go out to and come home from, as if it were a world completely different from that of home and family.

How can we reimagine the life of work? Let us imagine a participation in God's new creation of the world in Jesus Christ, in which the creative light comes forth from the center of the human person to work a transformation at once in the world and in the person. This transformation is into a *unitive* mode of being, into the new world of the body of Christ. The freedom and creativity of the Holy Spirit characterize this work, so that it brings freedom and newness into the world. The work always brings something new into the world, brings this Spirit itself into the world: a Spirit of freedom and peace. The work, then, is vessel and embodiment of this Spirit, its sacramental communication to the world.

Imagined in this way, work overflows the boundaries within which we usually conceive it, and this is right. We are brought inward to the roots of such a work, in the work of faith, hope, and love. Faith, hope, and love are the essential participation in the divine Act that brings the newness forth within this world. This work comprehends all of life, rather than only eight or twelve hours of the day spent at a particular "job." Emerging from its roots in faith, hope, and love, the work comes to expression in every situation and every encounter.

The eucharist, according to Teilhard de Chardin, takes up the work of all humanity into the body of Christ, into the transforming energies of the Christ-Omega. Teilhard sees work in function of the body of Christ, as human participation in a dynamic new creation. Bread and wine are not simply fruits of the earth but products of human work.

Bearing

Irenaeus makes a broad and profound use of the word *bear*.[43] This word, with its broad range of senses whether in Greek, in Latin, or in English, can embrace the notion of work that we have been developing. Among the meanings of *to bear* in English are: (a) to support, sustain; (b) to carry, bring (forward); (c) to suffer: *"passio"*; (d) to bear fruit, as a tree; (e) to bring forth from within, as a child. The vocation and responsibility of a human person is to bear the world.

Both the work of Adam and the work of Eve (Gn 3:16–19) are comprehended by this word. So also is the work of Jesus in his life and death, and our participation in the new creation as Paul sees it (see Rom 8:18–23; 2 Cor 4–5). The weight of suffering and the weight of glory are the two sides of Christian life, of Christian "bearing" for Paul (2 Cor 4:17; see Rom 8:18–23).

To "bear the world" (or bear Christ, or humanity, or even oneself, it all happens together) is therefore a polyvalent metaphor that seems to carry the whole meaning—both the weight of the old and the hidden, swelling potential of the new; both the masculine and the feminine sides of work. To bear the world, at least since the Incarnation, the coming of the God-man, is also to bear God. Here we immediately think of Mary. Irenaeus writes of the human person gradually learning and growing from childhood, being trained by God to bear the Holy Spirit, that is, to bear the weight of Divinity, the weight of the divine glory. This is the unitive terminus of work. The weight that we bear in this life is an initiation to the weight of God.

The image "to bear" is a dualistic one: We bear something that is outside us, on us, or something that is within us but other than ourselves. The terminus, however, must be unitive. And the bearing itself must be a progressive initiation into this unity, this participation in the One.

We are confronted with the choice between an acceptance or a refusal of this apprenticeship of bearing. At the heart of Mark's Gospel (8:34–38), Jesus presents this choice as that of taking up one's cross and bearing it after him. In his Letter to the Philippians (3:8–11), Paul exults in the unitive knowledge of Jesus Christ, by which he becomes Christ. By bearing the yoke of Jesus (see Mt 11:28–30), Paul himself becomes the tree of life, bearing the fruit of eternal life.

Jesus comes into the world as worker and as wood, as gardener (see Jn 20:15), as carpenter, and as the tree of life. In him we become this tree, this wood. The divine life (Holy Spirit, Grace, Sophia) flows up into us from within, at our inner roots, and then must flow outward into the world, with which we are unitively joined by our fruits, our work.

Artistic creation, in our contemporary culture, may seem only a diversion, an entertainment; often a pitiful cult of "originality." Art is a sign of great theological importance, however. The creative imagination expressed in art and poetry anticipates the "perfect work" of new creation, explores the far reaches of possibility, looks from within this confined, "fallen" world into the world of freedom, the world of resurrection, of the "glory of the children of God" (see Rom 8:21).[44]

From the subjective or personal viewpoint, genuine poetry and art are a realization of the inner self and its creative freedom: an experience of the unitive and generative core of the person. This central energy of creative freedom is then expressed in the world, brought out into the common consciousness as something new in the world. A glittering particle of new creation reflects the glory of the transfigured person. In this way, artistic creativity is prophetic. We find an explicitly prophetic poetry in the First Testament: already in Genesis and the other Books of Moses, and then in the Psalms, Song of Songs, and in the Prophetic books themselves, especially that of Isaiah. Much of the New Testament is a prophetic poetry looking forward to the kingdom of God, whether in Paul's rhapsodic singing of the Christ-mystery or in the parables and discourses of Jesus or in the gospel narratives themselves. Everywhere, the New Testament writings breathe the fragrance of the kingdom, of the new creation in progress.

Owen Barfield sees the emergence of the Romantic tradition of poetic creativity in the West as a fruit of the creative light and energy that came into the world in Christ, infused into humanity at the time of the incarnation of the Word.[45] Major works of art are "signs," epiphanies, something like the healing signs of Jesus. They are first fruits of the promised land: glimmering anticipations of a humanity that is healed, whole, free, and generative, and of a world full of the density and luminosity of God.

Bearing the World

Speaking of work in this century immediately opens issues of oppressive social and economic structures. From a Marxist perspective, our contemporary world is literally ruled by capital. One's profession or work is the key to one's social status, to one's slavery or freedom. From a Christian perspective, human work has to do with the progression or arrest of the kingdom in this world: with the achievement or failure of the *koinonia* that is the work of Christ.

To speak of work is to point to the weight that must be borne: the human weight, the whole weight of the old world, that is implicit in our metaphor "to bear." It is the people at the bottom who are bearing the rest of the world. We are being carried by the people at the bottom, by the people who are working "in the earth."[46] Truly, if a little too neatly, we can speak of the two great classes of people today as the *consumers* and the *consumed.*[47]

Jesus came into the world to bear the world, and taught his disciples to bear the world by carrying their cross after him (see Mk 8:31–37). Some people bear the world consciously, willingly, in Christian faith (or in a simple human faith). Others bear the world because they must: because they are at the bottom. And each of us bears the world in his or her own life, by bearing our own life, ourselves, and one another. To become mature means to bear rather than merely being borne. It means being parent rather than merely child. The mature tree bears fruit (see Jn 15:1–8).

The Christian and post-Christian West is hated by many other people because it has, since the age of colonialism, been borne by the rest of humanity rather than fulfilling its vocation to bear the world. This oppressive history is not absolved by the Western technology, which, while it promises to ease the burden for everyone, consolidates the grip of a dominant elite on the resources and lives of the rest of humanity.

The literally imperial style of the highest Roman Catholic authority has too often projected (despite the selflessly dedicated service of one pope after another) an institutional power that is borne by humanity rather than laboring to bring forth a new humanity. This symbolic confusion of kingdoms, together with the authoritarianism that it encourages, appears more and more clearly as an obstacle to the church in its mission of communicating the gospel.

The choice of bearing or being borne corresponds to the choice presented by the gospel: to descend or ascend. Jesus is decisively committed to the way of descent; again and again he insists on this way for his followers (see Phil 2:6–11; 1 Cor 1:17–31). Clearly, Jesus recognized that a self-gratifying ascent would be the great temptation for his apostles, and he strongly, repeatedly, warned them against it (see Mk 8:31–33, 34ff.; 10:35–45).

When Jesus, as the gospels tell us, washed the feet of his disciples and instituted the eucharist,[48] he symbolically destroyed the "old paradigm" of domination and instituted a new order of communion. This means mutual service, *bearing* one another (see Gal 6:2). Christians are ever learning to bear the world. The church suffers, through the ages and in a new way today, the pains of childbirth; something new, and larger than herself, comes forth from within her.

7. Mark's Gospel and the Cruciform Christ-Mystery

Our final geometry, the figure of the cross, is the center and summation of Mark's Gospel. Here all creation is drawn together at the point where the power and the wisdom of

God vanish into darkness and are reborn as the light and energy of new creation, moving outward into the whole universe. But in Mark's narrative, and in our own experience, this dynamic mystery is concealed beneath the surface of ordinary life.

At our fourth pole, we come to the first of the gospels to be written: the Gospel of Mark. Mark's Gospel is dominated by the cross, centered in the word of the cross and in Jesus' predictions of his own passion, death, and resurrection. Further, the actual structure of Mark is cruciform.[49] After fifteen centuries of neglect, Mark's Gospel has become a principal focus of study for biblical scholars during the past century and a half, because of its critical importance in understanding the genesis of the synoptic gospels as a whole.

It is in Mark's Gospel that the Christ-mystery is expressed most sparely. Mark leaves the Mystery in its shell: in the husk of more-or-less literal story. The later Evangelists will develop one or another aspect of the Mystery, opening it up to explicate the teaching of Jesus, or the work of the Spirit in this Messiah, or the unitive fullness of the Son of Man. While Mark seems simply to recount the series of events, his narrative contains compressed within itself the Christ-mystery in its fullness.

We are told at the very beginning of Mark's narrative (1:1) that Jesus is the Son of God. Yet the Markan Jesus is very much a man, with his feet on the earth. He appears as a seed that springs up from the ground, flourishes, dies, and returns to the earth. We follow his journey from the wilderness and baptism by John in the Jordan to that hole in the earth which is the empty tomb, and where the Markan veil gives way to the experience of baptismal fullness. If Mark was written as an Easter vigil reading in preparation for baptism,[50] the Christ-seed's descent and disappearance into the earth is to be followed by an opening of the fourfold blossom within the hearer, the believer, the neophyte. This figure of the cross is the baptismal mystery's intrinsic form as it is realized within the individual Christian and within the community. Mark leaves us, at the end of his gospel, in this world. The baptismal gift, and hence the Christ-mystery, is hidden like a seed beneath the surface of our ordinary human lives.

Mark as Political Manifesto

Ched Myers's *Binding the Strong Man: A Political Reading of Mark's Story of Jesus* is a radical reinterpretation of Mark's Gospel from the perspective of our fourth quadrant. Myers reads Mark from a political perspective (as "a manifesto of radical discipleship" in opposition to Empire), while setting aside the traditional theology of salvation. The drama of Mark's Gospel is viewed entirely within the context of this world, in the political arena of first-century Palestine, between the oppressed and poor of Galilee and the Roman and Jewish political and religious powers.

Jesus' essential teaching, according to Myers, is a nonviolent resistance to power and oppression (to Empire) equivalent to Gandhi's *satyagraha* (truth-power). The power of Jesus and of the gospel is the power of nonviolence.

Both the power and the restricted perspective of Myers's interpretation of Mark are evident in his treatment of the two exorcisms early in the gospel narrative: Jesus' first miracle in the Capernaum synagogue (1:23–28) and his expelling of the "Legion" (5:1–20).

> Thus the meaning of Jesus' struggle against the strong man is not reducible solely to his desire for the liberation of Palestine from colonial rule, though it certainly includes that. It is a struggle against the root "spirit" and politics of domination—which, Mark acknowledges matter of factly, is most clearly represented by the "great men" of the Hellenistic imperial sphere. (Mk 10:42)

> Mark believes that both parties of the colonial condominium are "possessed" by this spirit, and so assesses each in exactly the same terms. The discourse of "equation" is reflected at the outset in the parallelism between the two inaugural exorcisms, and again at the story's end in the double trial of Jesus. There Pilate is indicted along with the high priest for engineering the railroading of Jesus.[51]

Myers conjectures that it may have been from Daniel

> that Jesus came to his most revolutionary insight: namely, that the powers could only be defeated by the power of what we today call "nonviolence."... Domination would remain the law of the world order unless and until a people took upon itself to embrace the radical paradox: to lose life is to save life.... Jesus founded an apocalyptic community committed to the overthrow of the powers. It was not a secret society, but a way of life and death, and a hope of resurrection—the apocalyptic promise of vindication. (Dn 12:2f.)[52]

Mark intended his gospel, according to Myers, specifically for those "underneath."

> Mark's Gospel was written to help imperial subjects learn the hard truth about their world and themselves. He does not pretend to represent the word of God dispassionately or impartially as if that word were innocuously universal in its appeal to rich and poor alike. His is a story by, about, and for those committed to God's work of justice, compassion, and liberation in the world.[53]

Myers's reading of Mark exemplifies a theology that positions itself radically "from below." While overpolarized against theological tradition in excluding "spiritual" interpretations, his argument is frequently convincing on its own level. This is because the life and teaching of Jesus, and the Christ-event as a whole, issue forth in immediate political and economic consequences. The same immediate social bearing is evident in much of the Old Testament literature, which, nevertheless, is about much more than politics and economics. The social application (the imperatives of justice and of active compassion) are the immediate expression and application of the gospel on the plane of human life. They are not the whole of the Mystery, the Christ-event, however. The Act of God that is Jesus' life, death, and resurrection realizes itself in every dimension of reality, and throughout the cosmos (see Rom 8:18–23).

Let us bring together some of the suggestions both of earth (of "this world") and of quaternity that we find in Mark's

Gospel. Of the four Evangelists, Mark appears to remain closest to the brute facts of Jesus' story. It is a story that unfolds within the dark density of this world, of earth. Mark, according to tradition, is the associate of Peter, the "Rock," foundation of the church (though so named by Jesus in Matthew's Gospel rather than in Mark's Gospel). His Gospel was probably written for the church of Rome.

Jesus' way of *descent* (equivalent to the way of the cross) has a central place in Mark's Gospel (see Mk 8–10). It is in Mark that we see the seed falling into the ground. The imprint of the *cross* on the structure of Mark's Gospel[54] appears both in the overall structure of the narrative and in the explicit and emphatic introduction of the crucifixion-cross theme at its center (Mk 8:34–38).

The cruciform structure of Mark's Gospel is *geographical:* its four poles are specified by four distinct places on this earth.[55] We move, in the course of Mark's narrative, from wilderness to Galilee and then, by way of the central journey section, to Jerusalem and finally to the place of the tomb. These successive stations (the five places) are all profoundly symbolic. This symbolism, however, remains hidden within the simple geographical indications.

Jesus' divinity is veiled through most of Mark's narrative. His power flashes forth at a moment of healing or exorcism, when he multiplies bread for the crowd, walks on the sea, or is transfigured on the mountain. His wisdom is not expressed in long discourses or many parables. Mark's Gospel is a series of events, within which the identity of Jesus is concealed even as it is revealed. Jesus' repeated injunctions to silence, the atmosphere of *messianic secret,* recall this veil even at the revelatory moments. The somberness of Mark's narrative also serves as a veil for Jesus' divine wisdom and glory. This fullness is manifested but also concealed by Jesus' continual struggle with the powers of evil, which is accented by Mark so that it appears to be the central axis of his gospel. Jesus begins his ministry, after his temptation in the wilderness, by casting a devil out of a man in the synagogue. His struggle with the forces of evil (perhaps to be identified as cosmic powers) culminates in the darkness of the passion narrative, which dominates this gospel.

8. Eucharist and Omega

The New Testament envisions a transformation of the created universe: a "new heaven and new earth" (see Rv 21–22). As a cosmic perspective of vivid immensity is opened up for Christianity today by the new astronomy and physics, we are invited to reimagine the Christ-event in the dimensions of this larger universe.

Christianity's *eucharistic* dimension will not be fully realized until we see the circumference of the eucharist as widened to the full scope of humanity and planet earth, expanded in some way to the proportion of the universe itself. If our time is that of a dawning global consciousness,[56] it must also be the age of a new and larger eucharistic sense within Christianity: a global realization of the body of Christ.

Teilhard and the Fourth

The contribution of Pierre Teilhard de Chardin to our Fourth Quadrant is crucial. This is, first of all, because of his gravitation toward matter, earth, cosmos. Teilhard appears, in our time, almost single-handedly, to bring together Christ and cosmos, Christianity and cosmology, after many centuries of separation. This he does from his characteristic evolutionary perspective. Teilhard's sense of a dynamic cosmos, evolving within a field of Christ-energy, and his sense of the role of the feminine in this movement manifest his integration of "Three" into this vision. Finally, Teilhard brings together universe and eucharist: He is our contemporary prophet of a cosmic eucharist.[57]

Teilhard's Unitive Passion and Its Incarnation: Unitive Matter

Teilhard's thought is driven by a passion for the unitive, for a single thing that suffices and endures. As Teilhard describes his own development from childhood, he finds its central axis in the consistent experience of a "sense of plenitude" that we can identify with a unitive sense, unitive intuition. The unitive passion will express itself again and again in a very concrete fascination with matter.

> However far back I go into my childhood, nothing seems to me more characteristic of, or more familiar in, my interior economy than the appetite or irresistible demand for some "Unique all-sufficing and necessary reality." To be completely at home and completely happy, there must be the knowledge that "Something, essential by nature" exists, to which everything else is no more than an accessory or perhaps an ornament.[58]

This sense of plenitude will remain the central axis of his intellectual development and the key to the meaning of his work.

> Throughout all that I shall call in turn and indifferently "Sense of Consistence," "Cosmic Sense," "Sense of the Earth," "Sense of Man," "Christic Sense," everything that follows will be simply the story of a slow unfolding or evolving within me of this fundamental and "Protean" element which takes on ever richer and purer forms....

> While destined to culminate upon what is highest in the direction of Spirit, it started in the first place (as I know by evidence and direct proofs) from what is most tangible and most concrete in the Stuff of Things, later to make its way into and conquer everything.[59]

Teilhard describes this development, from its beginning in his love-affair with solid matter.

> I withdrew into the contemplation, the possession, into the so relished existence, of my "Iron God." *Iron,* mark you. I can still see, with remarkable sharpness, the succession of my "idols." In the country there was the lock-pin of a plough which I used to hide carefully in a corner of the yard. In town, there was the hexagonal head of a metal bolt which protruded above the level of the nursery floor, and which I had made my own private possession. Later, there were shell-splinters lovingly collected on a neighboring firing range.... I cannot help smiling, today, when these childish fancies come back to my mind; and yet I cannot but recognize that this instinctive act

which made me *worship*, in a real sense, a fragment of metal contained and concentrated an intensity of resonance and a whole stream of demands of which my entire spiritual life has been no more than the development.[60]

The density of reality that Teilhard found first in these bits of matter was later to expand to the dimensions of the universe; a universe that, for him, must be permeated by the energies and presence of Christ.

One way of visualizing the movement that Teilhard represents is to imagine him (on the background of our mandalic figure) as breaking out of the Western container of his time in two directions. First, from static to dynamic: Teilhard moves from static logos (both the logos of religious institution and theologizing and that of purely analytical scientific reason) to the dynamism of evolution, of the feminine and of human and cosmic energy. Christ, as Omega, becomes a dynamic center, a source of transformative energy. The surprising fact that Teilhard rarely mentions the Holy Spirit is probably a lingering symptom of the logos-bound Catholicism of his time.[61] Second, Teilhard represents a progression from spirit to matter, from a spiritualized Christianity to an incarnational Christianity, from isolated spirit to spirit in matter, from an isolated transcendent God to an immanent God.

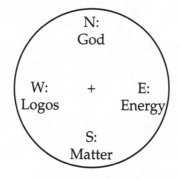

FIGURE 4.9

Thus Teilhard moves from the northwest hemisphere of our mandalic figure (logos and transcendent logos-bound Divinity) into the opposite southeast hemisphere of energy and matter (see Figure 4.9). Western Christianity (indeed all of surviving Christianity in East and West) had long dwelt very largely in that first (NW) hemisphere. The forward movement of contemporary Western thought and spirituality (e.g., the "New Paradigm" thought), despite its complexity and ambiguities, is a progression into the second (SE) hemisphere. Teilhard was a pioneer in this revolution.

Teilhard understood his own intellectual journey largely in terms of a quest to integrate the Fourth: cosmic reality or matter. He had at first accepted from his education and his religion a dichotomy between matter and spirit, body and soul, unconscious and conscious mind. Spirit, as long as it was opposed in this way to matter, was a term nearly without meaning for him. It was the principle of evolution that enabled him to see matter and spirit as but two sides of one dynamic reality.

> Looked at not metaphysically, but genetically, Spirit was by no means the enemy or the opposite pole of the Tangibility which I was seeking to attain: rather it was at its very heart.[62]

Here we see a double transformation of the customary Western and Christian view: both the shift from dichotomy (of spirit and matter) to unity and the shift from a static to a dynamic (evolutional) view. This is Teilhard's single but two-pronged subversion of the Greek philosophical perspective, which Western Christianity had inherited.

Teilhard sees this cosmic, or evolutional, realization as the first stage of development of his vision. The next phase is his discovery of "The Human, or Convergent."

> Today Man (or, to speak more correctly, the *Human*) forms the pivot upon which the whole structure of my interior Universe rests, around which its links are formed and it coheres and moves.[63]

The third and final stage of this development was Teilhard's realization, in cosmic proportions, of the "Christic, or the Centric." He speaks of the "two loves" that ruled his life: Christ and the cosmos:

The cosmic sense and the christic sense: these two axes were born in me quite independently of one another, it would seem, and it was only after a long time and a great deal of hard work that I finally came to understand how, through and beyond the Human, the two were linked together, converged upon one another, and were in fact one and the same.[64]

The two principles manifest a convergent movement, as if through an inner affinity:

On one side—in my "pagan" ego—a Universe which was becoming personalized through convergence.

And on the other side—in my Christian ego—a Person (the Person of Christ) who was becoming universalized through Radiation.[65]

Inevitably, Teilhard experienced a conflict between his emerging vision and the conventional Western view, prevalent even among the mystics, that God can be attained only by leaving behind all earthly realities, and "to be spiritualized = to be dematerialized."[66] This gradually articulated itself as a tension between a static transcendence and a dynamic immanence.

In the inmost depths of my soul a struggle, between the God of the Above and a sort of new God of the Ahead was, through structural necessity, being produced in the definitive coexistence and the irresistible meeting in my heart of the cosmic Sense and the Christic Sense.[67]

Gradually the two realities came together, and within this movement of convergence Teilhard recognized his own vocation.

To Christify Matter: that sums up the whole venture of my innermost being.[68]

It was to be the task and the never-ending delight of the next twenty years to see, as I looked around me, how—step by step, and in step with one another—the two Densities came to reinforce one another: the Christic Density, and the cosmic Density of a World.[69]

Teilhard repeatedly places an emergent sense of the *feminine* at the heart of his vision. The feminine is inseparably related to matter, to the cosmos. He sees the feminine principle as the great attractor, the unitive force of cosmic and human evolution.

Eucharist and Cosmic Evolution

The Christic divinization of all things, Teilhard suggested in his earlier works, occurs through the *eucharistic* action.

> Since first, Lord, you said, *"Hoc est corpus meum,"* [This is my body], not only the bread of the altar but (to some degree) everything in the universe that nourishes the soul for the life of Spirit and Grace, has become *yours,* has become *divine*—it is divinized, divinizing, and divinizable. Every presence makes me feel that you are near me; every touch is the touch of your hand; every necessity transmits to me a pulsation of your will.[70]

The world in its becoming is eucharist.

> But the offering you really want, the offering you mysteriously need every day to appease your hunger, to slake your thirst is nothing less than the growth of the world borne ever onwards in the stream of universal becoming.[71]

The body of Christ, and hence the eucharist, is the total human and cosmic *unity.*

> Nothing, Lord Jesus, can subsist outside of your flesh.... All of us, inescapably, exist in you, the universal milieu in which and through which all things live and have their being.[72]

Teilhard's unitive passion for matter has grown to the dimensions of this vision of the universe as body of Christ. He knows this truth of the great convergence to be the essence of his own message.

> For me, my God, all joy and all achievement, the very purpose of my being and all my love of life, all depend on this one basic vision of the union between yourself and the universe.

Let others, fulfilling a function more august than mine, proclaim your splendours as pure Spirit; as for me, dominated as I am by a vocation which springs from the inmost fibres of my being, I have no desire, I have no ability, to proclaim anything except the innumerable prolongations of your incarnate Being in the world of matter; I can preach only the mysteries of your flesh, you the Soul shining through all that surrounds us.

It is to your body in this its fullest extension—that is, to the world become through your power and my faith the glorious living crucible in which everything melts away in order to be born anew; it is to this that I dedicate myself.[73]

We can observe in Teilhard the epochal transition in Christian consciousness and spirituality from a "baptismal" to a "eucharistic" vision. In moving away from a first wisdom, which he sees as a quest for spirit through separation from matter, Teilhard explicitly seeks the eucharistic pole of a Unitive realized in matter, and in the matter of the whole cosmos. In this he is the major contemporary prophet within Christianity of what we have called the Second Wisdom.[74]

FIGURE 4.10

From our mandalic perspective (see Figure 4.10), Teilhard's emerging vision manifests a strong presence of "Two" (his basically scientific mind and language, the central importance of human intelligence and of reflection for him). Here we also find "Three" (his basically dynamic conception of the universe as evolving, his frequent focus on cosmic and human energy, the "redshift" toward love that we have observed, the centrality of a universal feminine principle) and "Four" (Teilhard's basic cosmological perspective and his enduring passion for matter). "One" (unitive Spirit or nondual reality) does not appear in Teilhard in its pure form, despite his many years in the East. It is characteristic of his vision that the Unitive is manifest in its incarnate form: in matter.

Teilhard sees the universe as being continually transformed into the body of Christ, a unitive body. Universe and eucharist converge in this process, which is a unitive creation, a unitive transformation. Teilhard insists on the material reality of the process. His vision of a cosmic eucharist converges with Ewert Cousins's conception of a new global consciousness[75] (emerging at the "Second Axial" moment) as a communion not only of people among themselves, but of humanity and cosmos.

Humanity, and the human person, requires a *saving transformation*. We need to be affirmed, and yet to be transformed. In this way, we humans recapitulate within ourselves the condition and drama of the universe—at least of the world that we know, this world that is passing away and can be restored only by a power beyond itself.

We know something of the transformations of science and technology, and something of the transformations of art. Both of them project us into a future that they cannot fulfill. We learn of the mythological transformations of the alchemists, largely from the psychotherapists who would lead us through a psychic alchemy, the process of individuation.

The ancient traditions, and patristic-medieval Christianity among them, believed in a transformation of the human person through asceticism and contemplation. For Christian ascetics who knew what they were doing, however, this journey could take place only within the transformation that had already taken place in the death and resurrection of Jesus Christ, and in which they participated through baptism and eucharist. *Resurrection and eucharist:* Here we seem to touch the deepest point of transformation. The transfiguration of Jesus on Mount Tabor, related by the synoptic gospels, had anticipated this changing of the body of flesh into the spiritual body, *soma pneumatikon.*

During the first four centuries of Christianity, a theological synthesis was developed that held the elements of this Mystery in a precarious unity, always subject to disintegration under the influence of human analytical and systematic thought. Spirit and intellect seemed ever to pull away from matter and body. Christianity, in its movement into the West and its progressive institutionalization, lost touch with essential dimensions of the Mystery. Crucial losses were sustained corresponding to our quadrants One, Three, and Four: loss of the unitive apophatic perspective; loss of an understanding of the dynamic movement of the Spirit, of the immanent divine energies; loss of the cosmic scope and bodily density of the Christ-event.

Eastern Orthodox Christianity, in its contemporary expressions, has conserved and further developed the sense of cosmos and body that had been realized (despite a perennial Platonic spiritualizing tendency) by patristic thought. This influence comes to us particularly through the writers who articulate the Russian tradition of religious philosophy.[76] We may be surprised to find a convergence with Teilhard de Chardin in their cosmological thought.

As we seek a final synthetic perspective from within our fourth quadrant, the risen body of Christ—and hence the eucharist—claims central place. From the New Testament viewpoint (which must be our final theological perspective), the personal and cosmic transformation is centered here.

It is, finally, with the *transformation of matter* that we are concerned. The confluence of Three and Four brings forth a further principle, a second wisdom,[77] that is peculiar to the Christian revelation, to the Christ-event. This second wisdom contrasts symmetrically with the first wisdom (or First Axial wisdom) that, in its Eastern and Western realizations, we have identified with One and Two.

What are the elements that come together in this vision of a cosmic transformation centered in Christ's eucharistic body? Among the essential components are "mystery," the sacramental body itself, the human person, the divine energies, martyrdom, human sexuality, the redshift, humanity as a whole, and human creativity.

First we must recognize that at the end, as at the beginning, we encounter *mystery*. In the density of earth, body, matter (even when matter is no longer opaque but transparent in spirit) we find an inverse or descending apophasis[78] that reflects the uncreated Mystery that is One. We shall not be able to contemplate this incarnate Omega in a single synthetic glance. We shall know it only when we have become it, for it is incarnation, a union in matter that surpasses wisdom while proving itself the ultimate wisdom, the incarnate Wisdom of God.

The *eucharistic body* of Jesus is the totality of this Omega. Matter has been, in this body, liberated from its confining role, from its opacity, its property of separation and isolation, to become the medium of union, of communion. This body expands gradually, to the full dimensions of humanity and *cosmos*, through a process of eucharistic transformation.

The *human person* as microcosm and image of God, as sovereign presence of God within the world (the person itself centered in Christ), is the center of this transformation. Here we must understand "person" as signifying transcendent freedom—a freedom that participates in the divine creativity through the immanent divine energies.

These *divine energies*, agents of new creation, are essentially the immanent divine Spirit working the change within the universe and particularly within the human person, the human body. From the beginning, these energies are present at the root of all created things, of all human persons.

In early Christianity, *physical martyrdom* was understood as a eucharistic consummation—a bodily participation in the paschal mystery of transformation; hence the eagerness of believers to possess physical relics of the martyrs. When persecution of Christians in the Roman Empire had ceased, the symbolic locus of transformation was transferred to the holy ascetics.

This unitive body of Christ is the terminus of *sexuality*, joining within itself masculine and feminine, Logos and Spirit, in "one flesh." Here may lie the key to a transfiguration of human sexual energy. Within this transformed energy, in turn, lies hidden the secret of cosmogenesis, of a new and unitive creation.

The movement from East to West and from the old to a new

wisdom is a *redshift*.[79] In this process of historical incarnation, the divine Unitive descends, becoming more and more manifest in matter. In a simultaneous ascending movement, history (as the feminine comes forth within it to be consciously integrated) becomes intelligible as a Christ-centered transformation.

All humanity (including all cultures and traditions) is to be brought together into this unitive body of Christ. Meanwhile the gospel imperative of justice works in the world. The eucharistic Christ-energy is a leaven within humanity that, through the struggle for justice and equality, gradually transforms social structures and the very fabric of human relationship in the direction of communion. The church, as eucharistic mystery, is the sacrament of God and of the divine energies and transformation within this world—a world created to become eucharist.

Human creativity is a participation in the divine creative act, and an incipient realization of the new creation, the eucharistic transformation of the universe. Western science and technology, with the desacralization of nature they presuppose, are at once a product of the Christ-event[80] and a "pre-Christian" phase of new creation, of the transformation of the world by the divine energies. If, in the postmodern West, the root of these human creative achievements is rediscovered in the risen Christ, they may find within themselves the lifeblood they lack in order to bring into being a truly human world.

On the astronomical scale of solar system, galaxy, and light-year, we observe the stately dance of planets and stars. On the submicroscopic level of atom and molecule, electrons whirl with incredible swiftness in their perpetual and inscrutable movement. Between these two worlds of incessant and impersonal dance lies the privileged speck of matter that is earth and, on its surface, the sphere of human existence. Here, in the burning bush of human flesh that painfully ripens into eucharist, the transformation is worked out.

> For the creation waits with eager longing for the revealing of the children of God; for the creation was subjected to futility, not of its own will but by the will of him who subjected it, in hope that the creation itself will be set free from its bondage to decay and will obtain the freedom of the

glory of the children of God. We know that the whole creation has been groaning in labor pains until now; and not only the creation, but we ourselves, who have the firstfruits of the Spirit, groan inwardly while we wait for adoption, the redemption of our bodies. (Rom 8:19–23, NRSV)

9. The Unity of Four: *Sophia*

Four, we have found, embraces a variety of themes. These tend to fall into three subgroups. It is when the body of Christ is viewed in relation to the immanent divine Feminine, Sophia, that the overall unity of this world of Four appears.

I The first group of issues has clamorously demanded attention in our time, often coupled with an indictment of Christian tradition (and of Western culture in general) for ignoring or even causing the related problems. This cluster is centered in the earth and the people of the earth: the poor, the oppressed, and particularly the indigenous and primal peoples; issues of liberation of the oppressed, of social justice, and of environment are joined in this theology "from below." Feminist and ecological positions are frequently allied. Mark's Gospel can be seen, with Ched Myers, from this perspective of social liberation as a manifesto of radical discipleship, of nonviolent resistance of the powers on behalf of the oppressed to whom the kingdom belongs. Following Ewert Cousins, we can see primal peoples as embodying, in their sense of tribal solidarity and communion with the earth, a key to the dawning global consciousness.

II A second constellation (which we have explored in the preceding section) outlines the Christian vision of body, earth, and cosmos, as expressed in the New Testament and the early theological writers. It is centered in the body of Christ, and salvation through this body. A theological body-axis is constituted by creation, incarnation (through Mary, the *Theotokos*), resurrection, divinization, eucharist. The risen body of Christ and the eucharistic body are seen as the firstfruits of the transformation of cosmic matter (in the human person) into its ultimate unitive state in God. In Teilhard, the cosmic perspective becomes dynamic, an evolutionary process centered in the Christ-Omega.

III A third subgroup of fourth-quadrant themes, emerging from the history of Christianity and of the West, can be joined under the common heading of "return to the ground." The arrival of a new wisdom can be understood as a return to nature, to the body, to earth and cosmos, after a long period of dualism and alienation. Emergence of the feminine is central to this development, which may be interpreted in terms of the unitive and universally immanent divine Feminine or Spirit. Art and poetry, in their rejoining of person and nature, anticipate the reintegration of body, senses, and cosmos in a new consciousness.

On reflection, the logic of a historical process emerges from these three groups of themes. Cluster I has come forth as protest, as prophetic criticism, as revolution, and as a critical counterassertion to historical Christianity. This voice is exemplified in Marxism, in the deep ecologists, in a contemporary revaluation of body, earth, indigenous and primal peoples.

Cluster II is equivalent to the "body-assertion" or Four-assertion of the New Testament itself: that is, the Christ-event understood as centered in the body of Jesus Christ. This corporeal character of the Mystery has not been adequately realized in the ensuing tradition of Christianity. Our first group of issues (Cluster I) may have come forth largely as a response to this inadequacy.

A naive criticism rejects Christianity as being hostile to body, earth, and cosmos, and as supporting structures of social privilege and oppression. A more differentiated criticism finds historical Christianity at fault for not realizing the principles that are either explicit or implicit in its own original revelation. These neglected principles regard stewardship of creation, participation in a new creation, human liberation, and the transformation of oppressive social structures.

Cluster III explicitly starts from the incompleteness of historical Christian (and Western) tradition, and moves toward a reconciliation of Western consciousness with nature; that is, with the earth-body-humanity elements of Cluster I. The two poles to be joined may be conceived as Word and nature, consciousness and nature, grace and nature, supernatural and natural, mind and body, Christ and cosmos, revelation and creation.

Elements that have been undervalued in the Christian West[81] include not only those belonging to "Four" (body, earth, environment, cosmos, the people of the earth), but also those related to our three other mandalic dimensions. These are the values of human freedom and development, creativity and its fruits, human reason and its autonomy, the feminine, sexuality, the Unitive itself. Liberation from the container involves an expansive movement in all these directions of the human compass. "The human," which includes all these dimensions, tends to associate itself with Four (as the secular or "natural" pole) when seen in opposition to the religious or "supernatural."

I have proposed that the dissociation of Christian tradition from *Four*, from the ground, both doctrinally and institutionally, is related to the marriage of Christianity with "Empire" from the time of Constantine. Sophia and Empire are opposed to one another as two great historical principles; the relation of Christianity to Four is largely determined by the struggle between them. Sophia, the immanent unitive divine Feminine (central to the Third Order), generates a Christianity of the ground: both thoroughly incarnate and virtually universal. Empire, on the other hand, generates (or institutes) a Christianity, a church, that is raised above the ground and enclosed within an impermeable container of doctrine, law, and institution. The Christianity of Sophia is dynamic and creative; the Christianity of Empire tends to be static, juridical, administrative. These crude strokes do not convey, of course, the complexity of the historical process.

Doctrinally, we can say that Trinity has been prioritized at the expense of Incarnation.[82] A central issue in the development of this Christian theological and spiritual tradition is the understanding of the body of Christ. The church fathers regarded both the eucharistic body and the ecclesial body with Paul's firm realism: the realism of a bodily *mystery*.

> The body of Jesus Christ, received in the faithful, produces between them a kind of union which is not merely moral but physical and natural, since it consists in the real union of

our body with that of Jesus Christ; by force of which it can be said that all the bodies with which Jesus Christ is joined through the eucharist constitute one body, since they have one and the same bond, which is the body of Jesus Christ.[83]

In the course of centuries, this physical *union* came to be understood either as a mere metaphor or as a purely spiritual communion (the "communion of saints"), abstracted from the body. Rather than retaining the vital tension of this bodily mystery, our conception of the body of Christ has relaxed into more comprehensible notions. The mystery's resonant energy field has been replaced by concepts of a moral body, a juridical body, an institutional body. Detached from our own bodily being, from the ecclesial community, from "body" as the human ground that is encountered in the poor and oppressed, from earth and cosmos, the "mystical body of Christ" has often been reduced to a collectivity without the concrete fullness and ineffable power of the mystery.

The body of Christ came to approximate the visible church, together with its invisible members in the other world. It began, indeed, more and more to resemble the Roman *civitas perfecta*, the institution of institutions.[84] Gradually the mystery and its numinous power recede as they become walled within the comprehensible. The body of Christ, that is, comes to be no more than an institutional church with its doctrines, laws, sacraments, and ritual. The larger and more dynamic dimensions of human bodiliness and of the body of Christ, which glow within the New Testament writings, become reduced to abstractions or "mere poetry."

The traditional body-of-Christ theology, in its Western development, tends insensibly to withdraw into the world of Two, having less and less to do with actual bodiliness. A parallel contraction is evident in the eucharistic rite. By the early twentieth century, the one species of bread (the wine/blood of Christ was no longer distributed to the people) had been reduced to a tiny, neat wafer, almost an abstraction. From within its own world, the traditional body-theology was perfect, complete. As long as we (unconsciously, no doubt) remain within its own logic, we cannot see its limitations. It is from outside, from the clamor of the neglected and excluded, that we become aware of the confinement of this theological vision. Then we must *imagine* a larger Christian body-vision to include that which has been excluded or ignored.

The traditional theology remained confined within its presuppositions rather than conversing with all the rest, with the totality of created reality with which the body of Christ has to do. Its presuppositions, once again, were of the order of Two: Word, Revelation, the seed of Christ. From our mandalic perspective, we can say that it did not sufficiently move out into the "other three worlds" of the unitive, of energy-feminine, of the body and cosmos. These other three dimensions are implicit within the body of Christ.

The body of Christ must be unitive not only intensively (joining many persons in communion), but also extensively. It must, that is, have a universal scope, in some way comprehending all creation. The body of Christ must be conceived not only as matter, but also as energy; not only as bread and body, but also as fire. This energy relates to the movement of history and to the movement of personal life, to sexuality as well as to spirituality and work. The body of Christ must be *body*, and related to our human physicality in its depth and breadth. What does it mean to realize the body of Christ in our own body?

The body of Christ must be body and matter openly and universally, and therefore beyond denominational bounds. It must be, in some way, inclusive of all humanity and the cosmos. Paradoxically, it must be body outside as well as inside the body. Closed body or open body? The body of Christ must be both. It must correspond to the sacramental organism of the church (the community of baptized believers in Jesus Christ) and it must be coextensive with all of humanity and all of creation.

Here again we must invoke Sophia. Can it be that this duality of circumscribed body and open body of Christ corresponds to the duality between revealed Logos and universally immanent Sophia? We can express this as the duality and interplay between Word and Spirit, but the feminine qualification of Sophia is important here. Sophia constitutes the invisible union of inside with outside, of explicit with implicit, of revealed with latent, of the circumscribed with the open, the ecclesial with the universal, institutional with cosmic. She is the unitive divine Feminine that is immanent everywhere and becomes explicit in the church, within the circle of revealed Christ-light. She draws humanity toward Christ, but at the same time, where Christ is not known, she makes him present in human persons. Those who listen to her and walk in her way are friends of God—and members of the body of Christ—wherever they are (see Wis 7:27).

It is Sophia, or the divine Feminine, who draws together our three clusters of themes. She appears most fully in the third cluster, within the movement toward reintegration of Word with nature, Christianity with the common ground of humanity, earth with cosmos. Sophia finds expression in the creativity of an art and poetry that move outside the scriptural enclosure into all of created reality, with the freedom of an inner unitive knowledge. As embodied in Mary, the bodily mother of Jesus, she is intimately involved in the whole mystery of body and of the body of Christ, which constitutes our second group of themes. She is the Spirit also of the church: the "Bride of Christ" who is Christ's body (see Eph 5:23). As "woman," she is identified with the spirit of the oppressed; as immanent divine Wisdom, she is earth-person, earth-woman, the divine "earth-spirit." As the Spirit of love, Sophia is revelation outside revelation, wisdom outside wisdom, Christ outside Christianity, the presence of God outside and beyond every representation of God and every boundary line.

Part Four brings our mandalic figure to completion. To conclude with a figure, however (even this symbolic figure of final integration), is not adequate. What we most urgently need is not the form but the *movement* of the whole. This divine energy that is Spirit or Sophia is the passion that has driven the entire search forward, as it drives forward the whole course of human development. This option for the energy, the movement itself, rejoins our quest for a new wisdom.[85] What can such a new sapiential Christianity be other than a fresh realization of the divine Wisdom itself: of *Sophia?* Sophia is the Spirit, the immanent divine energy that moves through image after image, figure after figure, formulation after formulation, toward the Fullness—a Fullness that cannot be described but only glimpsed.

Sophia's relation to the Logos-Bridegroom remains mysterious. From one viewpoint she is the effusion, the immanence of Logos; from another perspective she dwells within the "World Soul" and brings it to meet the Logos in Jesus Christ. This is suggested by the meeting between Jesus and the Samaritan woman in John's Gospel (4). Is the classical Christian nuptial spirituality to be opened to new dimensions by the emergence of Sophia, bringing Mary, church, and individual person to Christ the Bridegroom? Is Sophia to be discovered also as the bride of the human soul or spirit (see Gn 2:18, "It is not good that the man should be alone")? Is Sophia to be discovered in the passion itself that brings the two (Christ and the individual person) together, discovered as the Person who is the divine unitive energy within all things and especially within human hearts?

The golden thread that binds together all the varied threads of Four, drawing them together with its unitive magnetism, can be seen as Sophia, the divine Wisdom working in the world. Sophia, however, labors in the task of new creation, which takes place in history. She does this through the creativity of human persons, participating in her own light and energy. We have seen that the basic expression of this creativity is love.

If we identify Sophia with the energy of divinization, a parallel suggests the ultimate role of the feminine in this process.

1. Eve assents to the suggestion "You shall be as gods," and the drama begins (Gn 3:1–7).

2. Mary assents to the coming of the unique divine-human person, the God-man, within her own being (Lk 1:26–38).

3. The church responds in faith to this incarnate Word. As Bride of Christ and mother, she brings forth the divine-human Person in those who believe and are baptized.

4. Sophia realizes the divine humanity in all humanity. Immanent in every human person and in the whole cosmos, she labors to bring forth all creation in God (Rom 8:18–23). She is the immanent transforming Spirit, the divine "Affirmation," who

has been at work everywhere from the first moment of creation and who bears the whole creation toward its end.

We have seen that the second wisdom differs from the first wisdom largely in its affirmation of the human person, and of a larger, unitive Person who is Christ, growing toward completion in the world. This unitive Person is church, but church as open, all-inclusive, comprehending the outside as well as the inside, including cosmos as well as church as we know it.

Mary, embodiment of Sophia, is "person" in a very particular and emphatic way: While she does not play a significant role in most of the New Testament writings, tradition accords her increasing attention and veneration. Mary is "Person" in the capital and universal sense in which Jesus is Person. What does this mean, as we consider Spirit-Sophia as parallel to Word-Christ? If Jesus is the center, the point and the body of divinization, what is Mary's role on this larger scale? Perhaps Mary is Person in the order of divine *energy*, of the Holy Spirit, as is Sophia. Perhaps she is the one person who, in her transparency, becomes identified with the divine "Grace," or Spirit, which has come to dwell in her, so that she is associated with every realization of grace and divinization. Christian tradition recognizes some such role for Mary in the great stream of sacred history.

If Jesus is Person as Word and as Light, Sophia is Person as Love. This is the ultimate, unitive realization of person. Dwelling in human individuals, she bears them toward realization as persons-in-relation, within the great energy field of the divine *koinonia*. Dwelling in the church, she bears it toward its full realization as her embodiment: the one great "Person of Love" in this world.

If Sophia bears the world into its realization in God, she also dances. She dances in all of creation, anticipating the time when the creation itself will be delivered into its freedom (see Rom 8:21–23). Her dance is the living beauty all around us, in which we find the "already" of present fullness, of divine presence.

> When he marked out the foundations of the earth,
> then I was beside him, like a master-worker;
> and I was daily his delight,

rejoicing before him always,
rejoicing in his inhabited world
and delighting in the human race. (Prv 8:29–31, NRSV)

10. Four: A Meditation

After the dawn, the construction and the deconstruction, a four-petaled flower blossoms from the tomb. This bloom is the city of God and humanity, of God and creation. The stone rejected by the builders, when at last the temple made by men has been demolished, grows into its fullness and fills the whole earth like the marvelous stone in the book of Daniel (Dn 2:31–35).

Four is not a phase within process, but is that which has been hidden beneath and within the process from its beginning, and emerges into visibility and splendor now that the process has run its term. When human history has run its course, the cycle has been completed, this fullness appears from within, as from a hidden center.

Human constructions, in their invariable squareness, their rectangularity, imitate this hidden divine structure. They are four-shaped for solidity, for stability on their ground, for capaciousness and rationality. Man builds in squares; this is his strength. The square is the imposition of man's form and personality on nature. Cut stones, square temples, houses, and walls make sense of the world for him, create a rational space in the wilderness of creation.

Two is already rational: Human thought is linear. Four is a squared rationality, closed rationality, secure and habitable. We shall need, however, some windows and doors, albeit square ones.

We tire of this square world, but have forgotten how to feel along the irrational branch, to hear the bird's cry from outside the house, forgotten how to be wet. We move in and out of our house, but when we go outside we take our house with us. Our words have become square, like labels, name-plates, and we cover each thing with its label so quickly that we do not see the thing itself.

Within our minds we have installed a cubical container, a house; it silently dominates our consciousness, so that we see everything in cubes; we are unconscious cubists. So tight is the squareness of our thought that perception is shuttered out, or filtered through blinds. It comes through only in narrow, linear, horizontal slots.

The garden of childhood, the sun of infinity, the mother's smile, are eclipsed behind this rectangularity; we are no longer aware of the One enfolding us. Something has stopped; time has been squared and confines us like an endless, featureless corridor, an eternal subway. Possibility has given way to necessity; we are locked inside. Since there is no possibility but the determined possibility, there is no door in the corridor, in the blank room. We are compliant prisoners for the most part, unaware of our condition yet vaguely discontented.

Then come the cyclone, the earthquake, the fire, and the structure collapses around us. Miraculously we find ourselves still alive, but without meaning in this wilderness, without center or boundaries. In our desperation we pick up any bit of wreckage, any fragment of shape, any possibility of structure and order, but none of it quite shelters us from the angry, irrational wind.

A thousand quick messiahs bloom like mushrooms, with glossy smiles and toll-free numbers. The hungry shall eat! The blind shall walk, the dumb shall see: Just come and follow me.

We know only the light and the life that are in us; in this light and this life, incredibly, nothing is lacking. Within us is an abundance that is completely inexpressible, a knowledge that cannot be produced and packaged, a certainty that we are continually forgetting. Within this gentle light (and the light is around us as well as within us) there is a silent, infinite, and companionable wisdom, an assured good humor in the midst of all that happens. Within this light, which is not other than ourself, which is our true nature, there is hidden a knowledge of the restoration of all things. The light quietly urges us to pass the word on, to bring this great smile into the world.

The diamond body is there within, a single crystal that contains heaven and earth. From time to time we feel within us the absolute solidity of this ground, this diamond form; from time to time we experience the boundless light that glances from the facets of this stone.

Now that the temple is gone, we become aware of a brightness at the margins of the world, at the edges of our consciousness. There is nothing in particular to see; the light does not settle for long on any distinct thing. We seem to have a new relationship with the light, an intimate freedom that is indistinguishable from our own being and from the light itself. The season of disaster has left a glowing air, a subtle brightness in the mist. An unbounded possibility lingers in our emptiness and will not come to speech. Something endures, adamant and subtle. Is this only another mirage, more of our wishful fantasy? Is it truly something we can live from, or is it too thin? May it conceivably be that which we are, finally beginning to shine through the smoke of our destruction?

Our temple, and all the temples, are gone forever from the world. Now from within, from the center, the world itself is illuminated as temple, squared with an interior necessity, in the rightness of its essence. I myself, I am this absolute and indestructible form that rises into understanding and feeling, filled with the glory of God.

The music of the King sounds, beyond the ears' hearing, throughout this temple that is Christ. The one Child, the Son, has come into his fullness at the center of the world, and the world that exists in him is now illumined and glorified in him. From within this form that we know in its simple and final authority, filling it like the cloud in the old temple, there wells forth continually an abundance for which we have no name. The walls themselves dance in their precision of place, with this music that is life.

Epilogue

I have presented the Christ-mystery and its unfolding in four quadrants, corresponding to God, Word, Spirit, and cosmos/humanity. Now let us look back, for a moment, at the development of this Mystery during these two thousand years since the coming of Christ.

Our story began with a "first simplicity": that of the unitive Christ-mystery as expressed in the New Testament writings. The journey continued through a long period of diversification and confrontation during which the initial unity of the Mystery was eclipsed by the drama taking place in the foreground. The Mystery disappeared behind its successive objectifications and articulations and was forgotten in the noise and smoke of controversy.

Today, in the era of the Second Vatican Council, we find ourselves at the threshold of a third phase of this story: a *second simplicity*. The one Christ-mystery comes into view once again, but with a new transparency. Its essential form now appears, bearing enfolded within it all the dimensions of reality: the height and depth, length and breadth. The Mystery appears now in a global context: interacting with all of humanity and all human potential, in an open and expanding universe.

This book began with an enigma: the disappearance of a wisdom-consciousness (our "first simplicity") from the Christian West. The central thread of such a wisdom-consciousness in the world's spiritual traditions is the experience and knowledge of a unitive ultimate reality, an essentially participative experience and knowledge. We found that this unitive reality often appears in a quaternary expression in the spiritual traditions and decisively so in the New Testament. From this quaternary or mandalic perspective we have seen that Christianity (and, more broadly, the West) has remained confined largely within one quadrant of reality. We have named this sector "Two," the world of cognition, of knowledge, of rationality, of structure and institution.

"One," the divine Unitive, is experienced directly in contemplation. This experience belongs to Christian initiation and was abundantly present in the Christianity of the New Testament. The contemplative tradition within Western Christianity, while it continued to witness to this unitive reality, withdrew from the dynamic and incarnational dimensions of the Christ-mystery, becoming largely confined to the hemisphere constituted by One and Two. The contemplative tradition did not maintain within Christianity, therefore, an openness to the fullness of the Mystery or of reality.

During the past few centuries, a Faustian modern West has journeyed ever farther from its spiritual root in that infusion of divine Wisdom into humanity which was the Incarnation (or Christ-event). The modern West has abandoned spiritual wisdom for the more palpable benefits of rational-empirical thought. The gift of wisdom had come, as always, with its double challenge and potential: to open or to close. Heirs to successive Christian and secular ages, we find ourselves at the end of the twentieth century still largely within the thick-walled container of Two, but arrived at a moment when it has begun to break open on every side.

The emergence of a new Christian wisdom depends on an emergence from the "logos-box" of the rational-institutional quadrant that had closed in on itself. As consciousness breaks free of this container into the further dimensions of reality (which I have represented by the other three poles of the mandalic figure), it discovers itself once again as *participative.* This participation, no longer confined by the limits of doctrine or institution, or by the more subtle container of a single cultural complex, reaches outward into all reality.

Now we learn to recognize once again the wisdom that goes beyond wisdom (see 1 Cor 1:17—2:16), opening to a conscious and creative participation in human history, falling as a seed into the ground of humanity and of ordinary human life in the world.

Such a wisdom, now emerging once again as a second simplicity, is rooted in the subterranean streams of the divine Wisdom, Sophia, who is immanent in all of creation and who bears the creation toward its fulfillment. It knows, however darkly, the evolution of humanity and of the world, in all its turmoil and violence, as moving toward the eucharistic Omega that is the unitive Person. It knows already the *koinonia* of all persons in that new earth which is the body of Christ. [1]

Appendix I

From Old to New: Glossary of Terms

Frequently, throughout this book, the reader encounters the language "first wisdom," "second wisdom," "new wisdom," "second simplicity," "Third Order," "second faith," "third music," and so forth. Here I shall offer, in one place, some clarification on both the meaning and the relationship of these terms.

A. First and Second

I frequently speak of historical development in terms of two phases, *first and second;* thus, first and second wisdom, first and second simplicity, first and second faith. Sometimes instead of first and second, the language will be *old and new:* for example, old and new wisdom. The language of "Orders" (First, Second, Third, Fourth) is not directly parallel to these two-phase expressions (see E below).

Usually, when this language of first and second is used, a *three-phase process* is presupposed, with the intermediate phase being a time of division or alienation: a stage of transition during which an original ("first") fullness has been lost and a new ("second") fullness has not yet been attained. Usually the first phase will be located in the more or less distant past, the third phase (called "second," when only two phases are mentioned) in the future, and the intermediate phase in the recent past. In the present time (still dominated by the intermediate phase), both a continuing influence of the first phase and an emergence of the final phase are observed.

B. Simplicity

First simplicity: the original Christian sapiential vision as it is found in the New Testament (especially the Pauline and Johannine writings) and early patristic works. In using this term I ignore, for the moment, the pluralism that was intrinsic to this vision.

Second simplicity: I speak of the new wisdom as bringing a second simplicity in recovering the early unitive vision of the New Testament and early fathers, centered in the Christ-mystery.

C. Wisdom

First wisdom: the unitive consciousness and theological vision of early Christianity (equivalent to the "first simplicity" above). In a larger sense, this "contemplative" or unitive first wisdom embraces also the unitive spiritual and philosophical traditions of Asia: Hinduism, Buddhism, Taoism. This primordial unitive wisdom will sometimes be called a baptismal wisdom.

Second wisdom: a newly emergent consciousness that is both unitive and creative, highly personal and global. This second wisdom corresponds to the second simplicity. It will sometimes be called a eucharistic wisdom.

D. Faith

First faith: the unquestioning and obedient faith that corresponds to a precritical phase of development and therefore (loosely, however) to the first simplicity and first wisdom. This first faith may lack the unitive quality, the depth and transparency, of our first simplicity and first wisdom. The individual person—today, as ever—will also naturally go through the development from first faith to second faith.

Second faith: a postcritical faith that is associated with the development of personal autonomy, of a highly personal consciousness, and of personal creativity. This corresponds to second simplicity and second wisdom.

E. Music

Here the three-phase scheme becomes explicit, but in a language that is more generalized and metaphoric than other, related, terms.

First music: the spirit or "energy field" of youth, of a human and spiritual springtime, prior to the time of trials and the critical period. This first music corresponds to a first simplicity and, to some extent, to a first wisdom. In the gospels, the infancy narratives and early Galilean ministry of Jesus largely correspond to this first music.

Second music: this experience corresponds to a time of conflict, of discord, of a divided and alienated consciousness. Here the first music and first simplicity have disappeared, the first unitive light or first wisdom has been eclipsed. Here also is the period of critical consciousness, of demythologizing and deconstruction.

Third music: a final phase in which the conflict and division of the second phase give way to a new unity and resonance. The original unity, the first simplicity and wisdom, reemerges, but no longer circumscribed. Person, "other," community, and created world are known within the one divine Communion.

F. Order

First, Second, Third, Fourth Order: these terms refer not directly to successive historical phases, but to quadrants of reality (which appear together on the mandalic figure). Their prominence or suppression in a given culture, however (e.g., our Western culture) is related to the historical process represented by the two- or three-phase schemes. Some parallels will be observed, therefore.

First Order: the sphere or world of One (see Part I, *passim*), or a movement or phase determined chiefly by One.

Second Order: the sphere of Two (see Part II, *passim*). When this world becomes closed in on itself, we speak of a Two-container or Two-box.

Third Order: the sphere of Three (see Part III, *passim*). Associated with the emergence of this Third Order in history are the terms *Third Age, second simplicity, second wisdom, second faith, third music.*

Fourth Order: the sphere of Four (see Part IV, *passim*). This order emerges together with the Third Order, and its emergence is associated with the same terms.

Appendix II

Quaternity, Mandala

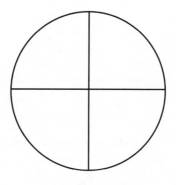

FIGURE 5.1

I swear it by the One who in our hearts engraved
The sacred Tetrad, symbol immense and pure,
Source of Nature and model of the Gods.[1]

Humanity is strongly inclined to understand reality as fourfold. In the philosophical and spiritual traditions, cosmos and humanity are often described in terms of four dimensions. In the human person, these dimensions may be interpreted as pure spirit, mind, feeling, and body, or as the ways of unitive experience, knowledge, love, and action. A universal spiritual anthropology is suggested here.[2]

> As compared with the trinitarian thinking of Plato, ancient Greek philosophy favoured thinking of a quaternary type. In Pythagoras the great role was played not by three but by four; the Pythagorean oath, for instance, says that the tetrakys "contains the roots of eternal nature." The Pythagorean school was dominated by the idea that the soul was a square and not a triangle. The origin of these ideas lies far back in the dark prehistory of Greek thought. The quaternity is an archetype of almost universal occurrence. It forms the logical basis for any whole judgment. If one wishes to pass such a judgment, it must have this fourfold

aspect. For instance, if you want to describe the horizon as a whole, you name the four quarters of heaven. Three is not a natural coefficient of order, but an artificial one. There are four elements, four prime qualities, four colours, four castes, four ways of spiritual development in Buddhism, etc. So too there are four aspects of psychological orientation....Schopenhauer proves that the "Principle of Sufficient Reason" has a fourfold root. This is so because the fourfold aspect is the minimum requirement for a complete judgment. The ideal of completeness is the circle or sphere, but its natural minimal division is a quaternity.[3]

Jung wrote repeatedly of the significance of *mandalic* figures as spontaneous symbols of the wholeness and balance of the psyche, or as symbols of the Self. [4]

As I have said, mandala means "circle." There are innumerable variants of the motif shown here, but they are all based on the squaring of a circle. Their basic motif is the premonition of a centre of personality, a kind of central point within the psyche, to which everything is related, by which everything is arranged, and which is itself a source of energy. The energy of the central point is manifested in the almost irresistible compulsion and urge to *become what one is*, just as every organism is driven to assume the form that is characteristic of its nature, no matter what the circumstances. This centre is not felt or thought of as the ego but, if one may so express it, as the *self*. Although the centre is represented by an innermost point, it is surrounded by a periphery containing everything that belongs to the self—the paired opposites that make up the total personality. This totality comprises consciousness first of all, then the personal unconscious, and finally an indefinitely large segment of the collective unconscious whose archetypes are common to all mankind.[5]

We encounter mandalic images today particularly in two spheres: in the ancient religious traditions and in the psychological experience of contemporary people.

In the sphere of religious practices and in psychology it [the word *mandala*] denotes circular images, which are drawn, painted, modeled, or danced. Plastic structures of this kind are to be found, for instance, in Tibetan Buddhism, and as dance figures these circular patterns occur also in Dervish monasteries. As psychological phenomena they appear spontaneously in dreams, in certain states of conflict, and in cases of schizophrenia. Very frequently they contain a quaternity or a multiple of four, in the form of a cross, a star, a square, an octagon, etc. In alchemy we encounter this motif in the form of *quadratura circuli*.[6]

Mandalic images are present in the biblical literature of both Testaments.

The "squaring of the circle" is one of the many archetypal motifs which form the basic patterns of our dreams and fantasies. But it is distinguished by the fact that it is one of the most important of them from the functional point of view. Indeed, it could even be called the *archetype of wholeness*. Because of this significance, the "quaternity of the One" is the schema for all images of God, as depicted in the visions of Ezekiel, Daniel, and Enoch, and as the representation of Horus with his four sons also shows.[7]

Spontaneous mandalic figures produced by the psyche surpass the traditional religious images in their variety and allusiveness.

Whereas ritual mandalas always display a definite style and a limited number of typical motifs as their content, individual mandalas make use of a well-nigh unlimited wealth of motifs and symbolic allusions, from which it can easily be seen that they are endeavouring to express either the totality of the individual in his inner or outer experience of the world, or its essential point of reference. Their object is the *self* in contradistinction to the *ego*, which is only the point of reference for consciousness, whereas the self comprises the totality of the psyche altogether, i.e., conscious *and* unconscious.[8]

According to Marie-Louise von Franz, mandalas make their appearance in the West at the time of the birth of Greek natural science, in the seventh and sixth centuries B.C.E. The figures reemerge vigorously at the end of the Middle Ages.

When the medieval masculine, spiritual god-image began to lose its vigor at the time of the Renaissance, that great period of cultural transformation, men turned toward the earth and the principle of matter. It was no accident then that it was just at that time—mediated by the Poimandres writings in the rediscovered *Corpus Hermeticum*—that the mandala once again began to occupy a special place as a model of the godhead and the cosmos.[9]

Like a compass of wholeness (see Figure 5.1), the mandala helps us to comprehend the phases and movements both of our own spiritual life and of that of our tradition and culture. At the pivotal moment in history, this figure took on new significance and power as an expression of the Christ-event in its totality.

Appendix III

The Christian Mandala
and Its Variants

As we have seen, the mandalic or quaternary form of the Christ-mystery expresses itself in various ways within the gospels and the Pauline writings.[1] Besides the fact of the existence of four gospels,[2] we find a group of four apostles singled out from the Twelve.

> And when they perceived the grace that was given to me, James and Cephas [Peter] and John, who were reputed to be pillars, gave to me and Barnabas the right hand of fellowship, that we should go to the Gentiles and they to the circumcised. (Gal 2:9)

Three of Jesus' twelve apostles constitute an inner circle around him, and accompany him at critical moments of his life. Peter, James, and John are with Jesus at the moment of light that is his transfiguration on the mountain, and at the moment of darkness in the garden when Jesus prays that the chalice of his passion may be taken away. When Paul joins these principal apostles, a four-pillared structure comes into being (see Figure 5.2).

The structure is a theological one: Worlds of meaning are condensed within its polarities. James and Paul constitute its horizontal axis, and their difference turns on Christian interpretation of the Jewish law and the progression from a Jewish

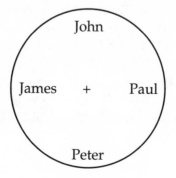

FIGURE 5.2

229

to a Gentile Christianity. James[3] represents a Jewish Christianity that is inclined to conserve the Torah. Paul, the Apostle to the Gentiles, leaves behind himself much of the structure of Jewish law in order to bring the gospel to those outside. Peter, between these two positions, becomes caught in the tension between them.[4]

This horizontal axis of the apostolic mandala is historical: Its polarity derives from the essential historical movement of the gospel from the center of Israel-Judaism-Jerusalem outward to all the peoples of the earth. The vertical axis, constituted by Peter and John, expresses a perennial spiritual polarity within Christianity rather than a historical movement. Peter, chief of the apostles, symbolically represents the external, institutional, and pastoral dimension of the church. John, most intimate disciple of Jesus, symbolizes the interior and unitive dimension of Christianity.

Exterior and interior, Jews and Gentiles: Each of these two axes of our figure has many parallels. The vertical axis is "ontological." It corresponds to a scale of the degrees of being that extends from the visible matter of this world to absolute divine Spirit. This axis or spectrum is both ontological and epistemological, cosmic and sapiential. The horizontal axis between James and Paul finds analogies on every plane of historical development.[5]

The Structure of Mark's Gospel

The cross or mandala figure, which represents the four gospels' mutual relationships, is also found in the structure of individual gospels. This can be demonstrated both in Mark (see Figure 5.3) and in John. When the structure of Mark[6] is diagrammed according to the geographical location of the narrative, it is found to consist of five parts, which form a center (Part III) and two axes. Four short "hinge" passages separate the five major parts.

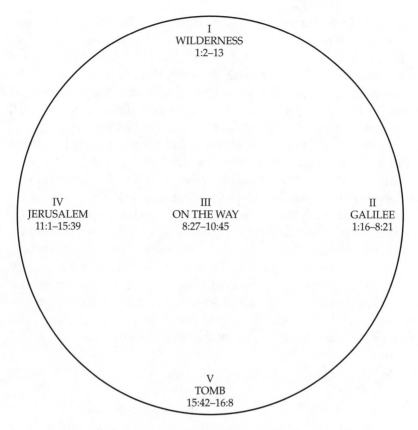

FIGURE 5.3

The locations of Parts I and V have much in common, as do those of II and IV. The horizontal axis, like that of the four gospels together, stretches symbolically between "Jews" and "World," the latter signified by the mixed (but largely receptive) population that Jesus encounters in Galilee. The vertical axis, which begins with the baptism of Jesus by John in the wilderness (I), concludes with the symbolic baptism of the disciple (V). Here Jesus' tomb and the baptismal font are symbolically identical, as Paul suggests (see Rom 6:3–4). In the central part (III), Jesus journeys with his disciples, teaching them to follow him on "the way" that will lead him to Jerusalem and his death.

The Christ-event, in this Markan structure, is once again

projected into quaternary form. While it is not certain precisely how we are to interpret the four poles of the figure, an approximation can be made. In the center (III) of the figure, Jesus' "word of the cross" (8:34–38) and his transfiguration (9:2–8) express the two sides of his paschal mystery of death and resurrection. The power of the Spirit manifested in Jesus' Galilean ministry (II) constrasts with the rigid law and its ministers, centered in Jerusalem (IV). At the beginning of Mark's Gospel (I), Jesus was baptized by John in the wilderness. At that moment the "heavens were opened" and Jesus was revealed to be the Son of God. From this initial peak we descend to the final scene of Mark's narrative (V) at the tomb—the opened earth—which had received his crucified body. This tomb was understood by the early community as symbolically identical with the baptismal font (see Rom 6:4), from which new life flowed forth at the Easter vigil liturgy. Mark's Gospel would have been read in its entirety as a preparation for this Easter baptismal event. The gospel narrative was opened and "brought home" as Jesus' baptismal illumination was personally experienced by the new child of God.[7]

Variants of the Christian Mandala

The mandalic figure, since it corresponds to the essential structure of human person, of cosmos and of Christ-mystery or Christ-event, appears in many different forms, many different places. Of special importance for our study is the scheme of the traditional "four senses of Scripture," or four levels of meaning in a biblical text: literal, allegorical, moral, and anagogical or mystical.[8] This scheme of four levels or dimensions of meaning in the Scriptures supplied the framework for the sapiential theology of Western Christianity from about 600 to 1300. It is, therefore, the principal medieval expression of the Christ-mystery's quaternary form. St. Gregory the Great was its first great proponent in the West, and was largely responsible for its widespread use in the Middle Ages.

> The words of Holy Scripture are square stones, for they can stand on all sides, because on no side are there rough spots. For in every past event they narrate, in every future event that

they foretell, in every moral saying that they speak, and in every spiritual sense they stand, as it were, on a different side.[9]

The classical verse of Augustine of Denmark (d. 1282) condenses the four levels of meaning.

Littera gesta docet, quid credis allegoria,
Quid agis moralis, quo tendis anagogia

The letter teaches what was done,
allegory what you should believe;
    the moral sense, what you should do,
    the anagogic, where you are heading.[10]

St. Thomas Aquinas witnesses to the centrality of this scheme in medieval theology when he explains the four senses and their relationship at the beginning of his *Summa*.[11]

The literal or historical sense is a text's basic meaning (intended by the human author), and from this can often (but by no means always) be educed a spiritual significance, which relates to the dual central Mystery of the New Testament: Christ and the church. From this "allegorical" sense of the text derive two other levels of meaning: our own participation in this Mystery (the moral or tropological sense) and the final realization of the Mystery at the end of history (the anagogical sense). Sometimes this final sense is also interpreted in terms of present spiritual experience; it may then be called the mystical sense.

The four senses may be represented by our basic mandalic figure.

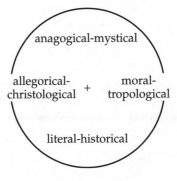

FIGURE 5.4

The four senses can be reinterpreted in the light of the four quadrants that we have been exploring in this book. These four levels of meaning of a biblical text open out into the four dimensions (One, Two, Three, Four) that pervade both the Scriptures and human life. These four dimensions, in turn, are rooted in the Trinity of divine Persons and in the creation, the "Fourth."

The *literal*-historical sense corresponds to *Four*, the dimension of concrete reality, and opens into such existential realities as the facts of economics, politics, and the environment. The *allegorical* sense, centered in the Christ-mystery, opens out also into the world of cognition, order, and wisdom that is *Two*. It is the third and fourth senses, however, that are most deepened and broadened by the mandalic interpretation. The *moral*-tropological sense opens into the personal-experiential and historical-dynamic dimension that we have explored as *Three*. The final *anagogical* sense becomes the *unitive* meaning of Scripture *(One)*. (See Figure 5.5) We have seen how these three further dimensions burgeon forth with the arrival of the New Testament.

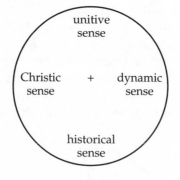

FIGURE 5.5

This development of the traditional scheme of the four senses of Scripture, opening it inwardly toward the trinitarian-cosmic mystery and outwardly into the dimensions of human life and experience, exemplifies the movement toward a new Christian wisdom proposed in this book.

A classical expression of four forms of Christian prayer (repentance, thanksgiving, petition, and praise) suggests an analogous structure.[12] Further parallels within spirituality can be found in the forms of meditation[13] and the classical Christian "ladder of contemplatives":[14] *lectio, meditatio, oratio,* and *contemplatio,* or reading, reflection, prayer, and contemplation. The fourfold pattern asserts itself again and again in the history of Christianity.

Notes

INTRODUCTION

1. A few preliminary descriptions of *wisdom*, as I am using the word, are: *experiential knowledge, unitive consciousness, unitive life*. The term is primordial and is used in various senses, and is therefore difficult to define. Nevertheless, its meaning in the context of this book should gradually become clear. The four perspectives that I shall develop are dimensions of wisdom; their articulation, however, is not precisely wisdom but a sapiential (wisdom) *theology*. Both Old and New Testaments speak of a divine Wisdom. This appears as *personified*, first simply as the "Sophia" of the Old Testament wisdom literature, and then as embodied in Jesus Christ in the New Testament writings. I shall capitalize the word *wisdom* when it is intended to denote this personified divine Wisdom.

2. *Sapientia* is the Latin word for wisdom. A sapiential consciousness is one that has the characteristics of wisdom. We shall understand it basically as a *unitive* consciousness.

3. See Part One, Section 2.

4. The quaternary structure of the Christ-mystery was expressed by patristic and medieval theology in the scheme of the *four senses of Scripture*: literal, allegorical, tropological, mystical. The internal structure of these four levels of meaning of a biblical text may also be represented by a mandalic figure. See Appendix II.

5. A mandala is a geometrical figure representing wholeness. The figure is both circular and quaternary (four-poled). See Appendix I.

6. This constellation of Trinity and creation appears frequently in the patristic writings. See McDonnell, *Baptism of Jesus*.

7. *Divinization*, or deification, is the union of God with the human person that brings about a divine humanity. This divine humanity appears first in Jesus Christ and then is communicated to other human persons by his death and resurrection and the imparting of the divine Spirit through baptism. Divinization was central to the

237

Eastern church fathers' vision of Christianity. See Lossky, *Mystical Theology*, pp. 154f., 196–216, 238; idem, *Image and Likeness*, ch. 5, "Redemption and Deification," pp. 97–110; Louth, *Origins*, pp. 73, 78, 124, 170, 197; McDonnell, *Baptism of Jesus*, ch. 9 and 10, pp. 128–55; Mantzaridis, *Deification of Man*; Pelikan, *Christian Tradition*, pp. 155, 233–34, 344–45; Thunberg, *Microcosm and Mediator*, pp. 454–59; *Dictionnaire de Spiritualite* art. "divinisation," vol. 3, cols. 1370–1459 (various authors).

8. The *perennial philosophy* is understood in this book to denote the unitive wisdom that is particularly characteristic of the great Asian traditions of Hinduism, Buddhism, and Taoism. This is the conception of ultimate reality as nondual: the *advaitan* doctrine of Hindu tradition. See Part One, Section 4.

9. Second simplicity: I speak of this new wisdom as bringing a *second simplicity* in recovering the original unity and simplicity of the Christ-mystery after many centuries of progressive differentiation and fission within Western Christianity. These complex and centrifugal developments have, for centuries, made it very difficult to perceive the original oneness and luminosity of the Mystery. See Appendix I.

10. Two and Three relate to one another as Word and Spirit, or masculine and feminine. This coordination of Word and Spirit, while rarely found in the tradition of Western Christianity, is at home in the East. We find it already in Irenaeus. In the contemporary Russian theologian Paul Evdokimov, the parallel correspondences Word-man and Spirit-woman become the basis for a theology of woman and of the sacramental union of woman and man. See *The Sacrament of Love* and *Woman and the Salvation of the World*.

11. See, e.g., Eph 2:11–22, 3:14–19; and see Part Four, Section 4, and Appendix II.

PART ONE

Introduction

1. Kabir, in White, *What Is Enlightenment?*, p. 34.

Section One

2. *Perennial philosophy*: see Introduction, note 8, and Part One, Section 4, below.

3. *Udana*, VIII, 1, quoted in Panikkar, *The Silence of God*, p. 42.

4. See Terrien, *The Elusive Presence*.

5. *Pseudo-Dionysius*: a Christian mystical theologian who wrote (probably in Syria) in the early sixth century and strongly influenced the theological traditions of both East and West. See *Pseudo-Dionysius, The Complete Works*.

6. On the dualism of Christianity and of the West, see Part Two *passim*, particularly Sections 5, 6, 7, 8, 9, 11.

7. Lossky, *Mystical Theology*, p. 26.

8. See Barfield, *Poetic Diction*. The relation of poetry to unitive wisdom will be further discussed in Part Three, Section 11.

Section Two

9. Griffiths, *Universal Wisdom*, p. 32.

10. *Tat tvam asi* (That art thou) is one of the four "Great Sentences" of the Upanishads that affirm that *brahman* (absolute reality) and the human self are one. This statement is found in the *Chandogya Upanishad*.

11. The *Axial period*: see Jaspers, *Origin and Goal of History*, pp. 1–21; Cousins, *Christ of the 21st Century*, pp. 4–7.

12. See Merton, *Seeds of Contemplation*, pp. 194–196; idem, *New Seeds of Contemplation*, pp. 267, 291–92; idem, *Zen and the Birds of Appetite*, pp. 67–68, 71–72, 80.

13. See Tanquerey, *The Spiritual Life*, par. 1386, p. 649.

14. Griffiths, *New Creation in Christ*, pp. 49–50.

15. Merton, *The Inner Experience*, quoted in Shannon, *Thomas Merton's Dark Path*, p.138.

16. Merton, *New Seeds of Contemplation*, pp. 291–92.

Section Three

17. Nicholas of Cusa, *Of Learned Ignorance*, ch. 2, p. 9.

18. *Shiva Nataraj*: the Hindu deity, lord of the universe, who is portrayed dancing in the midst of a ring of flames, representing the forces of nature. This cosmic dance of Shiva represents his five activities: creation, maintenance, destruction, embodiment, and liberation. See EEPR 243.

Section Four

19. Griffiths, *Universal Wisdom*, p. 8.

20. Huxley, *The Perennial Philosophy* (1944), quoted in White, *What Is Enlightenment?*, pp. 27–28.

21. Evagrius Ponticus (346–399): see Evagrius Ponticus: *The Praktikos and Chapters on Prayer*, and *The Mind's Long Journey to the Holy Trinity*.

22. Maximus Confessor (ca. 580–662): see *Maximus Confessor: Selected Writings*, and Thunberg, *Man and the Cosmos*.

Section Five

23. Griffiths, *Return to the Center*, p. 16.

24. Nyoshul Khenpo, *Natural Great Perfection*, p. 78.

25. See Merton, *New Seeds of Contemplation*, pp. 6–13, 47–51, 275–89.

26. See Coward, *Jung and Eastern Thought*.

27. Wilber: see his *The Atman Project, The Spectrum of Consciousness*, and *Up from Eden*.

28. *Monism* is the philosophical doctrine that insists that reality is one, disallowing any basic qualitative plurality or the existence of independent parts. An extreme monism may affirm that only the One is real, while all plurality is illusory.

Section Six

29. Panikkar, *Blessed Simplicity*, pp. 10–19.

30. Ibid., p. 15.

31. Ibid., p. 17.

32. Ibid., pp. 29–39.

33. See Part Two, Section 10.

34. See Mauser, *Christ in the Wilderness*.

35. *Ihidaya*: see Murray, *Symbols of Church and Kingdom*, pp. 13–16; idem, "Exhortation to Candidates for Ascetical Vows at Baptism," *passim*; Winkler, "Origins and Idiosyncrasies of the Earliest Form of Asceticism," pp. 27–37; Barnhart, *Good Wine*, pp. 368–71.

36. Winkler, "Origins and Idiosyncrasies," pp. 27–37.

37. DeVogue, *Rule of St. Benedict*, pp. 10–19 (especially 12–14), 284–85.

38. See Cassian, *Conferences*, Conference One: "On the Goal or Objective of the Monk," nn. 2–7, pp. 37–42.

Section Seven

39. See McDonnell, *Baptism of Jesus in the Jordan*; and "Jesus' Baptism in the Jordan."

40. See Stock, *Method and Message of Mark*, pp. 17–19; and Barnhart, *Good Wine*, pp. 321–58, especially pp. 330–44.

41. See Lao Tzu, *Tao Teh Ching*, ch. 1, p. 3; ch. 4, p. 9; ch. 6, p. 13; ch. 14, p. 29.

42. For the relation between the original creation and the baptism of Jesus in the Jordan, see McDonnell, *Baptism of Jesus in the Jordan*, pp. 55–57.

Section Eight

43. See Wilder, *Early Christian Rhetoric*, e.g; pp. xxx, 5–17, 128.

44. In Zen, a koan is a paradoxical saying that, defying rational comprehension, challenges the student to transcend thought in an intuitive leap beyond duality. See EEPR 182.

Part Two

Introduction

1. Being, in its higher realizations, possesses the intrinsic property of reflection or "luminosity." See Rahner, *Hearers of the Word*, pp. 31–44.

2. *Second Order*: this is the world of Two. Here it is being considered in a historical situation in which Two becomes dominant and exclusive, largely suppressing the operation and expression of One, Three, and Four. See Appendix I.

3. This modern Western mind is often referred to as "Cartesian." It is a dualistic consciousness that sees nature as external to mind, and proceeds exclusively by rational thought. See Tarnas, *Passion of the Western Mind*, pp. 275–80.

Section One

4. Pope, "Essay on Man."

5. See Part One, Section 5, "The Unitive Self."

Section Two

6. See Part One, Section 5 and n. 11.

7. Constitution on Divine Revelation, no. 2, Flannery pp. 750–51.

8. A claim to divine revelation characterizes many religious traditions, including Zoroastrianism and the Hindu Vedanta.

9. Buber, *Tales of the Hasidim*, p. 236.

10. See Introduction, n. 2 above.

11. See Part One, Section 4, "The Perennial Philosophy."

Section Three

12. *Flesh* (Greek *sarx*) : Paul sometimes uses this word in its neutral sense, as practically equivalent to "body." Often, however, he opposes *flesh* to *spirit*, and then flesh signifies the whole person outside the dominion of the spirit, dominated by the power of sin, or by the centrifugal energies of the outer self. See Gal 5:13–26.

13. See Malatesta, *Interiority and Covenant*.

Section Four

14. This transformation of consciousness, an aspect of the "new creation" that is implicit everywhere in the Pauline writings, becomes explicit for instance in Rom 8:5–10; Rom 12:2; 1 Cor 2:9–16; 2 Cor 3:15–18; Eph 4:22–24; Col 3:9–11. It is central to the mystagogical writings of the early patristic age.

15. *Logos*: see Pelikan, *Jesus Through the Centuries*, ch. 5, "The Cosmic Christ," pp. 57–70; idem, *The Christian Tradition*, pp. 186–89, 251–65; ODCC s.v. Logos; and Barnhart, *Good Wine*, pp. 399–400.

16. *Divinization*: see Introduction, n. 7.

17. Irenaeus, *Against Heresies* III, 19, 1, ANF vol. 1, p. 448, quoted in Clement, *Roots of Christian Mysticism*, pp. 37–38.

18. Maximus the Confessor, *Ambigua* (PG 91, 1360), quoted in Clement, *Roots of Christian Mysticism*, p. 40.

Section Five

19. Dulles, *Models of the Church*.

20. Rahner, "Basic Theological Interpretation of the Second Vatican Council," p. 83.

21. *Monotropic*: the word is used here to denote a Christianity that exists in only one authorized form, so that the natural richness, freedom and pluralism of gospel and Holy Spirit cannot be expressed.

22. See Part Two, Section 11 below.

23. See Brueggemann, *The Creative Word*, pp. 9–13 (an introductory summary of the three stages that Brueggemann will develop in the book).

24. This development of the third, "Wisdom" phase goes beyond Brueggemann's interpretation.

25. See Barfield, *Saving the Appearances*.

26. For example, biblical Fundamentalism and a reductive biblical criticism encounter one another as two opposing literalisms; neither perspective is open to the symbolic and unitive depths of a scriptural text.

Section Six

27. *Divinization*: see Introduction, n. 7 above.

28. [*The investiture struggle*: this was the dispute between popes and emperors over the right of kings to install bishops and abbots. It continued from about 1076 to the Concordat of Worms in 1122.]

29. Dolan in his Introduction to Nicholas of Cusa, *Unity and Reform*, pp. 35–37. See also the writings of Sherrard, especially *Church, Papacy and Schism*.

30. See Part Two, Section 5, pp. 56–7, and Part Two, n. 19.

31. Gilkey, *Catholicism Confronts Modernity*, pp. 46–47.

32. Rahner, art. *Grace, Sacramentum Mundi* 3, pp. 415–22 (ET 588–89); and Niermann, art. *Supernaturalism*, SM 6, pp. 191–93 (ET 1650–52).

33. Sherrard, "The Christian Understanding of Man," pp. 331–32.

34. Ibid., pp. 335–37

35. See Part One, Section 5.

Section Seven

36. *Christ-Quantum*: this expression is intended to represent the totality of the light and energy that came into the world with the coming of Christ and the new conferring of the Holy Spirit on humanity. This light and energy are conceived as remaining within the world, as if implanted in humanity itself, and bringing forth the progressive historical development that is observed in the world (and particularly in the West) since the resurrection of Christ.

37. Central to the progressive historical development of humanity during the past twenty centuries have been (1) the development of human reason, which has produced Western science, and (2) the growing communication and understanding between different peoples, which gradually moves toward a global human community. We are conceiving both of these developments as long-term fruits of the Christ-Quantum.

38. See White, "The Historical Roots of our Ecological Crisis," especially pp. 6–7.

39. Ibid., pp. 11–12.

40. See Jn 1:3; 1:9–10; Rom 8:19–23; Col 1:19–20; Eph 4:9–10; Rv 21:1; 21:5–6.

41. Before the time of Christ, a spiritual wisdom of very great depth had developed in Asia. See Part One above, especially pp. 17, 22, 25.

Section Eight

42. *Koinonia:* this Greek word denotes the *communion* that is the fundamental reality of the new Christian community. In early Christianity, this communion was understood as constituting the church (see Acts 2:42; 1 Cor 1:9). In the New Testament, this communion is understood as a participation in the divine life; that is, in God (see 1 Jn 1:3; 1:6–7). The sacred koinonia is actualized sacramentally in the eucharist (see 1 Cor 10:16).

Section Nine

43. The *old wisdom*: this expression is intended to denote the "precritical" Christian wisdom tradition in a general way, particularly in its later developments, which fell increasingly short of the fullness and dynamism of the New Testament wisdom. The *old wisdom* is, there-

fore, the *first wisdom,* but seen now from the perspective of its limitations and decline. See Appendix I.

Section Ten

44. The *first wisdom,* or old wisdom, corresponds to the Christian sapiential tradition of patristic and medieval times, before the age of rational-critical thought. The *second wisdom,* or new wisdom, denotes primarily a postcritical Christian wisdom that is emerging in our time and that, ideally, will embrace the totality of the Mystery I have represented in the mandalic figure. See Appendix I.

45. See Part One, Section 6.

46. Giancoli, *Physics,* p. 898.

47. *Hinayana* is the earlier Buddhist tradition that focuses on individual liberation. It was called the "Small Vehicle" (*Hinayana*) in contrast to the later *Mahayana* ("Great Vehicle") tradition, in which the well-being or liberation of all beings is sought as the goal of human life. See EEPR 215f.

Section Eleven

48. See Dunn: *Unity and Diversity in the New Testament,* ch. XIV, pp. 341–66.

Section Twelve

49. Yang-shan Hui-chi, in Suzuki, *Essays in Zen Buddhism,* p. 55.

PART THREE

Introduction

1. *New depth of subjectivity* is intended here to mean a deeper realization of personal identity that expresses itself in a deeper personal consciousness; a new personalization of values, ideas, and feelings; and a new freedom with respect to collective values and impersonal forces.

Section Three

2. Joachim conceived the age of the Father to extend until the coming of Christ, the age of the Son to continue from the time of Jesus until about 1260 C.E. (Joachim himself died in 1202), and a final age of the Spirit, to begin at that time. See ODCC, p. 878.

3. For the terms *first wisdom, second wisdo*m, see Part Two, n. 43 and 44, and Appendix I.

4. Richards, "That Supreme Point," in her *Imagine Inventing Yellow*, p. 78.

Section Four

5. See Capra, *The Turning Point;* Tarnas, *Passion of the Western Mind*, Epilogue, pp. 441–45.

6. Tarnas, *Passion of the Western Mind*, pp. 442–43.

7. See "Psyche: Lost and Discovered," later in this Section.

8. Jacobi, *The Psychology of C. G. Jung*, pp. 5–6.

Section Five

9. *The feminine*: the meaning of this term, in the general sense in which it is intended here, appears in the contrast between Third Order and Second Order, and in the contemporary emergences of the Third Order (see Part Three, Section 4 above). The emergence of woman and women's concerns is accompanied today not only by a women's liberation movement but by a broad reawakening to the reality of *psyche* and the transition from a mechanical to an organic vision of reality. In Christian tradition, the "shadow" side of woman and the feminine has been overaccented; today this imbalance begins to be addressed. See Evdokimov, *Woman and the Salvation of the World*, and idem, *The Sacrament of Love*.

10. The Russian "Sophiologists" include Vladimir Soloviev, E. N. Trubestkoi, Pavel Florensky, Sergius Bulgakov, and B. Zenkovsky. Nikolai Berdyaev has also written of Sophia.

11. See Solovyov, *Lectures on Divine Humanity*, pp. xiii–xv, 113, 118, 131–32, 138.

12. See Dulles, *Models of the Church*, and above, p. (##KW79)

13. *Tao of history* (see F. Capra, *The Tao of Physics*): the immanent principle and "order" of historical development. The concept reflects

Teilhard de Chardin's immanent "Christ-Omega," but proposes instead an immanent *feminine* principle.

14. Bohm, "Science, Spirituality and the Present World Crisis," p. 152.

15. *First wisdom, second wisdom*: see Appendix I and Part Two, n. 43 and 44.

16. See Barfield, *Rediscovery of Meaning* (Introduction), on the creative revolution introduced within humanity by the Incarnation.

17. I am conceiving this historical midpoint as the moment of transition from a first phase of revelation, predominantly through the solar masculine Logos, to a second phase in which revelation occurs primarily through the immanent feminine Spirit, or Sophia.

Section Six

18. *Sapiential*: see Introduction, n. 2.

19. Teilhard de Chardin, *Human Energy*, p. 121.

Section Seven

20. *First wisdom, second wisdom:* see Appendix I and Part Two n. 43 and 44. These terms, it should be recalled, do *not* correspond to First Order and Second Order.

21. *Divinization*: see Introduction, n. 7.

22. Modern secular humanism is the most explicit philosophical expression of this secular appropriation of "the divinity of man." See de Lubac, *The Drama of Atheist Humanism*.

23. See Boorstin, *The Discoverers*.

24. *Sapiential consciousness*: see Introduction, n. 2.

Section Ten

25. Wilbur, "A Christmas Hymn," in *The Poems of Richard Wilbur*, p. 57.

26. *Second wisdom*: see Part Two, n. 44, and Appendix I.

27. Sophia, as the divine Wisdom, animates every genuine wisdom: "first wisdom," "second wisdom," etc. I am proposing, as this second wisdom, however, a consciousness and vision that are more fully attuned to this "feminine" divine Wisdom, and in which Sophia herself begins to find explicit recognition.

28. See Sanders, *New Testament Christological Hymns*. Such theological poems, preexisting the New Testament texts themselves, have been proposed in Phil 2:6–11; Col 1:15–20; Eph 2:14–16; 1 Tm 3:16; 1 Pt 3:18–22; Heb 1:3; Jn 1:1–5 and 1:9–11. When we say *hymn*, of course, we imply an explicit musical setting and function at the origin of the text. In such a case the marriage of music and wisdom, of poetry and wisdom, is explicit.

29. See Moore and Gillette, *King, Warrior, Magician, Lover;* idem, *The King Within;* and Perry, *Lord of the Four Quarters*.

30. The biblical stories of David are to be found in 1 Sm 17–31, 2 Sm 1–24, and 1 Kgs 1–2, and in the parallel sections of 1 Chr. David was traditionally held to be the author of the Book of Psalms.

Section Eleven

31. Romanticism and Modernism were two successive movements (closely related and yet very different) toward creative freedom in the literature and art of Europe and America. The Romantic movement began, in reaction to Neo-Classicism and scientific rationalism, at the time of the French Revolution (1789) and continued, in some countries, to the middle of the nineteenth century. The Modernist movement began, in reaction to naturalism and realism, in the last decades of the nineteenth century and continued through the 1920s.

32. William Blake, in a letter to Thomas Butts (1802); see *Blake: Complete Writings*, p. 818.

33. Wallace Stevens, "The Man with the Blue Guitar," XXXII, *Collected Poems*, p. 183

34. *Maximal:* see Part One, Section 3.

35. *Second faith*: the movement from first to second faith is roughly parallel to the movement from first to second wisdom: These transitions are two aspects of the same process. See Part Two, n. 44, and Appendix I.

36. See Berdyaev, "Salvation and Creativity."

Section Twelve

37. See Fox, *Original Blessing*.

38. Stevens, "The Well Dressed Man with a Beard," *Collected Poems*, p. 247.

39. Stevens, "Of Bright & Blue Birds & the Gala Sun," *Collected Poems*, p. 248.

PART FOUR

Section One

1. See Fedotov, *The Russian Religious Mind*, ch. I, pp. 3–20; and Arseniev, *Russian Piety*.

2. Marie-Louise von Franz, *Jung: His Myth in our Time*.

3. Jung confronts the problem of the missing Fourth again and again in his writings. See *The Collected Works of C. G. Jung*, vol. 20, General Index, s.v. *quaternity, four, tetraktys, mandala*. In CW, vol. 11, *Psychology and Religion*, Jung discusses the problem of the Fourth at length in (1) "Psychology and Religion" (pp. 51–105), (2) "A Psychological Approach to the Dogma of the Trinity," pp. 164–92, and more briefly in (3) "Answer to Job," pp. 423–25.

4. Jung, "A Psychological Approach," p. 167.

5. Ibid., 178.

6. Ibid., pp. 178–79.

7. See Cousins, *Christ of the 21st Century*, pp. 6–7, 10, 132, 165–67.

8. See Washburn, *Ego and the Dynamic Ground*.

9. Jung, pp. 164ff.

10. Ibid., p.164.

11. Ibid., p. 176.

12. *Movements from below*: this expression is intended to comprehend both environmental and social movements—that is, not only the ecological but the various liberation movements of our time.

Section Two

13. See Part One, Section 4, p. 17.

14. Cousins, *Christ of the 21st Century*, pp. 5–6.

15. Ibid., pp. 4–6.

16. Ibid., p. 10.

17. Menchu, *I, Rigoberta Menchu*, p. 57.

18. See Jung, "A Psychological Approach," pp. 107–220, *passim*.

19. See von Franz, *Jung*, pp. 149–53.

20. See Gutierrez, *A Theology of Liberation;* and Nickoloff, *Gustavo Gutierrez: Essential Writings*.

21. See Cousins, *Christ of the 21st Century*, pp. 135–47.

22. See Suzuki, *Essays in Zen Buddhism, First Series*, "The Ten Cow-Herding Pictures", X, p. 376, and Plate X, opposite p. 193.

Section Three

23. *The flesh is the hinge of salvation*: this expression is Tertullian's. See Vagaggini, *The Flesh, Instrument of Salvation*.

24. *Church as sacrament*: this conception of the church is used definitively at the beginning of the Vatican II Constitution on the Church: "Since the Church, in Christ, is in the nature of sacrament—a sign and instrument, that is, of communion with God and of unity among all men..." (Flannery, p. 350). See also Rahner, *Foundations of Christian Faith*, pp. 411–13.

25. Teilhard de Chardin, "Mon Univers" (1924), in *Science and Christ*, New York: Harper and Row, 1968, pp. 56–57, quoted in Hale, *Christ and the Universe*, p. 80.

26. Ibid., p. 54, quoted in Hale, *Christ and the Universe*, p. 88.

27. Teilhard de Chardin, "The Priest" in his *Writings in Time of War*, p. 208; quoted by Hale, *Christ and the Universe*, p. 28.

28. Teilhard de Chardin, "The Spiritual Power of Matter" (1919), in his *The Heart of Matter*, p.74; quoted in Hale, *Christ and the Universe*, pp. 33–34.

29. Teilhard de Chardin, "The Spiritual Power of Matter" (1919), in his *The Heart of Matter*, p. 74.

30. See, for example, the "Hymn to Matter," which concludes Teilhard's "The Spiritual Power of Matter," in his *The Heart of Matter*, pp. 75–77.

Section Four

31. *Purusha-sukta*, Rig Veda X, 90, 3, quoted in Panikkar, *A Dwelling Place for Wisdom*, p. 31.

32. Eliade, *Patterns in Comparative Religion*, ch. 10, "Temple, Palace, Centre of the World," p. 371 (and see pp. 367–87).

33. Ibid., p. 373.

34. Ibid., p. 374.

35. See Appendix III for a fuller treatment of the Christian mandala.

36. The quaternity of three divine Persons and the cosmos appears in patristic developments of the gospel accounts of Jesus' baptism (see McDonnell, *Baptism of Jesus in the Jordan*). At this moment Jesus is understood to be *anointed* with the unitive divine Spirit, which he will impart to the world:

In the New Testament, the Father anoints Christ with the Spirit, and the Father in that Spirit-anointing binds from within Word, Church, world, universe. The finger of the Father reaching out to anoint the Christ with the Spirit also extends beyond the triune self to touch the world and the cosmos. The trinitarian dynamic is cosmic. (McDonnell, p. 127)

37. See above, Introduction, p. 4.
38. See Ez 1:4–14; 10:9–14; Rv 4:6–9.
39. See Appendix III.
40. Ibid.

Section Five

41. See Cousins, *Christ in the 21st Century*, p. 10.

Section Six

42. See Prv 8–9; Wis 7–9; Sir 1:1–20 and ch. 24; Bar 3:9–4:4.
43. See, for example, Irenaeus of Lyons, *Against Heresies*, Bk V, ch. 19, no. 1, ANF vol. l, p. 547 (*Roman Breviary* vol. 1, p. 244).
44. See Part Three, Sections 10, 11.
45. See Barfield, *The Rediscovery of Meaning*, e.g., Introduction, pp. 5–6.
46. See above, pp. 150–51.
47. Jonathan Swift, in his scathing social satire *A Modest Proposal for Preventing Children of Poor People from Being a Burden to Their Parents and to the Country* (1729), proposed that the poor people of Ireland (under a harsh British rule) raise their children as food for the rich.
48. See Bruteau, "The Holy Thursday Revolution," and "Neo-Feminism as Communion Consciousness." Both essays are collected in *Neo-Feminism and Communion Consciousness: Essays by Beatrice Bruteau.*

Section Seven

49. See Appendix III, pp. 230–32.
50. See Stock, *The Method and Message of Mark*, pp. 12–19.
51. Myers, *Binding the Strong Man*, p. 427.
52. Ibid., p. 446.
53. Ibid., p. 11.
54. See Appendix II, pp. 230–32 (sic).
55. See Part Four, Section 4.

Section Eight

56. See Cousins, *Christ in the 21st Century*, pp. 7–14.

57. See Hale, *Christ and the Universe*, especially pp. 23–29.

58. Teilhard de Chardin, *The Heart of Matter*, p. 16.

59. Ibid., p. 17.

60. Ibid., p. 18.

61. In Part Two (especially Sections 5 and 6), we have considered the tendency of Western consciousness and thought to remain within the world of "Two," that is, the logos-world. The theological tradition of Western Christianity has given relatively little attention to the Holy Spirit, in comparison with the efforts given to the development of Christology. Some Eastern Christian theologians (e.g., Vladimir Lossky) point out in Roman Catholicism a subordination of the Holy Spirit to Word, to doctrine, and to institutional structure and authority.

62. Teilhard de Chardin, *The Heart of Matter*, p. 28.

63. Ibid., p. 29.

64. Ibid., p. 40.

65. Ibid., p. 44.

66. Ibid., p. 45.

67. Ibid.

68. Ibid., p. 47.

69. Ibid., p. 48.

70. Teilhard de Chardin, "The Mystical Milieu," in *Writings in Time of War*, p. 146; quoted in Hale, *Christ and the Universe*, p. 24.

71. Teilhard de Chardin, "The Mass on the World," in his *The Heart of Matter*, pp. 120–121.

72. Ibid., p. 132. See also pp. 121, 123, 124, 125.

73. Ibid., p. 133.

74. *Second wisdom*: see Part Two, n. 44, and Appendix I.

75. See Part Four, Section 2, p. 155, and Cousins, *Christ of the 21st Century*, pp. 9–10.

76. These Russian authors include Vladimir Soloviev, Nikolai Berdyaev, Vladimir Lossky, and Paul Evdokimov; the contemporary French writer Olivier Clement continues this tradition of thought. See Bernhard Schultze, art. "Russian Religious Philosophy," SM, Vol. 5, pp. 372–74, and Olivier Clement, *Le Christ, terre des vivants*. This spiritual understanding of the material creation is often accompanied by a sensitivity to the feminine and to the spiritual potential of *eros*. See Evdokimov, *The Sacrament of Love*, and idem, *Woman and the Salvation of the World*.

77. *Second wisdom*: see Appendix I.

78. *Apophasis*: an approach to the Divine through mystery, unknowing. See Part One, Section 1.

79. *Redshift*: See Part Two, Section 10.

80. See Part Two, Section 7.

Section Nine

81. See Part Two, Sections 5 and 9.

82. See Part Four, Section 1; and Jung, "A Psychological Approach."

83. Quoted in de Lubac, *Corpus Mysticum*, p. 283.

84. See Dolan and Sherrard works in Part Two, n. 29.

85. *A new wisdom*: this corresponds to the "second wisdom" mentioned above. See Part Two, n. 44, and Appendix I.

EPILOGUE

1. Such a view of history may seem to be naively optimistic. This optimism, however, intends to express once more the perennial *good news* of the New Testament. While this good news reaches its fulfillment beyond history, it also works as a leaven within history. By looking toward its brightening horizon, we can participate consciously in its dawning.

APPENDIX II

1. From "The Golden Verses of Pythagoras," verse 25, quoted in Panikkar, *A Dwelling Place for Wisdom*, p. 32.

2. See, for example, Panikkar, *A Dwelling Place for Wisdom*, ch. 2, "*Quaternitas Perfecta*: The Fourfold Nature of Man," pp. 31–75.

3. Jung, "A Psychological Approach," p. 167.

4. See *Collected Works of C. G. Jung*, vol. 20. General Index, s.v. *mandala*. Jung's discussions of the mandala include "Concerning Mandala Symbolism," vol. 9/1, pp. 355–84; Appendix "Mandalas," vol. 9/1, pp. 387–90; "Commentary on *The Secret of the Golden Flower*," vol. 13, pp. 1–56 (+ plates). See also von Franz, *Jung*, ch. 7, "The Mandala," pp. 139–57; and Jacobi, *The Psychology of C. G. Jung*, pp. 136–41.

5. Jung, "Concerning Mandala Symbolism," p. 357.

6. Ibid., p. 387.

7. Ibid., p. 388.

8. Ibid., p. 389.

9. Franz, *Jung*, p. 150.

APPENDIX III

1. See Part Four, Section 4.

2. See Part Four, Section 4, pp. 169–71.

3. The *James* primarily intended here is the "brother of the Lord" who was a leader of the Jerusalem Christian community and known as a righteous man according to the Jewish law (see Gal 2:9). He is also the probable author of the Letter of James. By an opportune coincidence, the son of Zebedee and brother of John—a different person within the apostolic community, who is part of the trio of close associates of Jesus—bore the same name. See ABD, vol. 3, pp. 616, 620–22.

4. Writing to the Galatian Christians, Paul recalls Peter's defection from the freedom of the gospel to the "Judaizing" side of James (Gal 2:11–14).

5. See Part Three, *passim*, and Part Two, Section 10.

6. See Stock, *Method and Message of Mark*, pp. 19–32; Iersel, *Reading Mark*, pp. 20–26; and Barnhart, *Good Wine*, pp. 330–32.

7. See Part Four, Section 7, and Stock, *Method and Message of Mark*, pp. 12–19.

8. An account of the origin and history of the scheme of the four senses of Scripture is given by McNally, art. "Exegesis, Medieval," in *New Catholic Encyclopedia*, vol. 5, pp. 708–9. The scheme of the four senses has been summarized by St. Thomas Aquinas, *Summa Theologiae*, Pt. I, Q. 1, A 10, and by St. Bonaventure, *Breviloquium*, Prologue, 4:4, pp. 13–14.

A basic historical study of the scheme is de Lubac, *Exegese Medievale*. Part of this four-volume work is available in English in de Lubac, *Sources of Revelation*. De Lubac surveys the scheme's history briefly in "On an Old Distich."

9. Gregory the Great, Homily 9 on Ezekiel, no. 8, quoted in McNally, "Exegesis, Medieval," p. 708.

10. Quoted in ibid.

11. St. Thomas Aquinas, *Summa Theologiae*, Pt. I, Q.1, Art. 10.

12. See Rahner, art. "Prayer," in SM 5, p. 79 (ET 1273).

13. See Naranjo and Ornstein, *On the Psychology of Meditation*, pp. 16–18. To the three forms of meditation or consciousness mentioned here by Naranjo can be added, as fourth, an implicit recollection or "presence of God" that accompanies ordinary life and activity.

14. See Guigo II, *The Ladder of Monks*.

Bibliography

Abhishikhtananda (Henri Le Saux). *Saccidananda: A Christian Approach to Advaitic Experience*. Delhi: ISPCK, 1974.

Allchin, A.M. *The World Is a Wedding: Explorations in Christian Spirituality*. New York: Oxford, 1978.

The Anchor Bible Dictionary, 6 vols. New York: Doubleday, 1992.

The Ante-Nicene Fathers, 10 vols. (reprint). Grand Rapids, Mich.: Eerdmans, 1981.

Arseniev, Nicholas. *Russian Piety*. London: Faith Press, 1964.

Bacik, James J. *Apologetics and the Eclipse of Mystery: Mystagogy According to Karl Rahner*. Notre Dame, Ind.: University of Notre Dame Press, 1980.

Barfield, Owen. *Poetic Diction*. Middletown, Conn.: Wesleyan, 1973.

————. *The Rediscovery of Meaning and Other Essays*. Middletown, Conn.: Wesleyan, 1977.

————. *Romanticism Comes of Age*. Middletown, Conn.: Wesleyan, 1966.

————. *Saving the Appearances: A Study in Idolatry*. New York: Harcourt Brace Jovanovich, 1983.

Barnhart, Bruno. *The Good Wine: Reading John from the Center*. New York: Paulist, 1993.

————. "Monastic Wisdom and the World of Today." *Monastic Studies* 16 (1985): 111–38.

Bellah, Robert. *Habits of the Heart: Individualism and Commitment in American Life*. Berkeley: University of California Press, 1985.

Benedict, St. *RB1980: The Rule of St. Benedict*. Edited by Timothy Fry, OSB. Collegeville, Minn.: Liturgical Press, 1981.

Benet's Reader's Encyclopedia. 3d ed. Edited by Katherine Baker Siepmann. New York: HarperCollins, 1987.

Berdyaev, Nicholas. *The Meaning of History*. London: Geoffrey Bles, Centenary Press, 1936.

————. *The Meaning of the Creative Act*. New York: Collier, 1962.

————. "Salvation and Creativity." In *Historical Roots, Ecumenical Routes*, edited by M. Fox, 115–39. Notre Dame, Ind.: Fides, 1979.

Blake, William. *Blake: Complete Writings*. Edited by Geoffrey Keynes. London: Oxford 1969.

Bly, Robert. *News of the Universe: Poems of Twofold Consciousness*. San Francisco: Sierra Club, 1980.

Bloomsbury Guide to English Literature, The. Edited by Marion Davies. New York: Prentice-Hall, 1990.

Bohm, David. "Science, Spirituality and the Present World Crisis." *ReVision* 15, no. 4 (1993): 147–52.

————. *Wholeness and the Implicate Order*. London: Ark, 1983.

Bonaventure. *The Breviloquium (The Works of Bonaventure*, Vol. II). Paterson, N.J.: St. Anthony Guild Press, 1963.

Boorstin, Daniel. *The Discoverers: A History of Civilization*. New York: Random House, 1983.

Bouyer, Louis. *The Christian Mystery: From Pagan Myth to Christian Mysticism*. Petersham, Mass.: St. Bede Publ., 1995.

Bowman, John. *The Gospel of Mark: The New Christian Jewish Passover Haggadah*. Leiden: E. J. Brill, 1965.

Brock, Sebastian. *The Harp of the Spirit: Twelve Poems of Saint Ephrem*. Introduction and translation by Sebastian Brock (Studies Supplementary to Sobornost No. 4). London: Fellowship of St. Alban and St. Sergius, 1975.

————. *The Holy Spirit in the Syrian Baptismal Tradition*. Poona: The Syrian Churches Series, vol. 9, 1979.

————. *The Luminous Eye: The Spiritual World Vision of St. Ephrem the Syrian* (Cistercian Studies series no. 124). Kalamazoo, Mich.: Cistercian Publications, 1992.

————. "The Poet as Theologian." *Sobornost* 7, no. 4 (1977): 243–50.

————. "Studies in the Early History of the Syrian Orthodox Baptismal Liturgy." *JTS* 23 (1972): 16–64.

Brown, Raymond E. *The Critical Meaning of the Bible*. New York: Paulist, 1982.

————, et al., Eds. *The New Jerome Biblical Commentary*. Englewood Cliffs, N.J.: Prentice-Hall, 1990.

Brueggemann, Walter. *The Creative Word: Canon as a Model for Biblical Education*. Philadelphia: Fortress, 1982.

Bruteau, Beatrice. "The Holy Thursday Revolution." *Liturgy*, July 1978.

————. *Neo-Feminism and Communion Consciousness; Essays by Beatrice Bruteau*. Chambersburg, Penn.: Anima Publications, n.d.

————. "Neo–feminism as Communion Consciousness." *Anima*, Fall 1978.

Buber, Martin. *Tales of the Hasidim: The Early Masters.* New York: Schocken Books, 1947.

Bulgakov, Serge. *The Wisdom of God.* London: Williams & Norgate, and New York: Paisley Press, 1937.

Cady, Susan, Marian Ronan, and Hal Taussig. *Sophia: The Future of Feminist Spirituality.* New York: Harper & Row, 1986.

Cahill, P. Joseph, "The Johannine Logos as Center." *CBQ* 38 (1976): 54–72.

Capra, Fritjof, *The Tao of Physics: An Exploration of the Parallels between Modern Physics and Eastern Mysticism.* Berkeley: Shambala, 1975.

————. *The Turning Point: Science, Society and the Rising Culture.* New York: Simon and Schuster, 1982.

Cassian, John. *Conferences.* Translated by Colm Luibheid; Introduction by Owen Chadwick. New York: Paulist, 1985.

Clement, Olivier. *Le Christ, terre des vivants: Le Corps spirituel et Le sens de la terre, Essais theologiques.* Bégrolles-en-mauges (France), Abbey of Bellefontaine, 1976.

————. *The Roots of Christian Mysticism: Text and Commentary.* London: New City, 1993.

Cousins, Ewert. *Christ of the 21st Century.* Rockport, Mass.: Element, 1992.

Coward, Harold. *Jung and Eastern Thought.* Albany: SUNY Press, 1985.

Cross, F. L., & E. A. Livingstone, Eds. *The Oxford Dictionary of the Christian Church.* 3d ed. Oxford: Oxford University Press, 1997.

De Lubac, Henri. *Corpus Mysticum: L'Eucharistic et L' Église au Moyen Age,* 2d ed., Paris: Aubier, 1949.

————. *The Drama of Atheist Humanism.* New York: Meridian (New American Library), 1963.

————. *Exegese medievale: Les quatre sens de l'ecriture.* 4 vols. Paris: Aubier (Editions Montaigne), 1959–1964.

————. "On an Old Distich: The Doctrine of the 'Fourfold Sense' in Scripture." In his *Theological Fragments,* 109–27. San Francisco: Ignatius Press, 1989.

————. *The Sources of Revelation.* New York: Herder & Herder, 1968.

Danielou, Jean. *From Shadows to Reality.* London: Burns & Oates, 1960.

DeVogue, Adalbert. *The Rule of St. Benedict: A Doctrinal and Spiritual Commentary.* Kalamazoo, Mich.: Cistercian Publ., 1983.

Dulles, Avery. *A Church to Believe In: Imaging the Church for the 1980's—Discipleship and the Dynamics of Freedom.* New York: Crossroad, 1982.

————. *Models of the Church.* Garden City, N.Y.: Doubleday, 1974.

Dunn, James. *Unity and Diversity in the New Testament*. Philadelphia: Westminster, 1977.

Eckhart, Meister. *Meister Eckhart: The Essential Sermons, Commentaries, Treatises and Defense*. Translated and Introduction by Edmund Colledge and Bernard McGinn. New York: Paulist, 1981.

———. *Meister Eckhart: Sermons and Treatises*. Translated and edited by M. O'C. Walshe. 3 vol. Rockport, MA: Element Books, 1987–1991.

———. *Meister Eckhart: Teacher and Preacher*. Edited by Bernard McGinn, Frank Tobin, and Elvira Borgstadt. New York: Paulist, 1986.

Eliade, Mircea. *Cosmos and History*. New York: Harper, 1959.

———. *Patterns in Comparative Religion*. New York: Meridian (New American Library), 1963.

Ellis, Peter F. *The Genius of John: A Composition-Critical Commentary on the Fourth Gospel*. Collegeville, Minn.: Liturgical Press, 1984.

The Encyclopedia of Eastern Philosophy and Religion: Buddhism, Hinduism, Taoism, Zen. Ingrid Fischer-Schreiber, Franz-Karl Erhard, Kurt Friedrichs and Michael S. Diener. Boston: Shambhala, 1994.

Engelsman, Joan C. *The Feminine Dimension of the Divine*. Philadelphia: Westminster, 1979, and Wilmette, Ill.: Chiron Publ., 1989.

Ephrem, Selected Works. Series II, vol. 2, 167–341.

Evagrius Ponticus. *The Mind's Long Journey to the Holy Trinity: The Ad Monachos of Evagrius Ponticus*. Translated with an Introduction by Jeremy Driscoll, O.S.B. Collegeville, Minn.: Liturgical Press, 1993.

———. *The Praktikos and Chapters on Prayer*. Translated with Introduction and notes by John Eudes Bamberger, O.C.S.O. Spencer, Mass.: Cistercian Publications, 1970.

Evdokimov, Paul. *The Sacrament of Love: The Nuptial Mystery in the Light of the Orthodox Tradition*. Crestwood, N.Y.: St. Vladimir's Seminary Press, 1985.

———. *Woman and the Salvation of the World*. Crestwood, NY.: St. Vladimir's Seminary Press, 1994.

Fedotov, George. *The Russian Religious Mind*. New York: Harper & Row, 1946.

———. *A Treasury of Russian Spirituality*. Compiled and edited by George Fedotov. Belmont, Mass.: Nordland, 1975.

Ferguson, Marilyn. *The Aquarian Conspiracy: Personal and Social Transformation in the 1980's*. Los Angeles: Tarcher, 1980.

Flannery, Austin, O.P., Ed., *Vatican Council II: The Conciliar and Post-Conciliar Documents*. Northport, N.Y.: Costello, 1975.

Fox, Matthew. *Original Blessing: A Primer in Creation Spirituality*. Santa Fe: Bear & Co., 1983.

Giancoli, Douglas C. *Physics: Principles with Applications.* 3d ed. Englewood Cliffs, N.J.: Prentice-Hall, 1991.

Gilkey, Langton. *Catholicism Confronts Modernity.* New York: Seabury, 1975.

Glotfelty, Cheryl, and Harold Fromm, Ed. *The Ecocriticism Reader: Landmarks in Literary Ecology.* Athens, Ga.: University of Georgia Press, 1996.

Griffiths, Bede. *The New Creation in Christ.* Springfield, Ill.: Templegate, 1994.

———. *Return to the Center.* Springfield, Ill.: Templegate, 1976.

———. *Universal Wisdom: A Journey Through the Sacred Wisdom of the World.* London: HarperCollins, 1994.

Guigo II. *The Ladder of Monks: A Letter on the Contemplative Life, and Twelve Meditations.* Translated and Introduction by Edmund Colledge, O.S.A., and James Walsh, S.J. Kalamazoo, Mich.: Cistercian Publications, 1981.

Gutierrez, Gustavo. *Essential Writings.* Edited by James B. Nickoloff. Minneapolis: Fortress, 1996.

———. *A Theology of Liberation: History, Politics and Salvation.* Maryknoll, N.Y.: Orbis, 1973.

Hale, Robert, O.S.B. Cam. *Christ and the Universe: Teilhard de Chardin and the Cosmos.* Chicago: Franciscan Herald Press, 1973.

Heschel, A. J. *Quest for God: Studies in Prayer and Symbolism.* New York: Crossroad, 1982.

———. *The Sabbath: Its Meaning for Modern Man.* New York: Farrar, Straus & Giroux, 1951.

Hillman, James. *Re-Visioning Psychology.* New York: Harper & Row, 1975.

The Holy Bible, containing the Old and New Testaments. Revised Standard Version, Catholic Edition. Camden N.J.: Thomas Nelson & Sons, 1966.

The Holy Bible, containing the Old and New Testaments with the Apocryphal/Deuterocanonical Books. New Revised Standard Version. New York: Collins, 1989.

Huxley, Aldous. *The Perennial Philosophy.* New York: Harper & Row, 1944.

Iersel, Bas van. *Reading Mark.* Collegeville, Minn.: Liturgical Press, 1988.

Irenaeus of Lyons. *Against Heresies,* SC vols. 263, 264 (Book I), vols. 293, 294 (Book II), vols. 210, 211 (Book III), vol. 100 (2 parts: Book IV), vols. 152, 153 (Book V), English translation ANF vol. 1, pp. 315–567.

————. *Proof of the Apostolic Preaching*. Translated by Joseph P. Smith (Ancient Christian Writers No. 16). New York: Newman (Paulist), 1952.

Jacobi, Jolande. *The Psychology of C. G. Jung*. 8th ed. New Haven: Yale University Press, 1973.

Jaspers, Karl. *The Origin and Goal of History*. Translated by Michael Bullock. New Haven: Yale University Press, 1953.

Jones, Cheslyn, Geoffrey Wainwright and Edward Yarnold. *The Study of Spirituality*. New York: Oxford University Press, 1986.

Jung, Carl G. *The Collected Works of C. G. Jung* (cited as CW). Edited by Sir Herbert Read, Michael Fordham, Gerhard Adler, and William McGuire; translated by R. F. C. Hull (except vol. 2) (Bollingen Series XX). 20 vols. New York and Princeton: Princeton University Press, 1953–.

————. "Answer to Job." CW 11, pp. 355–470.

————. "Concerning Mandala Symbolism." CW 9/1, pp. 355–90.

————. "A Psychological Approach to the Dogma of the Trinity." CW 11, pp. 107–200.

————. "Psychology and Religion." CW 11, pp. 3–105.

Kapleau, P. *The Three Pillars of Zen*. Compiled and edited by Philip Kapleau. Boston: Beacon Press, 1967.

Keating, Thomas, Basil Pennington and Thomas Clark. *Finding Grace at the Center*. Still River, Mass.: St. Bede Publications, 1978.

Kelley, C. F. *Meister Eckhart on Divine Knowledge*. New Haven: Yale University Press, 1977.

King, Ursula. *Towards a New Mysticism: Teilhard de Chardin & Eastern Religions*. New York: Seabury, 1981.

Kuhn, Thomas S. *The Structure of Scientific Revolutions*. 2d ed. Chicago: University of Chicago Press, 1970.

Lampe, G. W. H. *The Seal of the Spirit: A Study in the Doctrine of Baptism and Confirmation in the New Testament and the Fathers*. 2d ed. London: SPCK, 1967.

Lao Tzu. *Tao Teh Ching*. Translated by John C. H. Wu. Boston: Shambhala, 1989.

Lawlor, Robert. *Sacred Geometry*. London: Thames & Hudson, 1981; New York: Crossroad, 1982.

Leclerq, Jean, O.S.B. *The Love of Learning and the Desire for God*. New York: Fordham University Press, 1961; rev. ed., 1974.

Leon-Dufour, Xavier, S.J., Ed. *Dictionary of Biblical Theology*. 2d ed. New York: Seabury, 1973.

Lossky, Vladimir. *In the Image and Likeness of God*. Crestwood, N.Y.: St. Vladimir's Seminary Press, 1974.

————. *The Mystical Theology of the Eastern Church*. Crestwood, N.Y.: St. Vladimir's Seminary Press, 1976.

————. *The Vision of God*. London: Faith Press, 1963.

Louth, Andrew. *The Origins of the Christian Mystical Tradition from Plato to Denys*. Oxford: Clarendon Press, 1981.

Loy, David. *Nonduality*. New Haven: Yale University Press, 1988.

Malatesta, Edward, S.J. *Interiority and Covenant: A Study of einai en and menein en in the First Letter of St. John*. Rome: Biblical Institute Press, 1978.

Mantzaridis, Georgios I. *The Deification of Man: St. Gregory Palamas and the Orthodox Tradition*. Crestwood, N.Y.: St. Vladimir's Seminary Press, 1984.

Matthews, Caitlin. *Sophia, Goddess of Wisdom: The Divine Feminine from Black Goddess to World-Soul*. London: Mandala (HarperCollins), 1991.

Mauser, Ulrich. *Christ in the Wilderness: The Wilderness Theme in the Second Gospel and Its Basis in the Biblical Tradition*. London: SCM Press, 1963.

Maximus Confessor: Selected Writings. Translated by George C. Berthold. New York: Paulist, 1985.

May, Gerald. *Will and Spirit: A Contemplative Psychology*. San Francisco: HarperCollins, 1982.

Mazza, Enrico. *Mystagogy: A Theology of Liturgy in the Patristic Age*. New York: Pueblo, 1989.

McDonnell, Kilian, O.S.B. *The Baptism of Jesus in the Jordan: The Trinitarian and Cosmic Order of Salvation*. Collegeville, Minn.: Liturgical Press, 1996.

————. "Jesus' Baptism in the Jordan." TS 56 (1995): 209–36.

McGinn, Bernard, and Meyendorff, John, Eds. *Christian Spirituality: Origins to the Twelfth Century*. New York: Crossroad, 1992.

McNally, R. E. "Exegesis, Medieval." In *New Catholic Encyclopedia*, vol. 5, pp. 707–12.

Menchu, Rigoberta. *I, Rigoberta Menchu: An Indian Woman in Guatemala*. New York: Verso Publ., 1984.

Mersch, Emile. *The Theology of the Mystical Body*. St. Louis: B. Herder, 1951.

————. *The Whole Christ: The Historical Development of the Doctrine of the Mystical Body in Scripture and Tradition*. Milwaukee: Bruce, 1938.

Merton, Thomas. "Hagia Sophia." In *The Collected Poems of Thomas Merton*, 363–71. New York: New Directions, 1977.

————. "The Inner Experience: Notes on Contemplation" (Parts I–VIII).

Cistercian Studies, vol. 18 (1983) pp. 3–15, 121–134, 201–216, 289–300; vol. 19 (1984), pp. 62–77, 139–150, 267–282, 336–345.

———. *Introductions East and West: The Foreign Prefaces of Thomas Merton*. Greensboro, N.C.: Unicorn Press, 1981.

———. *Mystics and Zen Masters*. New York: Farrar, Straus & Giroux, 1969.

———. *New Seeds of Contemplation*. New York: New Directions, 1972.

———. *Seeds of Contemplation*. New York: New Directions, 1949.

———. *Zen and the Birds of Appetite*. New York: New Directions, 1968.

Meyendorff, John. *St. Gregory Palamas and Orthodox Spirituality*. Crestwood, N.Y.: St. Vladimir's Seminary Press, 1974.

Mollenkott, Virginia R. *The Divine Feminine: The Biblical Imagery of God as Female*. New York: Crossroad, 1983.

Moore, Robert, and Douglas Gillette. *King, Warrior, Magician, Lover: Rediscovering the Archetypes of the Mature Masculine*. San Francisco: HarperCollins, 1990.

———. *The King Within: Accessing the King in the Male Psyche*. New York: Avon, 1992.

Murray, Robert. "An Exhortation to Candidates for Ascetical Vows at Baptism in the Ancient Syriac Church." *NTS* 21 (1974): 59–80.

———. *Symbols of Church and Kingdom: A Study in Early Syriac Tradition*. 2d ed. Cambridge: Cambridge University Press, 1975.

Myers, Ched. *Binding the Strong Man: A Political Reading of Mark's Story of Jesus*. Maryknoll, N.Y.: Orbis, 1988.

Naranjo, Claudio, and Robert E. Ornstein. *On the Psychology of Meditation*. New York: Viking, 1971.

Nasr, Seyed Hossein. *Knowledge and the Sacred*. New York: Crossroad, 1981.

New Catholic Encyclopedia. 15 vols. New York: McGraw-Hill, 1967.

Nicholas of Cusa. *Of Learned Ignorance*. New Haven: Yale University Press, 1954.

———. *Unity and Reform: Selected Writings of Nicholas De Cusa*. Edited by John Patrick Dolan. Notre Dame, Ind.: University of Notre Dame Press, 1962.

Nickoloff, James: see Gutierrez, Gustavo.

Nyoshul Khenpo. *Natural Great Perfection: Dzogchen Teaching and Vajra Songs*. Ithaca, N.Y.: Snow Lion Publications, 1995.

Oxford Dictionary of the Christian Church (ODCC): see Cross, F.L. and Livingstone, E.A.

Pannikar, R. *Blessed Simplicity: The Monk as Universal Archetype*. New York: Seabury, 1982.

————. *A Dwelling Place for Wisdom*. Translated by Annemarie S. Kidder. Louisville: Westminstery/John Knox Press, 1993.

————. *The Silence of God: The Answer of the Buddha*. Maryknoll, N.Y.: Orbis, 1989.

————. *The Vedic Experience: Mantramanjari, An Anthology of the Vedas for Modern Man and Contemporary Celebration*. Berkeley: University of California Press, 1977.

Patai, Raphael. *The Hebrew Goddess*. 3d ed., enlarged. Detroit: Wayne University Press, 1990.

Pelikan, Jaroslav. *The Christian Tradition: A History of the Development of Doctrine*, Vol.1, *The Emergence of the Catholic Tradition (100–600)*. Chicago: University of Chicago Press, 1971.

————. *Jesus Through the Centuries: His Place in the History of Culture*. New York: Harper & Row, 1987.

Perry, John W. *Lord of the Four Quarters: The Mythology of Kingship*. New York: George Braziller, 1966; New York: Paulist, 1991.

Pontifical Biblical Commission. *The Interpretation of the Bible in the Church*. Boston: St. Paul's Books & Media, 1993.

Pope, Alexander. "Essay on Man," Harvard Classics, vol. 40, 425–426. New York: Collier, 1910.

Pseudo-Dionysius: The Complete Works. Translated by Colm Luibheid and Paul Rorem; introductions by Jaroslav Pelikan, Jean Leclerq, and Karlfried Froehlich. New York: Paulist, 1987.

Rahner, Karl. "Basic Theological Interpretation of the Second Vatican Council," *Theological Investigations* 20 (1981): 77–89.

————. Ed. *Encyclopedia of Theology: The Concise Sacramentum Mundi* (cited as ET). New York: Seabury, 1975.

————. "The Experience of God Today," TI 11 (1974), pp. 149–65.

————. "Experience of Self and Experience of God," TI 13 (1975), pp. 122–32.

————. *Foundations of Christian Faith: An Introduction to the Idea of Christianity*. Translated by William V. Dych. New York: Seabury, 1978.

————. *Hearers of the Word*. Translated by Michael Richards. Montreal: Palm Publishers, 1969.

————. *Sacramentum Mundi: An Encyclopedia of Theology*, 6 vols. (cited as SM). Edited by Karl Rahner et al. New York: Seabury Press, 1968–1970.

————. *Theological Investigations* (cited as TI), vols. 1–20. London: Darton, Longman and Todd, 1961–1981, and New York: Seabury Press/Crossroad, 1974–1981.

Richards, Mary C. *Centering: In Pottery, Poetry, and the Person*. Middletown, Conn.: Wesleyan University Press, 1962.

————. *Imagine Inventing Yellow: New and Selected Poems of M. C. Richards*. Barrytown, N.Y.: Station Hill Literary Editions, 1991.

Roszak, Theodore. *Where the Wasteland Ends: Politics and Transcendence in Postindustrial Society*. Garden City, N.Y.: Doubleday Anchor, 1973.

Sanders, Jack T. *The New Testament Christological Hymns: Their Historical Religious Background*. Cambridge: Cambridge University Press, 1971.

Schipflinger, Thomas. *Sophia-Maria: Eine ganzheitliche Vision der Schöpfung*. Munich: Verlag Neue Stadt, 1988.

Schmemann, A. *Ultimate Questions: An Anthology of Modern Russian Religious Thought*. Edited and Introduction by Alexander Schmemann. New York: Holt, Rinehart and Winston, 1965.

Scholem, Gershom. *Major Trends in Jewish Mysticism*. New York: Schocken, 1961.

Scott, M. Philip, O.C.S.O. "Chiastic Structure: A Key to the Interpretation of Mark's Gospel." *BTB* 15 (1985): 17–26.

Scroggs, R., and K. I. Groff. "Baptism in Mark: Dying and Rising with Christ." *JBL* 92 (1973): 531–48.

Shannon, William H. *Thomas Merton's Dark Path: The Inner Experience of a Contemplative*. New York: Penguin, 1982.

Sheldrake, Rupert. *The Rebirth of Nature: The Greening of Science and God*. New York: Bantam, 1991.

Sherrard, Philip. "The Christian Understanding of Man." *Sobornost* 7–5 (Summer 1977): 329–43.

————. *Church, Papacy and Schism: A Theological Inquiry*. London: SPCK, 1978.

Soloviev (Solovyov), Vladimir. "Beauty, Sexuality and Love." In *Ultimate Questions*, edited by A. Schmemann, 73–134. New York: Holt, Rinehart and Winston, 1966.

————. *Lectures on Divine Humanity*. Revised and edited by Boris Jakim. Hudson, N.Y.: Lindisfarne Press, 1995.

————. *The Meaning of Love*. West Stockbridge, Mass.: Lindisfarne Press, 1985.

Stevens, Wallace. *The Collected Poems of Wallace Stevens* (cited as CP). New York: Knopf, 1954.

Stock, A. *The Method and Message of Mark*. Wilmington, Del.: Michael Glazier, 1989.

Suzuki, D. T. *Essays in Zen Buddhism*. First Series, London: Rider, 1949, and New York: Grove Press, 1961; Second Series, London: Rider, 1953; Third Series, London: Rider, 1953.

Suzuki, Shunryu. *Zen Mind, Beginner's Mind.* New York: Weatherhill, 1971.

Swidler, Leonard. *Biblical Affirmations of Woman.* Philadelphia: Westminster, 1979.

Tanquerey, Adolphe. *The Spiritual Life: A Treatise on Ascetical and Mystical Theology.* 2d ed. Tournai: Desclee, ca. 1930.

Tarnas, Richard T. *The Passion of the Western Mind: Understanding the Ideas That Have Shaped Our World View.* New York: Crown/Harmony, 1991.

Teilhard de Chardin, Pierre. *Activation of Energy.* New York and London: Harcourt Brace Jovanovich, 1970.

———. "Centrology: An Essay in a Dialectic of Union." In his *Activation of Energy,* 97–127. New York and London: Harcourt Brace Jovanovich, 1970.

———. *The Divine Milieu.* New York: Harper, 1960.

———. *The Heart of Matter.* New York: Harcourt Brace Jovanovich, 1978.

———. *Human Energy.* New York: Harcourt Brace Jovanovich, 1969.

———. *Writings in Time of War.* New York: Harper & Row, 1967.

Terrien, Samuel. *The Elusive Presence: The Heart of Biblical Theology.* New York: Harper & Row, 1978.

Thomas, Dylan. *The Collected Poems of Dylan Thomas, 1934–1952.* New York: New Directions, 1953.

Thunberg, Lars. *Man and the Cosmos: The Vision of St. Maximus the Confessor.* Crestwood, N.Y.: St. Vladimir's Seminary Press, 1985.

———. *Microcosm and Mediator: The Theological Anthropology of Maximus the Confessor.* Lund: C.W.K. Gleerup, and Copenhagen: Einar Munksgaard, 1965.

Tucci, Giuseppe. *The Theory and Practice of the Mandala.* New York: Samuel Weiser, 1970.

Turner, Victor. *The Ritual Process: Structure and Anti-Structure.* Ithaca, N.Y.: Cornell University Press, 1977.

Ulanov, Ann. *The Feminine in Jungian Psychology and in Christian Theology.* Evanston, Ill.: Northwestern University Press, 1971.

———. *Receiving Woman: Studies in the Psychology and Theology of the Feminine.* Philadelphia: Westminster, 1981.

Underhill, Evelyn. *Mysticism.* New York: Meridian, 1955.

Vagaggini, Cipriano, O.S.B. *The Flesh, Instrument of Salvation: A Theology of the Human Body.* New York: Alba House, 1969.

———. *Theological Dimensions of the Liturgy.* 4th ed. Collegeville, Minn.: Liturgical Press, 1976.

Vatican Council II: The Conciliar and Post-Conciliar Documents: see Flannery, Austin.

Von Franz, Marie-Louise. *C. G. Jung: His Myth in Our Time*. New York: G. P. Putnam's Sons for the C. G. Jung Foundation, 1975.

Washburn, Michael. *The Ego and the Dynamic Ground: A Transpersonal Theory of Human Development*. 2d ed. Albany: SUNY Press, 1995.

White, John W., Ed. *What Is Enlightenment? Exploring the Goal of the Spiritual Path*. New York: Paragon House, 1995 (originally published by J. P. Tarcher, Los Angeles, 1984).

White, Lynn Jr. "The Historical Roots of Our Ecological Crisis." In *The Ecocriticism Reader: Landmarks in Literary Ecology*, edited by Cheryll Glotfelty and Harold Fromm, 3–14. Athens, Ga., and London: University of Georgia Press, 1996.

Wilber, Ken. *The Atman Project*. Wheaton, Ill.: Theosophical Publishing House, 1980.

———. *A Brief History of Everything*. Boston: Shambhala, 1996.

———. *Eye to Eye: The Quest for the New Paradigm*. Garden City, N.Y.: Anchor Doubleday, 1983.

———. *The Spectrum of Consciousness*. Wheaton, Ill.: Theosophical Publishing House, 1977.

———. *Up from Eden: A Transpersonal View of Human Evolution*. Boulder, Col.: Shambhala, 1983.

Wilbur, Richard. *The Poems of Richard Wilbur*. New York: Harcourt Brace Jovanovich, 1963.

Wilder, Amos.*Early Christian Rhetoric: The Language of the Gospel*. Cambridge: Harvard University Press, 1971.

Winkler, Gabriele. "The Origins and Idiosyncrasies of the Earliest Form of Asceticism." In *The Continuing Quest for God: Monastic Spirituality in Tradition and Transition*, edited by William Skudlarek, O.S.B., 9–43. Collegeville, Minn.: Liturgical Press, 1981.

Wong, Joseph H. P. *Logos-Symbol in the Christology of Karl Rahner*. Rome: Libreria Ateneo Salesiano, 1984.

Abbreviations

I. Books of the Bible

Genesis	Gn	Proverbs	Prv
Exodus	Ex	Ecclesiastes	Eccl
Leviticus	Lv	Song of Songs	Sg (Song)
Numbers	Nm	Wisdom	Wis
Deuteronomy	Dt	Sirach	Sir
Joshua	Jos	Isaiah	Is
Judges	Jgs	Jeremiah	Jer
Ruth	Ru	Lamentations	Lam
1 Samuel	1 Sm	Baruch	Bar
2 Samuel	2 Sm	Ezekiel	Ez
1 Kings	1 Kgs	Daniel	Dn
2 Kings	2 Kgs	Hosea	Hos
1 Chronicles	1 Chr	Joel	Jl
2 Chronicles	2 Chr	Amos	Am
Ezra	Ezr	Obadiah	Ob
Nehemiah	Neh	Jonah	Jon
Tobit	Tb	Micah	Mi
Judith	Jdt	Nahum	Na
Esther	Est	Habakkuk	Hb
1 Maccabees	1 Mc	Zephaniah	Zep
2 Maccabees	2 Mc	Haggai	Hg
Job	Jb	Zechariah	Zec
Psalms	Ps(s)	Malachi	Mal

New Testament

Matthew	Mt	1 Timothy	1 Tm
Mark	Mk	2 Timothy	2 Tm
Luke	Lk	Titus	Ti
John	Jn	Philemon	Phlm
Acts of the Apostles	Acts	Hebrews	Heb
Romans	Rom	James	Jas
1 Corinthians	1 Cor	1 Peter	1 Pt
2 Corinthians	2 Cor	2 Peter	2 Pt
Galatians	Gal	1 John	1 Jn
Ephesians	Eph	2 John	2 Jn
Philippians	Phil	3 John	3 Jn
Colossians	Col	Jude	Jude
1 Thessalonians	1 Thes	Revelation	Rv
2 Thessalonians	2 Thes		

II. Other

ABD	Anchor Bible Dictionary
ANF	Ante-Nicene Fathers
BTB	Biblical Theology Bulletin
CBQ	Catholic Biblical Quarterly
CP	The Collected Poems of Wallace Stevens
CS	Cistercian Studies
CW	Collected Works of C. G. Jung
DBT	Dictionary of Biblical Theology (X. Léon-Dufour, ed.)
EEPR	Encyclopedia of Eastern Philosophy and Religion
ET	Encyclopedia of Theology
FOC	Fathers of the Church Series, Catholic University of America Press
Gr.	Greek
Heb.	Hebrew
IDB	Interpreter's Dictionary of the Bible
JBL	Journal of Biblical Literature
JTS	Journal of Theological Studies
LXX	Septuagint Greek Translation of Old Testament
NJBC	New Jerome Biblical Commentary
NPNF	Nicene and Post-Nicene Fathers, Series I and II
NRSV	New Revised Standard Version
NT	New Testament
NTS	New Testament Studies
ODCC	Oxford Dictionary of the Christian Church
OT	Old Testament
PG	Patrologia Graeca-Latina (Migne)
PL	Patrologia Latina (Migne)
RSV	Revised Standard Version
SC	Sources Chrétiennes
SM	Sacramentum Mundi
TDNT	Theological Dictionary of the New Testament
TI	Theological Investigations of Karl Rahner
TS	Theological Studies

Index of Authors

Index of Subjects

273